The Civilization of the American Indian Series

LAS MONJAS

JOHN S. BOLLES, a native of Berkeley, California, is Chairman of the Board of John S. Bolles Associates, Architects, San Francisco. He received the bachelor of science degree in civil engineering from the University of Oklahoma and the master's degree in architecture from Harvard University. In his work at Chichén Itzá he was the last of the excavators and explorers to serve under Sylvanus G. Morley. He is the author of *La Iglesia—Chichén Itzá* and of many technical papers in archaeology and city planning.

For many years Bolles was Chairman of the Board of the San Francisco Art Institute and for sixteen years owned San Francisco's foremost contemporary art gallery. He is persuaded of the inseparability of art and archaeology—exemplified by the discoveries at Las Monjas.

The author and a native assistant at Yaxchilán, Chiapas, Mexico, members of the Carnegie Institution expedition of 1931.

BOLLES, John S. Las Monjas: a major pre-Mexican architectural complex at Chichén Itzá, with new contributions by J. Eric S. Thompson and Ian Graham. Oklahoma, 1977. 304p ill map (Civilization of the American Indian series, 139) bibl index 75-16295. 35.00 ISBN 0-8061-1282-4. C.I.P.

Bolles has had a very distinguished career as engineer, architect, and archaeologist. During 1932–34 he was in charge of the excavations of the classic Maya building complex known as *Las Monjas* (The Nunnery). This abundantly illustrated volume is a complete and detailed report of the excavation of one of the most striking examples of Yucatan Maya architecture. The stone mosaic façade masks and previously unpublished murals are well described. The section on the ballcourt, with its many bas-relief carvings, is of particular interest. John Jennings provides a history of previous explorations of Chichén Itzá, the late J. E. S. Thompson discusses the hieroglyphic texts of *Las Monjas,* and Ian Graham contributes drawings and photographs of the lintels with explanatory material. This impressive volume is destined to join the list of classic accounts of Maya archaeology and should be included in all serious research libraries where it can be available to undergraduate and graduate students of archaeology and the Maya as well as of architecture.

LAS MONJAS

A Major Pre-Mexican Architectural Complex at Chichén Itzá

By JOHN S. BOLLES

Introduction by John H. Jennings

With new contributions by Sir J. Eric S. Thompson and Ian Graham

UNIVERSITY OF OKLAHOMA PRESS Norman

Library of Congress Cataloging in Publication Data

Bolles, John S
    Las Monjas: a major pre-Mexican architectural complex at
Chichén Itzá.

    (Civilization of the American Indian series 139)
    Bibliography: p. 301
    Includes index.
    1. Chichén Itzá, Mexico.   2. Mayas—Architecture.
3. Indians of Mexico—Architecture.   I. Title.   II. Series.
F1435.1.C5B64   722'.91   75–16295

Kenneth Conant, professor of the history of architecture at Harvard, was the first to acquaint me with the beauties of Maya art and architecture. Granted I was a dozing student in class, but his Maya lectures came just after his return from Yucatán in 1926. At that time I was a student in the graduate school of architecture, which then had an enrollment of possibly thirty in three-year courses.

I had a degree in civil engineering from the University of Oklahoma, where I had gone to avoid becoming an architect following my father's footsteps in San Francisco. In my third year at Harvard, the Oriental Institute of the University of Chicago, under James Breasted, asked for a student in architecture who could survey—and there was only one. And so I was soon off to Anatolia, which, the dean agreed, was somewhere in Asia Minor. At Alishar Hüyük, I received my baptism in archeology under the Prussian von der Osten, and the Bavarian Eric Schmidt.

Life in Turkey was fascinating for a young man out of Prohibition America. And then on to Egypt to work with Uvo Hölscher at Medinet Habu.

Egypt meant more sound training in German methods and practices, but it was full of life in other forms. The Oriental Institute under Breasted was the goal for all foreign dignitaries—kings and queens included—and for all those left of the 1929 depression who could and did afford the Cook's tours on the Nile and could also, perhaps, help subsidize Breasted's archeological efforts.

There followed a short period in Jerusalem, Beirut, and Damascus, where we measured "live" skulls in an effort to find Hittite traces. From there I went to Cluny, France, to survey the remains of what turned out to be the longest church ever built. This work was for Kenneth Conant and the Medieval Academy of America, and is now published and housed in the Loeb Library in the new Gund Hall at Harvard. Cluny was without question one of the great works of man and the culmination, under the Benedictines, of the Romanesque period of architecture and art.

Conant informed me, to my surprise and delight, that he had arranged with A. V. Kidder for me to go to Chichén Itzá to do some work on Maya art and architecture.

After a few months at school, I arrived in Yucatán, and there met Sylvanus G. Morley, Karl Ruppert, H.E.D. Pollock, and Gus Stromsvik. My first assignment was to survey El Caracol, on which Ruppert had completed excavations the year before. I remember Sylvanus Morley's unbounded glee when I confirmed the observatory's sight lines. However, the daily encounter with Las Monjas, walking by it several times a day going to the hacienda, and my insatiable desire to see and know all of Chichén convinced me that here was the most interesting complex in the city and obviously the one with the longest and by far the most continuous period of structural and artistic development.

Sylvanus Morley was not one to need much prodding when done with genuine enthusiasm; he too had long harbored a desire to excavate and repair Las Monjas. From an initial one-season

vii

project, the work carried through three, and even then only the surface was touched.

Following the tradition of nearly all "explorers" to Chichén Itzá, including Stephens, Maudslay, and Morley, we set up our field office in the sunny east room of the Second Story. In 1933, Gustav Stromsvik ran electricity to this "office" from the hacienda, and there Russell Smith, Fred Parris, and I had good light for our drawings. We also utilized electricity for work in our tunnels and for controlled night light for photographing bas-relief sculpture and lintels. This was only three years after electric lights were run into the Pyramid of Cheops to enable King Albert of Belgium to enjoy his visit better.

Using the surveying ability I had learned as a boy in Sonoma County, California, as well as the training in civil engineering, architecture, and the thoroughness in archeological methods taught me by the Germans, I went to work on Las Monjas with a precision heretofore not used in the Americas. The volumes of photographs, notes, and reams of surveys and drawings now in the Peabody Museum attest to this. This book is presented as an insight into one of the most important buildings in the Maya culture. For those needing to do detailed study of the progress of the work and its results, or who wish to continue the excavations, the files of the Carnegie Institution of Washington now repose in the Peabody Museum at Harvard and are available for students. Photocopies of the voluminous accounts of the excavations, details, and assumptions are available in several libraries devoted to the study of the Maya.

As the director of the work, my primary duty was to supervise and direct excavations and repairs and to make the surveys necessary for the orderly assemblage of information. Most of the beautiful, but precise, drawings were made by Russell T. Smith of Brookline, Massachusetts, and a classmate in the Harvard School of Architecture. Several drawings, such as those of the Ball Court sculpture, were by Fred Parris, also from Harvard, who shuttled back and forth from the then-embryonic University of Pennsylvania excavations at Piedras Negras. John O'Neil drew

several masks when he was not burdened by his survey started by Kilmartin for the environs of Chichén Itzá.

Bernard Tun, of Pisté, was my constant companion and *capitán*. Henry Roberts' work on the ceramics covered several months, and of course both Karl Ruppert and Sylvanus Morley were always available for guidance. Hermann Beyer worked on the rubbings of the lintels, which Jack Denison had originally made. E. Wyllys Andrews' first job in Yucatán was on the lintels of Las Monjas under our program.

Later, on Christmas, 1936, I was to meet Jack Denison in Damascus to discuss the Las Monjas lintels. He was ill in Aleppo, and we missed our connection. He joined the Red Cross in World War II for duty in North Africa, where he died during the campaign.

Each season in Chichén Itzá we went on exploratory trips, and on these I was the surveyor and sometime guide. Two trips were outstanding. These included Sylvanus Morley and his wife Frances, Karl Ruppert, and Gustav Stromsvik. The first was to Piedras Negras and Yaxchilán. Alden Mason and Linton Satterthwaite had just commenced work at Piedras Negras for the University of Pennsylvania. We spent several weeks at Yaxchilán, where I enlarged and rechecked the old Maler survey and had my first taste of discovery. Rumors of the new murals at Bonampak failed to excite us, since a trip there would have taken another week. Instead, we headed down the Usamacinta in dugout canoes, and on to Palenque.

The second year, we went to southern Campeche to "discover" Calakmul, about which there had been only rumors. There we found one of the largest of the Maya cities, and brought to light the largest number of hieroglyphic monuments of any Maya city then known.

Again, on the basis of a rumor among *chicleros*, Ruppert and I went east to "discover" La Muñeca, apparently not far from Río Bec. Unfortunately, Ruppert collapsed with fever about noon of the first day. A *chiclero* and I tied him on a mule, rolled him into water holes when we found them, and then, against the advice of

viii

my guide, I headed diagonally through the bush to reach our party. Luck was on my side, and after an all-night ordeal we finally got Ruppert to our expedition and then on to the coast and finally to Tulane, where he eventually recovered and returned later to go into Bonampak to study the murals there.

The training of the workers at Pisté, under Morley, Ruppert, Morris, and then me, led to a caste system in Yucatán somewhat similar to that around Luxor, Egypt. Thirty years later, I arrived about sunset at Dzibilchaltún to find the entrance closed. The guard's wife took one look, opened her arms and the gate, and called to her husband, "It's Señor Juan." And so again I met a former trainee from Pisté, the ruling class of excavators for Yucatán. Throughout the world, there are hundreds of Bernie Tuns who have become the petty officers and staff sergeants for the trained archeologists for whom they work. In Turkey, Egypt, Persia, and Mexico, they were the unsung, meticulous excavators who learned their trade and carried it on through their village system from one institution to another—even those two mischievous French boys at Cluny were still at work there years after I left, and now, as senior citizens, could undoubtedly give even Kenneth Conant a few points of importance he has overlooked.

The present volume on Las Monjas cannot be introduced without some explanation for its years in preparation. Most of the seasons' works were summed up either at the Laboratory of Anthropology in Santa Fe or at the Peabody Museum at Harvard. After the final season, Russell Smith and I were given an office in the Peabody, and appeared to be within final stages of reporting. However, the Oriental Institute of the University of Chicago called me back into service, and I was sent to Persepolis to excavate and survey, again under Eric Schmidt, who was then in charge of their Persian operations. The agreement was that I could continue my work on the Las Monjas manuscript; a large amount of that work was, accordingly, done at Persepolis.

With the death of James Breasted and deteriorating world economic conditions, I returned to London to complete my Persepolis papers and to do more work on Las Monjas. There I made the decision finally to become an architect and returned to San Francisco, which I had left eighteen years before, and became the sole employee and associate of my father. Again, I devoted six months to Las Monjas, and then gradually was drawn more and more completely into my livelihood.

I sometimes wonder if I overworked my father with my drive to feed a growing family. At any rate, he passed away just as our business began to grow and my time became more and more involved in art and architecture and less and less in archeology.

I made a number of trips to Yucatán, became involved in new aspects of Las Monjas, and believed that the present study could obviously improve with more study, more work. For example, at the time of our excavations carbon-14 testing was not known, and we were endeavoring to relate our structures by construction methods, art forms, hieroglyphs, and ceramics. In 1961, my son David went to Yucatán to work with E. Wyllys Andrews at Dzibilchaltún. They obtained permission from the Mexican government to take samples of beams in La Iglesia and La Casa Colorada. The results of the carbon-14 tests gave positive seventh-century dates, plus or minus, to these structures. Since then carbon testing has become more refined. Then too, J. Eric S. Thompson's dating of the lintels would not have been accepted in an earlier period.

Perhaps in the future, we will have newer and more precise and convenient methods for dating artifacts and hieroglyphs. This offers some excuse for delay in publishing—and probably a poor excuse—but does unquestionably add to the strength of my training by German tutors to remove, or excavate, minimally so that a maximum of undisturbed evidence is left for future studies using more sophisticated techniques. I sincerely hope and trust that readers, students, and professionally trained excavators will find our work of interest for the period within which it was accomplished.

I want especially to acknowledge my thanks to Kenneth Conant, Sylvanus Morley, A. V. Kidder, Eric Schmidt, James

Breasted, and a host of others. My wife Mary typed much of the manuscript at Persepolis in the 1930s. John Jennings, who did the editing and design on my *La Iglesia*, has edited the present work. The production and design have been in the capable hands of the University of Oklahoma Press. Karen Kleiderman has typed and retyped all the scribblings and notes. Sarah Bolles spent weeks clarifying the drawings of La Iglesia, the East Wing, and the Southeast Annex. Katherine Edsall has patiently held on to all the data in the Peabody Museum of Harvard University, which is the repository for the Carnegie Institution of Washington files and has granted the rights to use material furnished through them.

The new contributions by the late J. Eric S. Thompson and by Ian Graham have added immeasurably to this effort. Henry Roberts worked on the ceramics, but because of his illness most of the carefully labeled specimens were lost. A few strategic test pits in undisturbed areas would doubtlessly be rewarding to future students of ceramics.

Most of the photographs herein were taken by me. In addition, Raul Cámara of Mérida made many of the beautiful comprehensive photographs. All drawings and photographs have been reproduced herein through the courtesy of Peabody Museum, Harvard University, which is the repository for these Carnegie Institution of Washington materials, except as otherwise noted in the legends.

The watercolor of the mural in Room 22 has been reproduced through the kindness of Jean Charlot as well as of the Peabody Museum. Similarly, the drawing by A. Breton came from the Peabody Museum.

JOHN S. BOLLES

San Francisco, California

x

CONTENTS

LAS MONJAS

ARCHITECTURE: General Description

The first recorded mention of Chichén Itzá, at least in any European language, was Diego de Landa's brief description in his *Relación de las cosas de Yucatán*. Writing about 1566—only some forty years after Cortés' Conquest—Landa said: "Chichen Itza is a very fine site, ten leagues from Izamal and eleven from Valladolid. It is said that it was ruled by three lords who were brothers who came into that country from the west, who were very devout, and so they built very beautiful temples."

Landa's work did not appear as a book, and was consequently unknown, until it was published in Paris in 1864 as *Relation des choses Yucatan—texte espagnol et traduction française—par l'Abbé Brasseur de Bourbourg.*

Emmanuel von Friederichsthal is said, by Victor Wolfgang von Hagen, to be "the first European to visit Chichén Itzá," and is mentioned by Stephens (see below). Friederichsthal's brief (some twenty pages) *Les Monuments de l'Yucatan* (Paris, 1841) contains the first published mention of Chichén Itzá.

In February, 1842, the American Benjamin N. Norman spent about a week at Chichén Itzá. Norman, an amateur adventurer and traveler, had already made a trip to Cuba and other nearby islands. Enthused by the wide success of Stephens' published account of his first journey to Middle America, *Incidents of Travel in Central America, Chiapas, and Yucatan* (1841), and personally encouraged by Stephens, Norman made a trip of his own to Yucatán. His *Rambles in Yucatan* was published in 1843. Both his text and illustrations are highly fanciful and inaccurate, and

are of interest for our purposes only because he was the first both to describe and to illustrate Las Monjas.

It was on the morning of the 10th of February that I directed my steps, for the first time, toward the ruins of the ancient city of CHI-CHEN. . . .

The names by which I have designated these ruins, are such as were suggested to me by their peculiar construction, and the purposes for which I supposed them to have been designed. . . .

Situated about three rods south-west of the ruins of the Dome [El Caracol] are those of the HOUSE OF THE CACIQUES [Las Monjas]. I cut my way through the thick growth of small wood to this sublime pile, and by the aid of my compass was enabled to reach the east front of the building. Here I felled the trees that hid it, and the whole front was opened to my view, presenting the most strange and incomprehensible pile of architecture that my eyes ever beheld—elaborate, elegant, stupendous, yet belonging to no order now known to us. The front of this wonderful edifice measures thirty-two feet, and its height twenty, extending to the main building fifty feet. Over the door-way, which favors the Egyptian style of architecture, is a heavy lintel of stone, containing two double rows of hieroglyphics, with a sculptured ornament intervening. Above these are the remains of hooks carved in stone, with raised lines of drapery running through them; which, apparently, have been broken off by the falling of the heavy finishing from the top of the building; over which, surrounded by a variety of chaste and beautifully executed borders, encircled within a wreath, is a female figure in a sitting posture, in basso-relievo, having a head-dress of feathers, cords, and

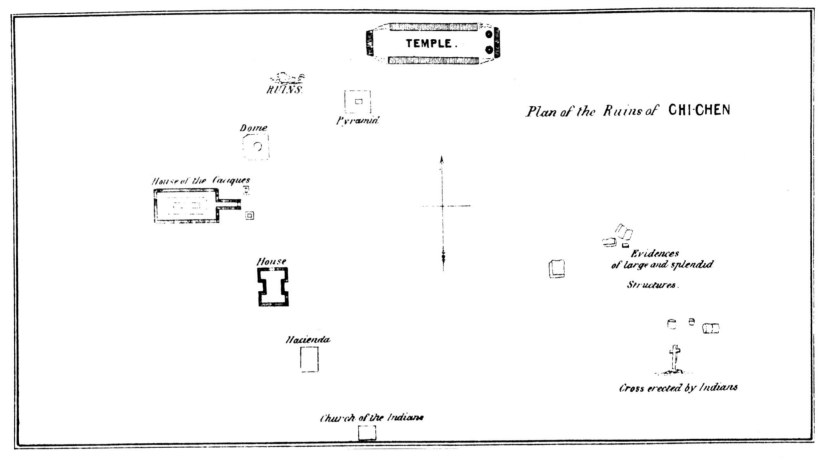

First published plan of Chichén Itzá. From Benjamin N. Norman, *Rambles in Yucatan* (1843). Courtesy American Antiquarian Society.

tassels, and the neck ornamented. The angles of this building are tastefully curved. The ornaments continue around the sides, which are divided into two compartments, different in their arrangement, though not in style. Attached to the angles are large projecting hooks, skilfully worked, and perfect rosettes and stars, with spears reversed, are put together with the utmost precision.

The ornaments are composed of small square blocks of stone, cut to the depth of about one to one and a half inches, apparently with the most delicate instruments, and inserted by a shaft in the wall. The wall is made of large and uniformly square blocks of limestone, set in a mortar which appears to be as durable as the stone itself. In the ornamental borders of this building I could dis-

First published illustration of Las Monjas. From Benjamin N. Norman,
Rambles in Yucatan (1843). Courtesy American Antiquarian Society.

cover but little analogy with those known to me. The most striking were those of the cornice and entablature, *chevron* and the *cable* moulding, which are characteristic of the Norman architecture.

The sides have three door-ways, each opening into small apartments, which are finished with smooth square blocks of stone; the floors of the same material, but have been covered with cement, which is now broken. The apartments are small, owing to the massive walls enclosing them, and the acute-angled arch, forming the ceiling. The working and laying of the stone are as perfect as they could have been under the directions of a modern architect.

Contiguous to this front are two buildings, as represented in the plan. The one on the right, situated some twenty-five feet from it, (about two feet off the right line,) has a front of about thirty-five feet, its sides ten wide, and its height twenty feet, containing one room similar in its finish to those before described. The front of this building is elaborately sculptured with rosettes and borders, and ornamental lines; the rear is formed of finely cut stone, now much broken. Near by are numerous heaps of hewn and broken stones, sculptured work and pillars.

The other building on the left, is about eight feet from the principal front, measuring twenty-two feet in length, thirteen in width, and thirty-six in height. The top is quite broken, and has the appearance of having been much higher. The *agave Americana* was growing thriftily upon its level roof. On all sides of this building are carved figures, broken images, in sitting postures; rosettes and ornamental borders, laid off in compartments; each compartment having three carved hooks on each side and angle. This building contains but one room, similar to that on the right. A soil has collected on the tops or roofs of these structures to the depth of three or four feet, in which trees and other vegetation are flourishing.

From these portions of the ruins I worked my way through the wild thicket, by which they are surrounded, to the north side of the main building, in the centre of which I found a flight of small stone steps, overgrown with bushes and vines, which I cut away, and made an ascent by pulling myself up to the summit, a distance of forty feet. This platform is an oblong square, one hundred by seventy-five feet. Here a range of rooms were found, occupying about two-thirds of the area; the residue of the space probably formed a promenade,

6

which is now filled up with crumbling ruins, covered with trees and grass. These rooms varied in size; the smallest of which measured six by ten, and the largest six by twenty-two feet.

The most of these rooms were plastered, or covered with a fine white cement, some of which was still quite perfect. By washing them, I discovered fresco paintings; but they were much obliterated. The subjects could not be distinguished. On the eastern end of these rooms is a hall running transversely, four feet wide, (having the high angular ceiling,) one side of which is filled with a variety of sculptured work, principally rosettes and borders, with rows of small pilasters; having three square recesses, and a small room on either side. Over the doorways of each are stone lintels three feet square, carved with hieroglyphics both on the front and under side. The western end of these rooms is in almost total ruins. The northern side has a flight of stone steps, but much dilapidated, leading to the top; which, probably, was a look-out place, but is now almost in total ruins. The southern range of rooms is much broken; the outside of which yet shows the elaborate work with which the whole building was finished.

I vainly endeavored to find access to the interior of the main building. I discovered two breaches, caused, probably, by the enormous weight of the pile, and in these apertures I made excavations; but could not discover any thing like apartments of any description. It seemed to be one vast body of stone and mortar, kept together by the great solidity of the outer wall, which was built in a masterly manner, of well-formed materials. The angles were finished off with circular blocks of stone, of a large and uniform size. (Pp. 108, 111, 119–23.)

In March, 1842, one month after Norman's visit, John Lloyd Stephens arrived in Chichén Itzá for the first time. By that time he was already widely known as both world traveler and published author (*Incidents of Travel in Egypt, Arabia Petraea, and the Holy Land* (2 vols., 1837), *Incidents of Travel in Greece, Turkey, Russia, and Poland* (2 vols., 1838), and, especially, *Incidents of Travel in Central America, Chiapas, and Yucatan* (2 vols., 1841).

On this 1842 trip, as on the earlier one to Middle America, Stephens was accompanied by Frederick Catherwood, an Englishman who had illustrated the 1841 volumes. Stephens and Catherwood had met in London. Of this meeting, Victor Wolfgang von Hagen says, in his *Maya Explorer: John Lloyd Stephens and the Lost Cities of Central America and Yucatán,* "From this meeting of an American and an Englishman was to come one of the most romantic episodes in the history of man's exploration of his past—the rediscovery of the Mayas and the beginnings of American archaeology" (p. 59).

Catherwood, painter, architect, archeologist, had spent considerable time in the Near East, where he had made many renderings of famous ruined structures, eventually becoming architectural adviser to the viceroy of Egypt, to whom he was responsible for the repair and preservation of mosques in Cairo. With his background and professional experience, he was the ideal illustrator for Stephens' two greatest works. Stephens and Catherwood had not seen Chichén Itzá on their earlier trip, although they had studied other nearby sites, including Uxmal, at that time.

In 1842, they spent about three weeks in Chichén Itzá. Their observations were published in 1843 in the two-volume *Incidents of Travel in Yucatan:*

> The ruins are nine leagues from Valladolid, the *camino real* to which passes directly through the field. The great buildings tower on both sides of the road in full sight of all passers-by, and from the fact that the road is much travelled, the ruins of Chichen are perhaps more generally known to the people of the country than any other in Yucatan. It is an interesting fact, however, that the first stranger who ever visited them was a native of New-York, whom we afterward met at Valladolid, and who is now again residing in this city....

Plan of Chichén Itzá. From John L. Stephens, *Incidents of Travel in Yucatan* (1843).

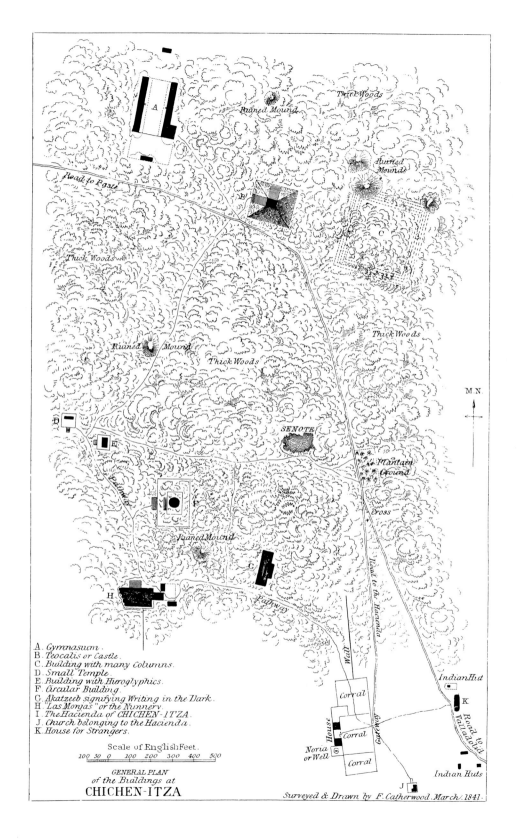

A. Gymnasium.
B. Teocalis or Castle.
C. Building with many Columns.
D. Small Temple.
E. Building with Hieroglyphics.
F. Circular Building.
G. Akatzeeb signifying Writing in the Dark.
H. "Las Monjas" or the Nunnery.
I. The Hacienda of CHICHEN-ITZA.
J. Church belonging to the Hacienda.
K. House for Strangers.

Scale of English Feet.
100 50 0   100   200   300   400   500

GENERAL PLAN
of the Buildings at
CHICHEN-ITZA

Surveyed & Drawn by F. Catherwood. March. 1841.

East Wing with La Iglesia on right. From John L. Stephens, *Incidents of Travel in Yucatan* (1843).

Las Monjas. From John L. Stephens, *Incidents of Travel in Yucatan* (1843).

In 1838 Mr. [John] Burke came from Valladolid to the village of Cawa, six leagues distant from Chichen. While making excursions in the neighbourhood, one of the young men told him of old buildings on this hacienda, from one of which Valladolid was visible. Mr. Burke rode over, and on the fourth of July stood on the top of the Castillo, spy-glass in hand, looking out for Valladolid. Two years afterward, in 1840, they were visited by the Baron [Emmanuel von] Fr[i]ederichstahl, and by him first brought to the notice of the public, both in Europe and this country; and I take occasion to say that this visit was made in the prosecution of a route recommended to him by me after my return from my former interrupted journey of exploration among the ruins of Yucatan. . . .

[Here is] the general plan of the ruins of Chichen. This plan is made from bearings taken with the compass, and the distances were all measured with a line. The buildings are laid down on the plan according to their exterior form. All now standing are comprehended, and the whole circumference occupied by them is about two miles, which is equal to the diameter of two thirds of a mile, though ruined buildings appear beyond these limits. . . .

Following the path indicated in the map . . . we reach a modern stone fence, dividing the cattle-field of the hacienda, on the other side of which appears through the trees, between two other buildings, the end façade of a long, majestic pile, called, like one of the principal edifices at Uxmal, the Monjas, or Nuns; it is remarkable for its good state of preservation, and the richness and beauty of its ornaments, as represented in the plate. . . . The view comprehends the corner of a building on the right, at a short distance, called the Eglesia, or Church. The height of this façade is twenty-five feet, and its width thirty-five. It has two cornices of tasteful and elaborate design. Over the doorway are twenty small cartouches of hieroglyphics in four rows, five in a row, barely indicated in the engraving, and to make room for which the lower cornice is carried up. Over these stand out in a line six bold projecting curved ornaments, like that presented from the House of the Governor at Uxmal, resembling an elephant's trunk, and the upper centre space over the doorway is an irregular circular niche, in which portions of a seated figure, with a head-dress of feathers, still remain. The rest of the ornaments are of that distinctive stamp, characteristic of the ancient

American cities, and unlike the designs of any other people, with which the reader must now be familiar. The tropical plants and shrubs growing on the roof, which, when we first saw it, hung over the cornice like a fringe-work, added greatly to the picturesque effect of this elegant façade.

The [next] plate represents the front of the same building. It is composed of two structures entirely different from each other, one of which forms a sort of wing to the principal edifice, and has at the end the façade before presented. The whole length is two hundred and twenty-eight feet, and the depth of the principal structure is one hundred and twelve feet. The only portion containing interior chambers is that which I have called the wing. This has two doorways opening into chambers twenty-six feet long and eight feet deep, behind each of which is another of corresponding dimensions, now filled up several feet with mortar and stones, and appearing to have been originally filled up solid to the ceiling, making again casas cerradas, or closed houses. The whole number of chambers in the wing is nine, and these are all the apartments on the ground floor. The great structure to which the wing adjoins is apparently a solid mass of masonry, erected only to hold up the two ranges of buildings upon it. A grand staircase fifty-six feet wide, the largest we saw in the country, rises to the top. On one side of the staircase a huge breach, twenty or thirty feet deep, has been made by the proprietor, for the purpose of getting out building stone, which discloses only solid masonry. The grand staircase is thirty-two feet high, and has thirty-nine steps. On the top of the structure stands a range of buildings, with a platform of fourteen feet in front extending all round.

From the back of this platform the grand staircase rises again, having the same width, fifteen steps to the roof of the second range, which forms a platform in front of the third range; this last is, unfortunately, in a ruinous condition, and it is to be observed that in this, as in all the other cases, these ancient architects never placed an upper building on the roof of a lower one, but always back, so as to rest on a structure solid from the ground, the roof of the lower range being merely a platform in front of the upper one.

The circumference of this building is six hundred and thirty-eight feet, and its height, when entire, was sixty-five feet. It seems to have been constructed only with reference to the second range of

La Iglesia. From John
L. Stephens, *Incidents
of Travel in Yucatan*
(1843).

apartments, upon which the art and skill of builders have been lavishly expended. It is one hundred and four feet long and thirty feet wide, and the broad platform around it, though overgrown with grass several feet high, formed a noble promenade, commanding a magnificent view of the whole surrounding country.

On the side of the staircase are five doorways, of which the three centre ones are what are usually called false doors, appearing to be merely recesses in the wall. The compartments between the doorways contained combinations of ornaments of unusual taste and elegance, both in arrangement and design. The two extreme doorways open into chambers, in each of which are three long recesses in the back wall, extending from the floor to the ceiling, all of which, from the remains still visible, were once ornamented with paintings. At each end of the building was another chamber, with three niches or recesses, and on the other side, facing the south, the three centre doorways, corresponding with the false doors on the north side, opened into an apartment forty-seven feet long and nine deep, having nine long niches in the back wall; all the walls from the floor to the peak of the arch had been covered with painted designs, now wantonly defaced, but the remains of which present colours in some places still bright and vivid; and among these remains detached portions of human figures continually recur, well drawn, the heads adorned with plumes of feathers, and the hands bearing shield and spears. All attempt at description would fail, and much more would an attempt to describe the strange interest of walking along the overgrown platform of this gigantic and desolate building.

Descending again to the ground, at the end of the wing stands what is called the Eglesia, or Church, a corner of which was comprehended in a previous view, and the front of which is represented herewith. It is twenty-six feet long, fourteen deep, and thirty-one high, its comparatively great height adding very much to the effect of its appearance. It has three cornices, and the spaces between are richly ornamented. The sculpture is rude but grand. The principal ornament is over the doorway, and on each side are two human figures in a sitting posture, but, unfortunately, much mutilated. The portion of the façade above the second cornice is merely an ornamented wall....

The whole of this building is in a good state of preservation. The interior consists of a single apartment, once covered with plaster, and along the top of the wall under the arch are seen the traces of a line of medallions or cartouches in plaster, which once contained hieroglyphics. The Indians have no superstitious feelings about these ruins, except in regard to this building; and in this they say that on Good Friday of every year music is heard sounding. . . . This chamber, by-the-way, was the best we had found for our Daguerreotype operations. Having but one door, it was easily darkened; we were not obliged to pack up and carry away; the only danger was of cattle getting in and breaking; and there was no difficulty in getting an Indian to pass the night in the room and guard against this peril. (Vol. II, pp. 283–84, 290–97.)

Désiré Charnay, the French archeological explorer, visited Chichén Itzá in 1872 and again in the 1880s. His *Ancient Cities of the New World: Being Travels and Explorations in Mexico and Central America from 1857–1882* (1887) contains a chapter devoted to Chichén Itzá, including a description of Las Monjas:

"El Palacio de las Monjas," or Nuns' Palace, is one of the most important monuments at Chichen-Itza, and possesses a greater number of apartments than any other. Whether the name is due to this circumstance, or from its traditionary appellation, is uncertain; but we know from Mexican writers that it was the custom among the Aztecs to dedicate girls of noble birth to the service of the gods, on their attaining the age of twelve or thirteen. Some remained there until they were about to be married; some few took perpetual vows; others, on account of some vow they had made during sickness, or that the gods might send them a good husband, entered the Nunnery for one, two, three, or four years. They were called deaconesses or sisters; they lived under the superintendence of staid matrons of good character, and upon entering the convent, each girl had her hair cut short. They all slept in one dormitory, and were not allowed to undress before retiring to rest, that they might always be ready when the signal was given to rise. They occupied their time with weaving and embroidering the tapestry and ornamental work of the temple. They rose in the night to renew the incense in the braziers, a matron leading the procession; the maidens with eyes modestly cast down filed up to the altar, and returned in

East Wing. From Désiré Charnay, *Ancient Cities of the New World* (1887).

Second story detail. From Désiré Charnay, *Ancient Cities of the New World* (1887).

North facade, East Wing. From Désiré Charnay, *Ancient Cities of the New World* (1887).

the same manner; they fasted often, and were required to sweep the temples and keep a constant supply of fresh flowers on the altars. They did penance for the slightest infringement of their religious rules by pricking their tongues and ears with the spines of the maguey plant. Death was the punishment of the Mexican maiden who violated her vow of chastity.

It has been supposed, from the latter custom, that an order of Vestals, similar to those in Rome, existed in America, but the analogy is more apparent than real. According to Clavigero, priesthood was not binding for life among the Mayas. Of the different male and female religious orders, those dedicated to Quetzalcoatl deserve particular mention; their members had to submit to the strictest observances, but in compensation the people paid them almost divine honours, whilst their power and influence were boundless. Their chief or superior bore the name of Quetzalcoatl, and never walked abroad except to visit some royal personage. Thus the Nunnery may very well have been a convent and a priestly abode. It is not a considerable pile, the façade measuring only some 29 feet by 19 feet 6 inches high, while its grotesque, heavy ornamentation reminds us in its details of a Chinese carving. The base up to the first cornice is occupied by eight large superimposed idols, and four of these figures are enclosed within two very salient cornices. The door is crowned with a medallion representing a cacique or priest with the usual head-dress of feathers, the inscription of the palace and stone spires, some of which have entirely disappeared, while the outline of the rest is much defaced. The whole length of the frieze of the north façade has a row of similar gigantic heads, bearing the general characteristics of the ornamentation observable throughout this structure. The Nunnery is typical of the Toltec calli.... The left wing is but 26 feet wide, by 13 feet deep, and about 32 feet high; it consists of three cornices, with two friezes interven-

La Iglesia. From Désiré Charnay, *Ancient Cities of the New World* (1887).

ing in which the same designs are repeated; the first two high-reliefs represent stooping figures, one having his body locked in a tortoise shell, while the centre and the sides of the frieze are decorated with grotesque figures like those of the main façade, which, with small variations, are the same throughout the peninsula. As we have seen in a former chapter, these monstrous masks have been called elephants by Waldeck and others, who wished to claim a fabulous antiquity for these monuments, but the types they most resemble are the Japanese or Chinese. Here, as at Palenque, the upper portion of the wall is ornamented so as to enhance the effect of height.

The main body of the Nunnery rests on a perpendicular pyramid, the platform of which is occupied by a solidly constructed building, intersected with small apartments having two niches facing each other, traversed by a corridor running from east to west of the pyramid. Over this is a smaller structure or third story. The first platform is reached by a steep, broad stairway 50 feet wide, which continues with additional steps to the second platform, where the apartments of the ruined building were but cells. The ornamentation of the first story differs from that of other buildings at Chichen; it consists of small sunk panels, having in the centre a large rose-like device, framed with exquisitely moulded stones. The lintels, likewise of stone, were covered with sculptures and inscriptions now fallen into decay; we could only collect three, and even these are much defaced. In this building are curious traces of masonry out of character with the general structure, showing the place to have been occupied at two different epochs.

This second construction, or rather restoration, was effected with the materials of the ancient building, as is seen in the fragments of sculptured stones which in the later construction are identical with those of the first, save that they were put up haphazard, so that the systematic ornamentation of the older structure is no longer reproduced, but in places a thick plaster coating was laid over the whole. The rebuilding may have been the work of the aborigines, since we know that Chichen was abandoned and reoccupied towards the middle of the fifteenth century; or, more likely still, the clumsy restoration may have been the work of the Spaniards during their sojourn in the city, when the Nunnery, from its elevated position, constituted a valuable fortress. (Pp. 331–34.)

Although his prose in this passage, particularly that concerning the inhabitants of the Nunnery, may give the impression that Charnay was simply another popular nineteenth-century writer of travel and adventure, he was a serious and dedicated archeologist. For example, later in the same chapter, Charnay says, in describing El Castillo:

It was in this temple that the striking analogy between the sculptures and the bas-reliefs of the plateaux [of central Mexico] with those at Chichen was first revealed to us; and since the dates of the Toltec emigrations are known, we can fix approximately the age of these monuments. We know, on the other hand, that the Aztec civilisation was but a reflex directly derived from the Toltecs, so that in some of their manifestations the two civilisations must resemble each other; from all which it may be seen that these monuments are both Toltec and recent. The balustrade on the grand staircase consists of a plumed serpent like those forming the outer wall of the temple in Mexico; an emblem of Quetzalcoatl, a deity common to the Toltecs, the Aztecs, and the Mayas. (Pp. 341–43.)

Charnay was one of the first to recognize the Toltec (Mexican) influence on the later Maya structures at Chichén Itzá and elsewhere.

Augustus Le Plongeon, in his *Sacred Mysteries among the Mayas and the Quiches 11,500 Years Ago: Their Relation to the Sacred Mysteries of Egypt, Greece, Chaldea, and India* (1886), says:

I will endeavor to show you that the ancient sacred mysteries, the origin of Free Masonry consequently, date back from a period far more remote than the most sanguine students of its history ever imagined. I will try to trace their origin, step by step, to this continent which we inhabit,—to America—from where Maya colonists transported their ancient religious rites and ceremonies, not only to the banks of the Nile, but to those of the Euphrates, and the shores of the Indian Ocean, not less than 11,500 years ago. (P. 22.)

17

Later in the same volume, Le Plongeon describes La Iglesia:

On the façade of the building at Chichen Itza called by the natives *Kuna*, the house of God, to which Stephens, in his work on Yucatan, gives the name of *Iglesia*, is a tableau representing the worship of that great pachyderm, whose head, with its trunk, forms the principal ornament of the temples and palaces built by the members of king Can's family.

This tableau is composed of a face intended for that of the mastadon. Over the trunk and between the eyes formerly existed a human head, which has been destroyed by malignant hands. It wore a royal crown. This is still in place. On the front of it is a small portrait cut in the round of some very ancient personage. On each side of the head are square niches containing each two now headless statues, a male and a female; they are seated, not Indian fashion, squatting, but with the legs crossed and doubled under them, in a worshiping attitude. Each carries a symbol on their back; totem of the nation or tribe by which the mastadon was held sacred. Under these figures, are two triangles ⟁ emblems of offerings and worship in Mayax as in Egypt. So also was the other symbol ⬡ image of a honey-comb, an oblation most grateful to the gods, since with the bark of the Balche tree, honey formed the principal ingredient of *Balche*, that beverage so pleasing to their palate: the same that under the name of nectar, *Hebe* served to the inhabitants of Olympus. It is the *Amrita*, still enjoyed, on the day of the full moon, by the gods, the manes and the saints, according to the Hindoos; although it was the cause of the war between the gods and the Titans, and is the origin of many sanguinary quarrels among the tribes of equatorial Africa even in our days.

These symbols leave no doubt as to the fact that the personages represented by the statues are in the act of worshiping the mastadon.

The corona of the upper cornice, that above the mastadon's head, is formed of a peculiar wavy adornment often met with in the ornamentation of the monuments erected by the Cans. Emblematic of the serpent, it is composed of two letters *N* juxtaposed, monogram of Can 〰 . The corona of the lower cornice is made of two characters ⌐⌐ that read in Maya *Ah am*, He of the throne—the monarch. (Pp. 93–95.)

This same volume contains a photograph of the east elevation of the East Wing of Las Monjas complex. The legend for the photograph reads, "Tableau of the creation, from the east façade of the palace at Chichen-Itza." Accompanying the illustration, the text reads:

The creation of the world, according to their conceptions, is sculptured, and forms an interesting tableau over the door-way, on the east façade of the palace at Chichen-Itza.

It might serve as illustration for the relation of the creation, as we read it at the beginning of the first chapter of the Manava Dharma Sastra, or ordinances of Menu; a book compiled, says the celebrated indianist, H. T. Colebrooke, about 1300 years before the Christian era, and from other and more ancient works of the Brahmins. Said relation completed, however, by the narrative of the myth according to the Egyptians as told by Eusebius in his work *Evangelical Preparations*.

Effectively, in the tableau we see represented a luminous egg, emitting rays, and floating in the midst of the waters where it had been deposited by the Supreme Intelligence. In that egg is seated the Creator, his body painted blue, his loins surrounded by a girdle; he holds a sceptre in his left hand; his head is adorned with a plume of feathers; he is surrounded by a serpent, symbol of the Universe. (Pp. 71–72.)

Augustus Le Plongeon, the author of all this, can best be described by referring to Robert Wauchope's fascinating *Lost Tribes and Sunken Continents*:

Who was this highly imaginative, fire-breathing dragon, so cantankerously defying his enemies, both real and imagined? Strangely enough, of this eloquently voluble and widely traveled mystic, who became embroiled in so many verbal and legal battles and who wrote voluminous letters to any who would read them, we know very little of his pre-archeological career. Born on the island of Jersey in 1826—his maternal great-uncle was Lord Jersey—and having attended military college at Caen and the Polytechnic Institute of Paris, he and a fellow student acquired a yacht, which they sailed to the west coast of South America. Off the coast of Chile a violent storm arose. For many tortuous hours they battled the fierce winds and heavy seas, vainly seeking a haven along that treacherous shore. Finally in a sustained roar of near-hurricane intensity, the monstrous waves engulfed the small vessel and as she foundered, it was every man for himself. Whatever can be said of Le Plongeon's passionate mind, his colossal conceit, and his perverse obstinacy, one must grant him also a tremendous courage. He pitted his own strength, which must have been great indeed to carry him through so many years in the fever-ridden tropics, against the raging sea, and he won. Of that entire company only Le Plongeon and his co-captain survived; the Frenchman staggered ashore battered, exhausted, half-drowned, but still very much alive and, within a short time, his old confident, egotistical self.

It is typical of Le Plongeon's stubborn will that instead of returning dejected to France and home, he saw in this new land a test of his wits and his initiative. He obtained a job teaching drawing, mathematics, and language at a college in Valparaiso, and it comes as no surprise to anyone who studies the single-minded intensity of the man to learn that when he started out again, it was not as a timid traveler who had forsworn sailing the seas again forever, as many a person might under similar circumstances, but again as a skipper, in command of a vessel bound for California. Nor does it arouse too much wonder in those who have followed his subsequent violent career to read that this second voyage also encountered formidable storms; as his widow recorded later, "the ship was reduced to a pitiable condition." This was still the era of great risk on the high seas. Frederick Catherwood, the gifted English architect who immortalized himself and focused worldwide interest on the Maya ruins of Yucatan and Central America with his masterly lithographs of the ancient cities visited by him and his companion, John Lloyd Stephens of New York, was lost at sea in a similar voyage from Panama to California and at about the same period. But this time Le Plongeon and his ship made port together.

San Francisco was another challenge to Augustus Le Plongeon. Apparently well schooled in drawing and mathematics, he eventually became City and County Surveyor. He made a valuable acquaintance in Stephen J. Field, afterward a Justice of the United States Supreme Court. But he could not settle down, and he returned to Europe and England. Again the urge to move seized him, and he sailed to the island of Saint Thomas, then to Veracruz, and later crossed Mexico to Acapulco on horseback. "Upon his return to San Francisco," his wife, Alice, wrote matter-of-factly in a necrology, "Dr. Le Plongeon took up the practice of law and was successful; but certain occurrences attracted him to the practice of medicine, in which he quickly made a name for the remarkable manner in which he restored various patients who had been pronounced incurable." Since Mme Le Plongeon, in her fairly detailed account of her husband's earlier schooling, mentions no particular law school or medical college, it seems fair to infer that Augustus Le Plongeon actually had very little formal training in either law or medicine and may have conferred the degrees M.D. and LL.D. on himself. In his writings he invariably referred to himself as Dr. Le Plongeon. When he was later commissioned to study archeology in Peru, he established there a private hospital, where, according to his widow, "he introduced the application of electricity in medicinal baths, and effected notable cures." In Yucatan he is said to have endeared himself to the natives by treating them for yellow fever, having survived a bout with it himself and considering himself at least partially immune to the dread disease.

In Peru Le Plongeon also became interested in earthquakes, invented a seismograph and seismometer by which, his wife tells us, he could foretell the approach and direction of an earthquake, and published articles on this subject in *Van Nostrand's Magazine*, New York. After more travel in New York, London, and Paris, he returned in 1875 to Yucatan, "at the peril of his life," Alice Le Plongeon wrote, "for the war of the races was very active at that time." For over thirty years more he explored the ruined Maya cities of the peninsula, published his spectacular theories, and waged a verbal war with American anthropologists and Mexican government officials, the latter of whom he accused of illegally confiscating the antiquities he excavated.

Le Plongeon went overboard seemingly for every notion that occurred to him or to anyone else. He was utterly incapable of critically examining either the factual or the logical evidence bearing on any theory he wanted to believe. When he found a line across a sculptured lintel in an ancient ruin in Yucatan and noticed some zigzag motifs near it, he immediately decided that the prehistoric Maya communicated by means of electric telegraph wires! . . .

A letter to the Honorable John W. Foster, Minister of the United States at Mexico, dated May 1, 1877, at the Island of Cozumel . . . shows Le Plongeon's mind churning with questions, speculations, and notions of every kind. In the middle of an epistle that must have been thirty handwritten pages long, doubtless composed by candlelight or torch, we find the following passages:

These inner edifices belong to a very ancient period, and among the debris I have found the head of a bear exquisitely sculptured out of a block of marble. It is in an unfinished state. When did bears inhabit the peninsula? Strange to say, the Maya does not furnish the name for the bear. Yet one-third of this tongue is pure Greek. Who brought the dialect of Homer to America? Or who took to Greece that of the Mayas? Greek is the offspring of Sanscrit. Is Maya? or are they coeval? A clue for ethnologists to follow the migrations of the human family on this old continent. Did the bearded men whose portraits are carved on the massive pillars of the fortress of Chichen-Itza belong to the Mayan Nations? The Maya language is not devoid of words from the Assyrian. . . .

The customs, religion, architecture of this country have nothing in common with those of Greece. Who carried the Maya to the country of Helen? Was it the Caras or Carians, who have left traces of their existence in many countries of America? They are the most ancient navigators known. They roved the seas long before the Phoenicians. They landed on the North-East coasts of Africa, thence they entered the Mediterranean, where they became dreaded as pirates, and afterwards established themselves on the shores of Asia Minor. Whence came they: What was their origin? Nobody knows. They spoke a language unknown to the Greeks, who laughed at the way they pronounced their own idiom. Were they emigrants from this Western continent? Was not the tunic of white linen, that required no fastening, used by the Ionian women, according to Herodotus, the same as the *uipil* of the Maya females of to-day even, introduced among the inhabitants of some of the Mediterranean isles?

These words pouring from his pen on that faraway tropical island show how uncritically Le Plongeon accepted any similarity as evidence of historical contact, how he assumed unquestioningly that his own identifications (of the bear, for example) were correct (which it was not), and how, instead of questioning his own theories when he confronted a mass of contrary evidence, he merely admitted bewilderment and walked calmly away from the subject, still convinced of his original hypothesis.

Although he foresaw with ample reason the opposition that his writings would meet, or, worse, that they would simply be ignored, Augustus Le Plongeon rushed to meet his unseen foes with anticipated counterthreats.

If the perusal of this book fails to awaken in this country an interest in ancient American civilization and history, then I will follow the advice said to have been given by Jesus of Nazareth to his disciples when sending them on their mission of spreading the gospel amoung the nations: "And whomsoever [*sic*] shall not receive you, nor hear you, when ye do part hence, shake off the dust under your feet. . ." St. Mark, chap. vi, verse 11—for I shall consider it useless to spend more time, labor, and money on the subject in the United States, remembering the fate of Professor Morse, when he asked Congress for permission to introduce his electric telegraph in this country.

In 1881, speaking before the American Antiquarian Society in Worcester, he said, ". . . since I felt that I was abandoned by ALL, notwithstanding ALL wanted to procure from me GRATIS what had cost me so much time, labor and money to acquire, I made up my mind to keep my knowledge, so dearly purchased, to destroy some day or other my collections, and to let those who wish to know more about the ancient cities of Yucatan, do what I have done. . . ." As a matter of fact, Le Plongeon actually did something of this sort in retaliation against Mexican officials who had confiscated the monuments, statues, and other relics that he found in Yucatan. After his death in 1908, his widow revealed: "Another great statue which he found and hid again, is yet concealed, its whereabouts being known only to the present writer." (Pp. 14–19.)

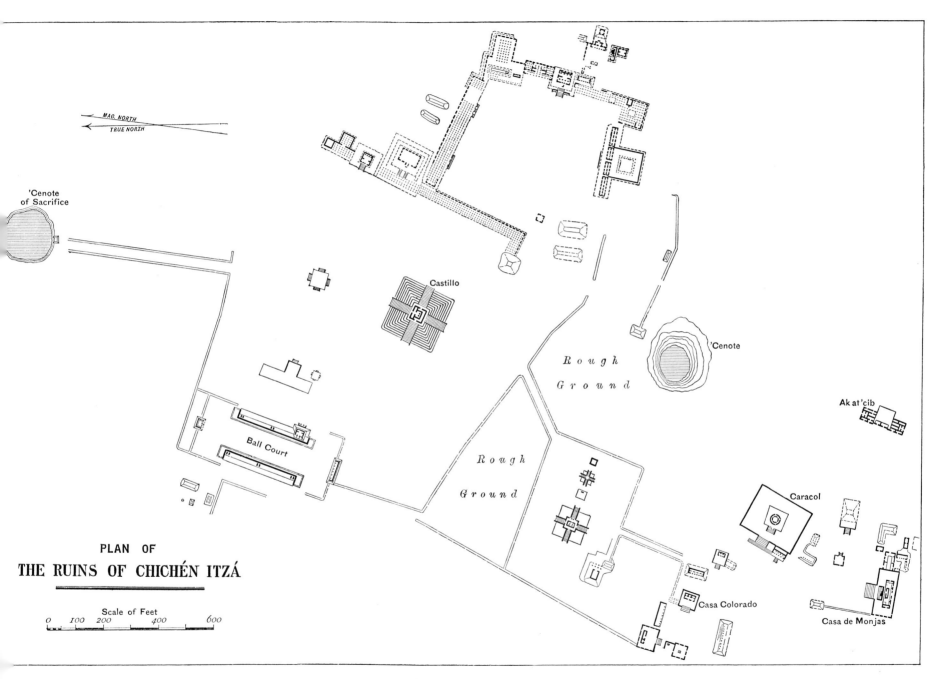

PLAN OF
THE RUINS OF CHICHÉN ITZÁ

Scale of Feet

0   100   200   400   600

'Cenote
of Sacrifice

MAG. NORTH
TRUE NORTH

Castillo

Rough Ground

'Cenote

Rough Ground

Ball Court

Ak at'cib

Caracol

Casa Colorado

Casa de Monjas

From Anne Cary Maudslay and Alfred Percival Maudslay, *A Glimpse at Guatemala* (1899).

In the early 1880s, Alfred Percival Maudslay made the first of seven explorations of Middle America. Robert Wauchope, in *They Found the Buried Cities*, says of Maudslay: "Immediately after graduation, with a 'great desire to see a tropical forest,' he went to the West Indies, Panama, and Guatemala. Later he visited Iceland, and served five years as a colonial administrator in Fiji, the latter assignment resulting in a book called *Life in the Pacific Fifty Years Ago*." (P. 185.)

In 1920, Sylvanus G. Morley wrote, "Maudslay's indefatigable labors, covering many years in an adverse environment, easily constitute the most important contribution to Maya archaeology" (Wauchope, p. 185). In 1946, this time in his preface to his own definitive work *The Ancient Maya*, Morley wrote: "Since Stephens' time many institutions as well as individual students have engaged in piecing together different parts of the Maya picture-puzzle. To mention all would expand this preface beyond reasonable limits, but the three most important should be noted: (1) the English archaeologist, Sir Alfred P. Maudslay, the results of whose fifteen years in the Maya area (1881–1894) were published in the magnificent section on Archaeology of the *Biologia Centrali-Americana*, the first scientific publication about the Maya civilization." (P. vii.)

Victor Wolfgang von Hagen, in *Maya Explorer*, calls Maudslay "a discerning English amateur."

In addition to *Archaeology. Biologia Centrali-Americana* (five volumes, 1889–1902), Maudslay, in collaboration with his wife Anne, published a more popular work, *A Glimpse at Guatemala, and Some Notes on the Ancient Monuments of Central America* (1899). In that book, the authors describe Las Monjas:

La Iglesia. From Anne Cary Maudslay and Alfred Percival Maudslay, *A Glimpse at Guatemala* (1899).

I had shifted my quarters from the Casa Colorada to the building known as the "Casa de Monjas," or the Nunnery. This is a fine structure, raised on a solid basement of masonry, 165 feet in length, 89 feet wide, and 35 feet high. A magnificent broad stairway of forty-nine steps leads to the level top of this basement, on which stands a house with eight chambers. One of the chambers had been filled in and sealed so as to form a secure foundation to an upper story which is now in ruins; but the remainder were in good condition, and made a most comfortable lodging for us. The interior wall-surfaces had formerly been coated with plaster and covered with paintings; but of this decoration only a few fragments two or three inches square remained. (Pp. 202–203.)

Maudslay's work may be called the real beginning of American archeology. Between 1888 and 1915, the Peabody Museum of Archaeology and Ethnology of Harvard University sponsored many expeditions to the Maya area. From 1915 until the late 1930s, the Carnegie Institution of Washington did extensive major work in the field, including large-scale excavation and restoration, under the general supervision of Sylvanus G. Morley, at Chichén Itzá—for example, The Temple of the Warriors, under the leadership of Earl H. Morris; El Caracol, of Karl Ruppert; and Las Monjas, of John S. Bolles. Mr. Bolles' final report was never issued by Carnegie, whose publishing activities had terminated about the time his material was completed in manuscript form. The present work is the first publication devoted entirely to Las Monjas.

While all the archeological work was going on at Chichén Itzá and elsewhere in the Maya area, there was an ever increasing throng of less professional visitors, some of whom later published books describing their "adventures" and even attempting more "serious" subjects.

One of these visitors was Theodore A. Willard, a wealthy American who manufactured storage batteries. In his preface to *The Lost Empires of the Itzaes and Mayas: An American Civilization, Contemporary with Christ, Which Rivaled the Culture of Egypt* (1933), Willard writes:

A. P. Maudslay at work in Las Monjas, 1889. From Anne Cary Maudslay and Alfred Percival Maudslay, *A Glimpse at Guatemala* (1899).

23

Las Monjas East Wing
and La Iglesia about
1910. (Photograph by
Guerra)

24

Las Monjas. From Anne Cary Maudslay and Alfred Percival Maudslay, *A Glimpse at Guatemala* (1899).

Each year's exploration discloses new records, new mysteries, and hitherto unknown cities. A number of reports and monographs, dealing in technical language with scientific details, have been published, but have little appeal for those outside the field of scientific archaeological research. A growing interest has been manifested by the general reading public, and has created a demand for a more popular and readable account of these intensely interesting people and their advancement in civilization. Several of these have been written by casual visitors whose researches were of a very superficial nature, and so contain considerable erroneous and misleading information.

The author of this volume has spent a large part of the past twenty-five years in Yucatan and adjoining territories conducting archaeological research, and has been present at the important investigations carried on in the Itza-Maya ruined cities. In this volume he has made an effort to correct some errors, and to present, in an interesting and readable manner, a record of the facts so far discovered. The writer does not attempt to support any particular theory, of which there are many, but rather to narrate what has been disclosed by excavation, research, and exploration, and to present the facts as recorded by early Spanish writers whose volumes are now rare and difficult of access. (Pp. 13–14.)

So far, so good. But the unsuspecting reader comes upon Willard's description of Montejo the elder in Chichén Itzá:

The size and number of the marvelous stone structures amazed them, it is related, and Montejo exclaimed to his captain, "It is even more grand than we were told! These splendid marble-like walls, while not of solid silver as the natives told us, remind me of the buildings of my native land."

Towering above all was the great pyramid of Kukulcan, now erroneously called the *castillo*. Its nine terraces, crowned with a holy temple, were then almost obscured by the rank growth of vegetation, large trees, and tangled vines.

"There was once the dwelling place of the false priests, sons of pagan gods," the general told his followers, "but we shall soon erect on the lofty temple a cross, the emblem of our true faith. It is

25

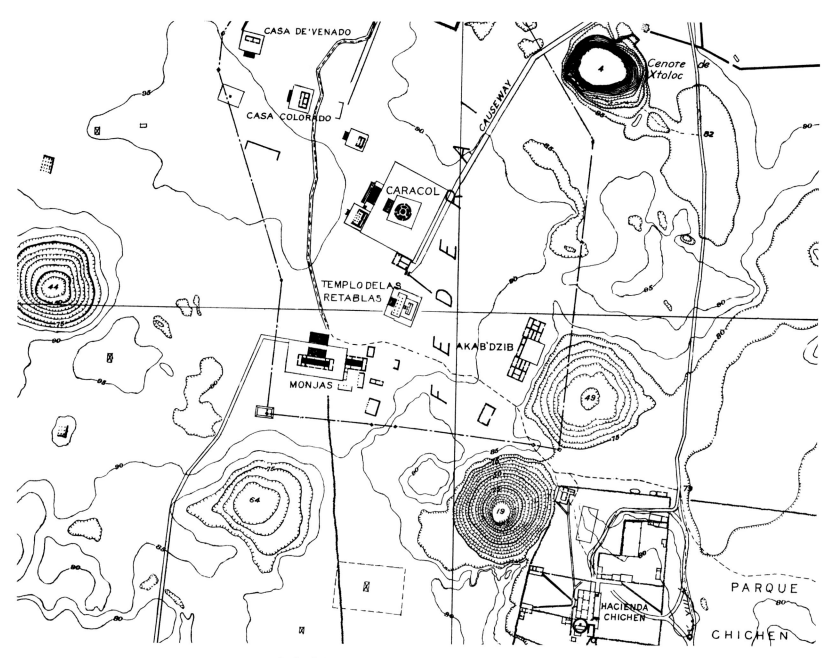

Portion of Chichén Itzá (Carnegie Institution of Washington Plan).

very ancient," he continued with increasing optimism, his plans developing as they do in the fertile minds of all conquerors, "but no older than the dreams of our people who have realized them."

It is related that Montejo erected an altar and shrine on top of the great pyramid between the serpent pillars on the north side and on the exact spot where once stood the sacrificial stone. Montejo's orders, no doubt, caused the stone to be thrown down and broken into many pieces. The bases of the pillars which were monolithic serpents' heads similar to those seen in front of the tiger temple, have been marred and broken. They no longer bear resemblance to the head of the rattlesnake, which they were supposed to have represented. The erection of an altar was probably a clever scheme of Montejo's, who desired to see his soldiers exercise properly each morning. They had to climb ninety-one steps every day in order to attend mass. . . .

To the amazement of his soldiers and the natives, Montejo rode his favorite horse up the broken stairway of the pyramid. This was done presumably to impress the Indians, who were fearful of horses, some time after the arrival of Montejo and his men.

Upon their entry, weary and footsore, the Spaniards were concerned with finding comfortable and safe quarters for the night. The city promised these and more. Montejo knew he had found an ideal spot. He thought the temple on the pyramid would be a good storehouse for the gold they would wrest from the inhabitants, as it was quite inaccessible and could be guarded easily. Into the center of the city they marched, their minds intent upon the wealth this adventurous campaign would yield them.

"Why not?" they reasoned. "Had not some of them just come from the army of Pizarro and the gold of the Incas? Surely the builders of such cities as this had left gold hidden somewhere, and if it were concealed in the huts of the natives, all was well. It would be a simple matter to find and confiscate it."

On they tramped, to the cheerful staccato of their drums, until before them loomed a massive three-storied building with terraced front. In the center was a broad stairway having balustrades covered with many carved stone rings. As the company came abreast of the imposing structure, Montejo called a halt and permitted the men to rest while he and his captains ascended the grand stairway to the first terrace.

"What purpose did this building serve?" the general asked his faithful guide, who had come with them from Tabasco where he had learned the language of the conquerors in a few short months.

"*Quien sabe*; who knows? Perhaps it was the king's palace, or the temple of the virgins," he suggested.

This may have been the correct name for the building, as it is now known as *la casa de las monjas*, the house of the nuns. The soldiers discovered a long building with a high arched roof, on the first terrace. Colored paintings of buildings, domestic scenes, warriors attacking a walled city, and sacrifices covered the walls. Within the building was a room which was very long for its width. On each end there were three smaller rooms. "Just the things," the enthusiastic leader decided. The end rooms were presented forthwith to his favorite officers, while he retained the larger central one.

Ascending by a narrow stairway to the second terrace, they found a smaller structure. "What could be better for a lookout?" he asked. "Here shall be the abode of the captain of the guards." . . .

Nearest to the house of the nuns is a small and handsomely decorated structure, now called *la iglesia*, or the church. Perhaps it was so named by Montejo. (Pp. 106–109.)

Willard's account lacks only a wide screen and color. A much more reliable account of Montejo in Chichén Itzá can be found in *The Conquest of Yucatan* (1936), by Frans Blom, at the time director of the Department of Middle American Research (now the Middle American Research Institute) at Tulane University. In his book, Blom says: "It is most unfortunate for our story that Montejo did not have historians to tell about his adventures, as Bernal Diaz, Salazar, the Anonymous Conqueror, Gomara, and others who wrote about Cortes" (p. 63). How even more unfortunate that Willard made his attempt! And as to Willard's "'Had not some of them just come from the army of Pizzaro and the gold of the Incas?'" compare Blom: "Just before leaving on this venture, they had heard rumors of Pizarro's conquest of the land called Peru, where one waded in gold" (p. 68). Both authors are speaking of Montejo and his men in Chichén Itzá.

To bring this brief historical sketch to a conclusion, it seems

F

L

fitting to quote from J. Eric S. Thompson's *The Rise and Fall of Maya Civilization* (1954):

Other research centers—University Museum of the University of Pennsylvania, the Middle American Research Institute of Tulane University, the Instituto de Antropología e Historia of Mexico, the British Museum, and The Chicago Natural History Museum—have also contributed greatly to our knowledge of the Maya. Research has turned from surface exploration to detailed excavation; from the general to the particular. As a result of this intensive work more has been learned and published about the Maya in the past twenty-five years than in the previous century and a half, with the result that now research tends to shift again from the particular to the general. (P. 37.)

Now, in 1976, some twenty years after Thompson wrote these words, it seems that, once again, research is shifting, this time from the general back to the particular. Undoubtedly the most important work being done at this time in the Maya area comprises that of Ian Graham, who is undertaking the monumental task of compiling in the field a complete catalog, using both photography and the most precise drawings, of all hieroglyphs still in situ, and that of J. Eric S. Thompson, who is continuing his lifetime work of interpreting and correlating these hieroglyphs. (See the contributions by both Ian Graham and J. Eric S. Thompson later in this volume.)

1. ARCHITECTURE: General Description

Las Monjas complex may be divided into four general components: (1) the basal terraces, supporting the main platforms and the outlying buildings; (2) the platforms, which formed the nucleus of the complex; (3) the basements to the superstructures, whether built on the basal terraces or on the platforms; and (4) the buildings which were of one or more rooms built upon terraces, platforms, or basements. Generally a low plinth course established the floor level, and on this the room walls were built.

The basal terraces provided a level area above the irregular surface of the bedrock upon which the complex was built, and functioned as basement courses to the main platforms.

The platforms served somewhat the same purpose as did the basal terraces, in that both functioned as foundations of buildings.

The basements were actually the first, or ground, floor level of buildings, upon which the walls were built.

The plinth course found beneath the Southeast Court and the low walls just west of La Iglesia probably represented the earliest building remains of the site. The nature of the building in the Southeast Court area was problematic. The width of the plinth was too great for a single range of rooms and too narrow for a double range.

A low plinth and remains of a wall were found west of La Iglesia, the floor from the plinth passing beneath the East Wing Basement Addition supporting La Iglesia.

EAST WING

The East Wing, the most interesting and beautiful construction in the complex, was a thirteen-room building, consisting of three east-west ranges of four rooms each and a single north-south room at the east end. All rooms had single entrances, with the exception of the east rooms of the north and south ranges, each of which was entered by two doorways and had a third opening into the east room. The central rooms were entered from either the south or the north rooms.

The construction of Platform 3 buried the three west rooms, and before the construction of Platform 4 the central range of rooms was filled in. After the erection of Platform 4, only five of the original thirteen rooms remained open.

LA IGLESIA

One of the best-preserved buildings in Chichén Itzá was La Iglesia. Except for the probably intentional destruction of some of the sculpture and of the band of plaster glyphs in the interior and the comparatively recent collapse of part of the flying facade, the building was considered to be in excellent condition.

The plain wall zone of the building rested on a low plinth. The upper zone was faced on all sides with well-designed decorative cornices and vertical surfaces. The west face of the building was topped by a flying facade with three mask panels of reused material.

La Iglesia was constructed before the so-called Mexican period, but its exact time relationship to other buildings in Las Monjas complex could not be determined.

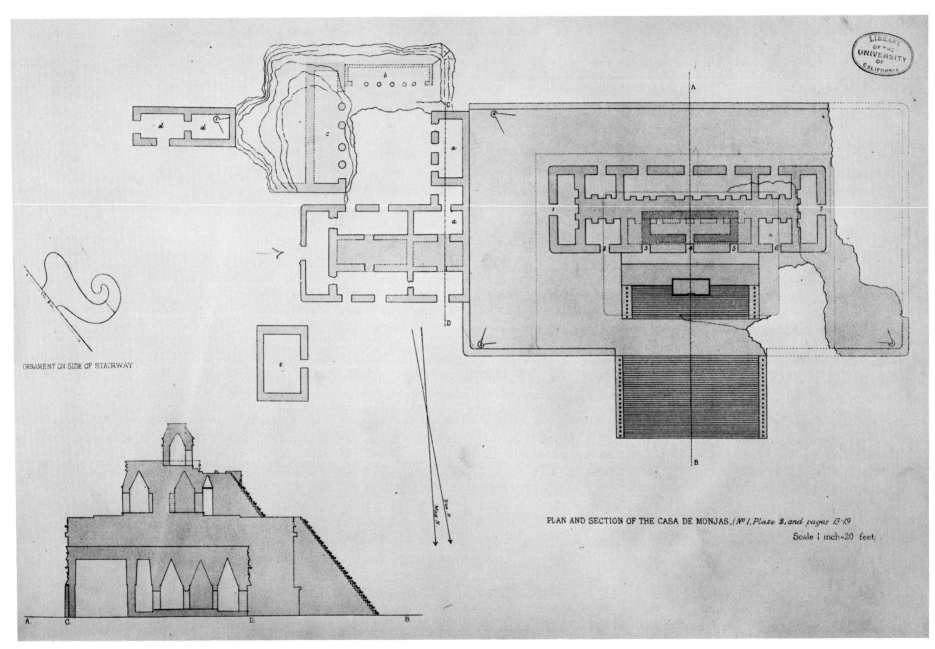

ORNAMENT ON SIDE OF STAIRWAY

PLAN AND SECTION OF THE CASA DE MONJAS, (Nº 1, Plate 2, and pages 13-19

Scale 1 inch = 20 feet

Plan and Section (A. P. Maudslay)

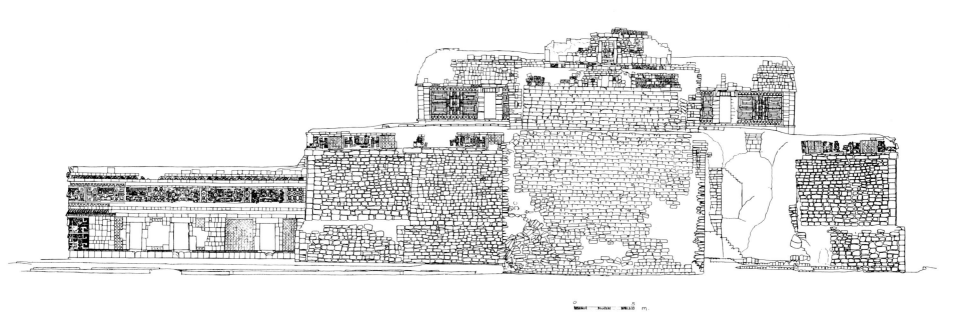

North elevation

SOUTHEAST ANNEX

Southeast of the East Wing was the two-room building called the Southeast Annex, or La Casita. Like La Iglesia and the South Addition, the Southeast Annex retained much the same elevation profile as that of the East Wing. The building rested on a low plinth, like those of the two small buildings, and had a plain wall surface. Only the surface between the medial and upper cornice bands on the north elevation was decorated, and this with mask panels.

The building was probably originally built as a two-room structure but was later added to at either end. Then these additions were, in turn, torn down, or they may have collapsed and were removed. Changes were probably effected in the vault and walls during these alterations.

EAST BUILDINGS

During the excavation of the East Building, traces of walls were found beneath the level of the East Court. These had been built on terraces of the time of, or earlier than, Basal Terrace 3. Those found between the Southeast Annex and the East Building had doubtlessly been built later than Basal Terrace 3; two periods were represented directly in front of the East Building. The earlier walls of this group were supported by the so-called East Court Terrace; the later buildings to the west were built on what was probably an early stage of Basal Terrace 3.

The East Court did not acquire its present arrangement until the Mexican period. The buildings beneath the present East Building may have served to form a courtyard on the east of the East Wing.

33

South elevation

The first building of the group of three forming the north and east sides of the court was the East Building, which had six rooms. The full width of the west facade was occupied by the entrance portico, with four columns supporting the wooden lintels. On the east side of the portico, with two columns similar to those of the entrance portico, was an opening into the vestibule. A doorway on the east side of the vestibule entered a hallway, which, in turn, opened into rooms on the north, south, and east.

The vestibule, hall, and east room were all of the same size and were side by side; the north and south rooms had east and west axes, and extended along the ends of the other three. The north chamber was also entered by a doorway in the north wall of the building near the northeast corner.

All the openings had been covered by wooden lintels. None of these lintels was found, but their positions were clearly marked in the walls at a number of places.

The building had a battered base motif, or talus, above which the wall rose vertically to the cornice. Remains of a decorative cornice motif and low-relief sculpture from the upper zone were found in the debris.

East Building First Addition. A single-room building was added onto the north face of the East Building, with its west end flush with the west facade of that building. To support the vault of this building, three columns had been set into the talus of the north face of the East Building, and beams of wood carried east and west on these. The eastern end of the north elevation was a wall; the northwest corner and part of the north elevation were supported by two columns.

Northeast Annex to the East Building. The Second Addition to the East Building was composed of the Northeast Annex and its continuation along the north of the East Building.

34

West elevation

The Northeast Annex closed the East Court on the north. Its south elevation—the front—was in line with the north face of the East Building. Two east and west vaults covered the building, being supported along the center line by a row of four columns. The entrance had four columns to support the lintels.

The building was unusual in having a talus only on its front elevation. Little remained of the building, so that such features as the height of the spring of the vault were not determined.

The north wall of the Northeast Annex was continued east to the line of, and then south to tie in with the northeast corner

35

Las Monjas from north, 1934 (Photograph by Raul Cámara)

Las Monjas from northwest, 1934 (Photograph by Raul Cámara)

Las Monjas from southwest, 1933 (Photograph by Raul Cámara)

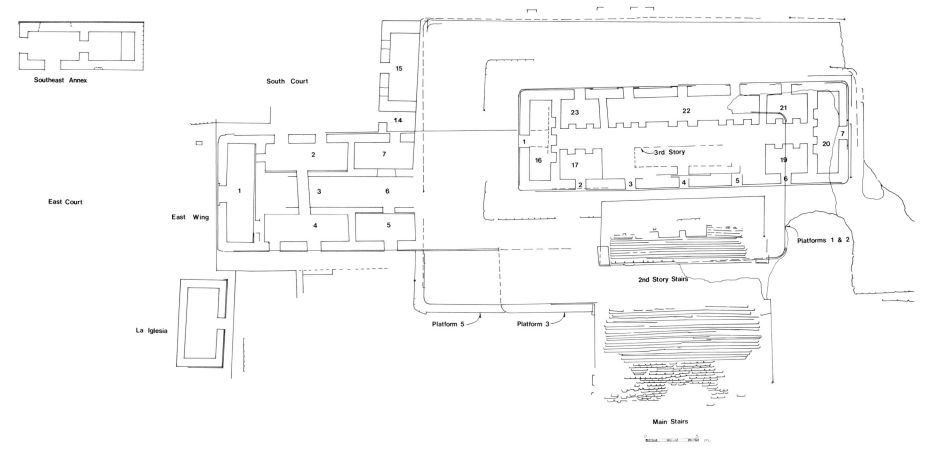

Plan at beginning of work—1932

of, the East Building. This wall enclosed the First Addition to the East Building; the East Addition had two rooms, the east one being L-shaped. A doorway opened out through the north wall at the north center line of the west room. The east room had been later divided into two separate chambers by a small east-west wall with a doorway. At some phase of the additions, the north door to the East Building was blocked in.

SOUTHEAST COURT

The south and east sides of the Southeast Court were formed by two so-called Mexican type buildings; on the north and west sides were the East Wing and its South Addition. The courtyard could be entered by passageways to the northeast and southwest as well as through the East Wing and the South Building of the court.

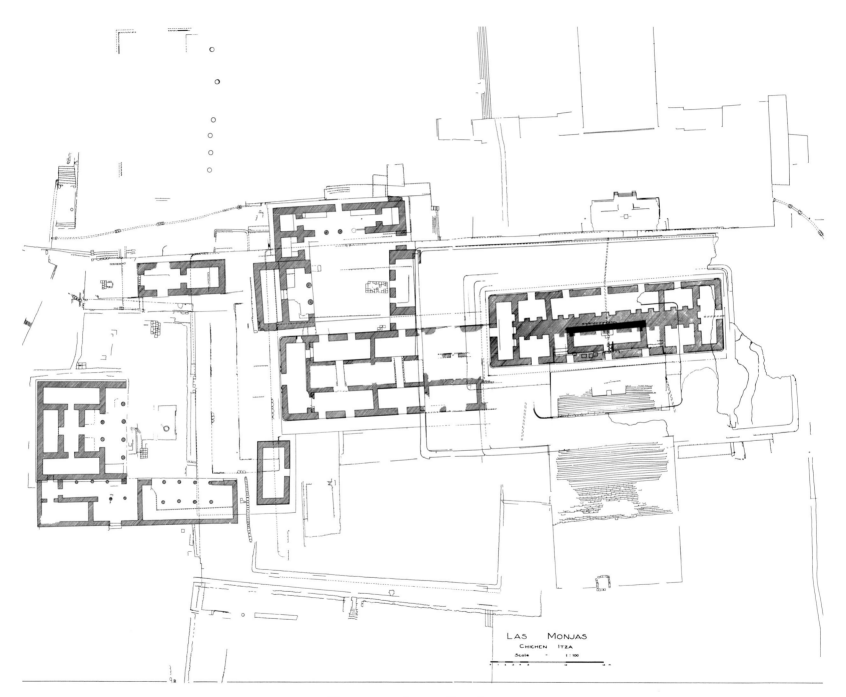

LAS MONJAS
CHICHEN ITZA
Scale — 1 : 100

Plan at completion of work—1934

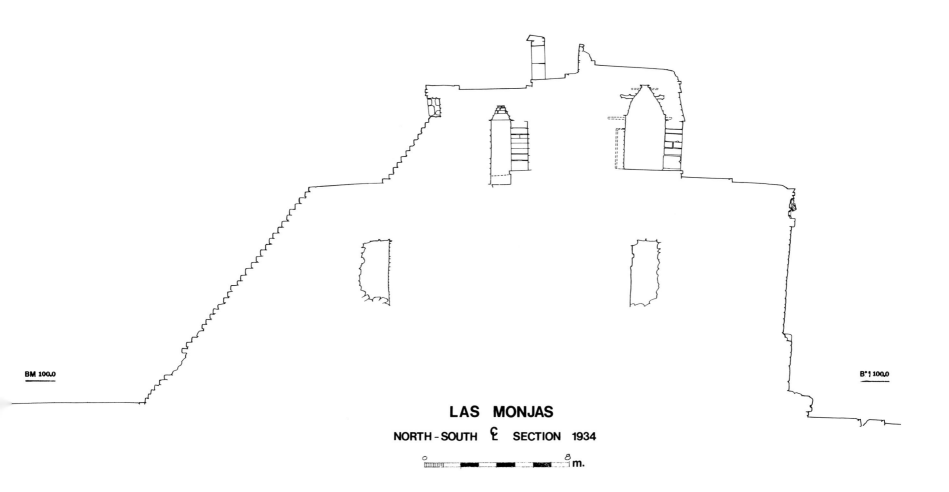

BM 100.0

B°¡ 100.0

LAS MONJAS

NORTH - SOUTH Ⅼ SECTION 1934

8 m.

North-south section, 1934

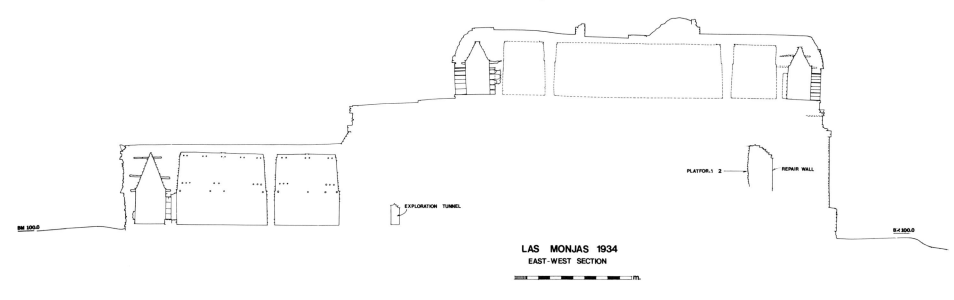

LAS MONJAS 1934
EAST-WEST SECTION

East-west section, 1934

Of the two buildings, the east building was the earlier. It had a two-columned entrance portico on the west, with a room of approximately the same size, but on a higher level, behind it. At first, the west room probably stood alone, the east room being an addition. The peculiar projection to the east from the original northeast corner was inexplicable, and just what arrangement the cornices would have assumed about this projection was even more puzzling.

Part of the medial cornice band along the south wall was in position where it had been abutted by the South Building. Several stones of the spring line of the vault were also still in position. The building apparently had had no sculptured decoration.

The Southeast Court Terrace was built to accommodate the South Building of the court. An L-shaped building on the east connected it with the south wall of the East Building of this court.

A long room, with a three-columned opening, occupied the center of the building. These columns, unusual in that there was an odd number of them, were decorated in low relief, as were

their square capitals and the jambs. On the south wall was a small door in line with the central column; similar doors from either end of the room opened onto two, small, almost square rooms.

Low benches ran along the east and west thirds of the south wall of the large room, the one to the east having its sides sculptured in low relief. Each of the smaller rooms had a bench against its rear wall.

The addition to the east faced onto the courtyard and was similar to those flanking the long room. Sections of the cornice were found where they abutted the East Building. The east and northeast room vaults ran north and south.

A passageway had been built in the space between the west end of the South Building and the south face of the South Addition to the East Wing. South of the west room, another passage was built against the structure, perhaps beneath a former stairs ascending to the roof of the South Building.

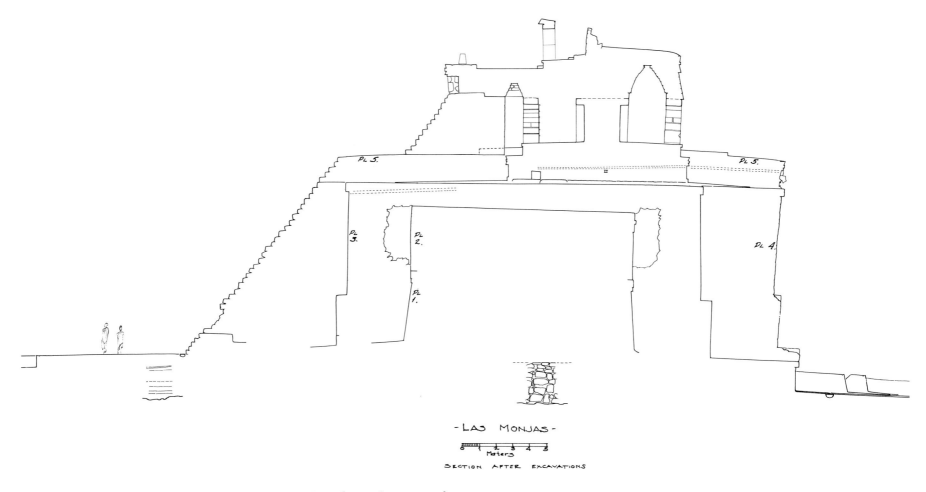

- LAS MONJAS -

SECTION AFTER EXCAVATIONS

North-south section after excavation

NORTH BUILDING

The walls directly north of the Northeast Terrace had probably been part of a building of the Mexican period. At the east end, north of the Northeast Annex, were traces of the north wall of the structure. Jamb stones and a single column base, probably one of a two-columned entrance, marked the entrance to a room with a north exposure. No definite west limit of the building was found; it may have extended east of the explored room.

The plan seemed to indicate that it had been a balancing motif to the structures along the south side of El Caracol, but it

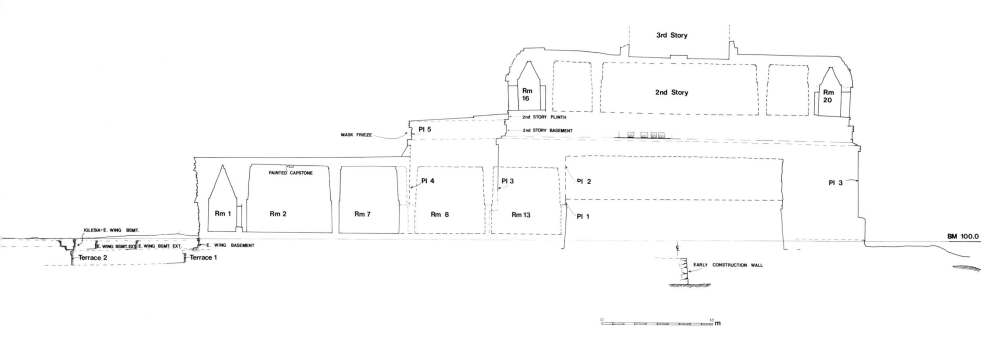

3rd Story

2nd Story

Rm 16

Rm 20

2nd STORY PLINTH
2nd STORY BASEMENT

MASK FRIEZE

Pl 5

Pl 4

Pl 3

Pl 2

Pl 3

Pl 1

PAINTED CAPSTONE

Rm 1

Rm 2

Rm 7

Rm 8

Rm 13

BM 100.0

IGLESIA-E. WING BSMT.

E. WING BSMT. EXT. E. WING BSMT. EXT.

E. WING BASEMENT

Terrace 2

Terrace 1

EARLY CONSTRUCTION WALL

10 m

Longitudinal section, 1935

was of an earlier level, corresponding to that of the sub-building floor found to the north and south of the Temple of the Wall Panels. There may well have been a similar series of buildings at this level beneath El Caracol South Annex.

STRUCTURE WEST OF THE MAIN STAIRS

Remains of the buildings built against the platforms on the west side of the Main Stairs were almost too scant for conjecture as to their use. Since almost no debris from walls and vaults was found, any hypothetical building must have been removed before the collapse of the northwest corner of Platform 3 and the subsequent formation of the large cave in the Platform 3 hearting.

BALL COURT

Against the south side of Las Monjas was the Ball Court, with its axis north and south. The court was of the late type, similar to the large ceremonial Ball Court of the great Mexican Plaza of Chichén Itzá.

A stairs was found on the east side of the east wall. Demolition was so complete on the west that nothing remained there.

Like the large Chichén Itzá Ball Court, this one apparently had had a north temple. Only the remains of the terraces supporting this building were found.

A marker extended from bench to bench at either end of the playing zone, and two plain plaques were set in the floor on the main axis. Another plaque was found on the main axis beneath the first North Temple Terrace. Openings in the end zone walls provided access to the playing area.

The sloping sides of the playing benches were decorated with four panels of low-relief sculpture. There were panels at the north, south, and center lines, as in the large, later Ball Court, and an additional panel centered at some distance from the north end. The panel at the south end of the east bench was missing.

Fragments of two rings were found in the fill in front of the north quarter-point panels, indicating that the rings had been on the walls above these panels, rather than at the center line, as was customary.

The areas to the east and west of the Ball Court had been filled to the height of the end zone walls. Six risers of the east stairs of the Ball Court were buried in the fill, and so were preserved. At a later period, the Ball Court was demolished and the end areas and playing zone filled in to make a terrace level just above the base of the cornice band of Basal Terrace 1. This terracing had probably never been completed, since no surfacing for it was found.

The destruction of the Ball Court during the life of the city presented an interesting clue to the time of the collapse of the southwest corner of Platform 4. Mask elements, probably from the fallen part of Platform 5, were found in the material used to fill the Ball Court; some of the sculptured stones definitely from the Ball Court playing benches were found at the site of the fallen corner of Platform 4.

SOUTHEAST BUILDING

South of the Southeast Annex was a large, unexcavated building. This building had an eight-columned entrance portico on the west. The base of the wall had a talus base supporting a plain vertical surface. Fragments of a heavy-relief serpent design for the cornices were lying about the surface of the mound.

Between this Southeast Building and the Ball Court were traces of other small buildings, extending south as far as the south line of the Ball Court.

SOUTHWEST BUILDING

West of the Ball Court was a natural rise upon which a construction had been undertaken. No evidence of building walls was found on the surface. On the north slope of the hillock, a small cave in the limestone was cleaned in the hope that it was a cistern or a storage cave. Considerable ceramic and some skeletal material was found there.

NORTHWEST BUILDING

Extending north from the northwest corner of Platform 4 was a low ridge, cut through at only one place. No traces of construction, other than fragments of floors and a possible west edge of a terrace, were found. The rise above the terrain level, following what is now merely a stone wall, could not be accounted for. To the north, this ridge tied in with a small mound that had probably been a platform or a building.

BURIAL VAULTS

The small burial chamber built into the late terrace fill north of the Northeast Terrace and the small chamber cut into the base of the east stairs of the Ball Court may have been constructed either at the time of the filling of those areas or later. Each had its vault cap near the present surface. Only a few fragments of a redware plate and some human hand bones were found in the Ball Court Tomb. The Northeast Terrace Tomb revealed fragments of at least forty skeletons, doubtlessly secondary burials, and several interesting complete ceramic objects.

2. BASAL TERRACES

BASAL TERRACE 1

Foundations. The early terrace was built on a foundation of bedrock and rough stone fill. Where the fill on the bedrock occurred, large, loose rubble was laid to the approximate level required, and then more or less a construction level was obtained by using smaller stones to fill the upper interstices and to which gravel and soscob were added. The vertical wall of the basal terrace had been built on this surface, and later a lime mortar floor was laid over the small stone and gravel up onto the lower edge of the first stone course.

How far beneath the terrace edge the construction level was carried could not be determined. It was not encountered in any of the pits dug within the area enclosed by the terrace. In all probability it was used only for the wall and surrounding plaza level, while within the basal terrace the rubble carried down to bedrock.

Rubble. The rubble work of the terrace was similar to that of the construction level supporting its confining walls. The stone used was clean, buff-colored, and undressed. No evidence of lime plaster was found on any of the material, nor were cast-off facing or sculptured stones found, with the exception of the metate fragments from the shaft beneath Platform 1.

Beneath Platform 1, a crude wall with a west face was found. This may have been a task or section wall in the construction of Basal Terrace 1. Its surface coincided with the top of the first

46

basal, and its base had been built on the bedrock. What was apparently a construction level, of smaller stone and some gravel, extended both east and west at the top of this rough terrace face. The face of the wall had only a slight batter. The wall was seven and eight courses high. The tenons on the stones were comparatively short.

No mortar was used in the wall. Only spalls were employed, apparently just sufficient to hold the stones in position during construction. Such a wall was generally never intended as an exposed surface.

Floors. The floor on the basal terrace was found in several places. At the southwest corner of Platform 3, it was continuous from the cornice of the basal to the base of the platform, but did not carry beneath Platform 3 as it did beneath Platform 4. In the Southeast Court, the low plinth course was supported by Basal Terrace 1, and the floors tying in with its sides were those of the basal. They did not pass under this plinth; a pit within the plinth showed its rubble to be continuous with that of the terrace. The floors found here had a dull red color.

To the north of the East Wing were several floors, but none that could be definitely said to have belonged to the basal terrace. The wall remains west of La Iglesia rested on a construction level that may have been the surface of Basal Terrace 1. It seemed more than likely that terraces and platforms were not given finished floor surfaces until the completion of the buildings upon them, and they were often torn out with the building. This would account for the seeming lack of floors to help define the sequences of construction.

Floors secondary to that tying into the base of Basal Terrace 1 were found at the north end of the Ball Court and at the northeast corner of the terrace.

Facing. The vertical wall section of the terrace was built of rough-dressed ashlar masonry laid in lime mortar. The stones varied considerably in size on their faces. The chinks were large or small, depending on the regularity of the wall stone. Spalls were used freely. As throughout the earlier phases of the complex, the masonry was laid horizontally and was kept well to courses. The smaller stones and larger spalls were used increasingly at the top of the wall to give a more or less level bedding for the cornice.

The cornice was of a single course of well-dressed stones. The ends of the stones were set together, obviating the use of spalls.

The cornice stone tenons varied nearly as much in length as did their faces. No sections were cut through the wall, but, where exposed, the tenons were roughly equal in length to the breadth of the face of the stone. Generally these butts narrowed toward their stub ends, as was true of all the facing masonry of the complex. This type of cutting facilitated the lining and tying in of the wall stones. The face of the wall and cornice was covered with a coat of plaster of a deep buff color, which covered the joints and followed the surface irregularities rather than arriving at a plane finish. Most of this plaster was missing.

Only the southeast corner was in position. The stones were better dressed than was most material for this basal terrace. At this corner, the single coat of plaster was in good condition. At the northeast corner, the bedding mark in plaster of a round cornerstone was found.

The south side of the basal terrace extended west to the west wall of the Ball Court north playing zone and was then torn out. Part of the cornice of the terrace was missing, as was part of the top course of stone of the wall. The Ball Court wall was standing to what had been its full height at the point of intersection, this being the approximate line of the base of the basal terrace cornice.

The Ball Court wall was definitely built against the basal terrace. The latter, however, extended only a few centimeters west of the east face of the former; the west face of the Ball Court wall ended north of the line of the terrace. A floor of Ball Court level was found at the base of the wall on the west, and it too passed to the north of the basal terrace line. Either the southwest corner of the basal terrace was east of this, or the floor, which seemed to be the same as that laid to the base of the terrace, was built after the basal terrace was torn out.

The depth to which the mortar-bound masonry was carried was not investigated, but a pit dug into the basal terrace at the southwest corner of Platform 3 revealed only loose rubble near the face of the terrace. Also, in Room 1 of the East Wing, a pit revealed only loose stone near the east face of Basal Terrace 1. From these observations, it would seem certain that only the facing stones, with perhaps a single row behind them, had been set in lime mortar. This would then provide the same shell type of construction as in Platforms 1, 2, and 3.

Stairs. A break in the cornice line, attributed to a stairs location, was the only one in the cornice of the long south line of Basal Terrace 1. The top of the wall here was level with the top of the cornice on the west side of the break; at the center and on the east, it rose slightly above it. At this point, the bedrock extended through the floor, and there were no signs of an attempt to level or cover it with plaster. The masonry of the wall was the same as that of the remainder of the terrace, and had been laid in six courses well to line.

Since no plaster remained to either side on floor or wall, to act as a clue, and since no stairs side wall remains were found, it was impossible to say that they definitely represented the location of a stairs. A similar break occurred on the north face of Platform 3 at the stairs location. The stairs had probably been torn out after the construction of Platform 4, when it became useless, or remained until the building of the Ball Court, when it may have been an impediment in the north playing zone.

BASAL TERRACE 2

Foundation. Where it joined the southeast corner of Basal Terrace 1, the base line of the second was above that of the first. The floor at the base of this corner of the first basal terrace had been covered with only a single layer of large rubble and then small rock and gravel. There was considerable debris on the floor. On this foundation, the vertical face of Basal Terrace 2 was built.

At its southeast corner, Basal Terrace 2 was built on a construction level similar to that beneath Basal Terrace 1, the rubble being clean and buff-colored. The two south corners were the only places at which the foundations for the second basal were exposed.

Rubble. Several pits were dug in the area covered by Basal Terrace 2. One of the most interesting was one just east of the northeast corner of the East Building of the Southeast Court. Below the surface, at a floor level belonging to one of the East Wing Basement additions, a definite change in the rubble was noted, this level being that of the surface of Basal Terrace 2. There were considerable small stones of fist size marking the construction level for the top of the basal terrace; below this, the normal, large, clean, buff-colored rubble was found.

At the bottom of the pit, a riser faced east. On the floor of this, some debris had accumulated before the rubble of Basal Terrace 2 was laid. The step was in front of the east face of Basal Terrace 1, and its top level was on an approximate line with the base of the southeast corner of that basal.

Two pits were dug east of the northeast corner of the East Wing. Both encountered the same construction level at the old surface line of Basal Terrace 2; below that, there was large rubble. In the pit next to Basal Terrace 1, the rubble of the second basal rested on well-packed debris on the floor and bedrock extending east from the terrace face.

48

In the second pit, east of the northeast corner of the East Wing, the basal terrace rubble was of the same color, and was free from dirt and plaster.

In these three pits, the rubble above the basal terrace level was a dirty white, as though it had been formerly bedded in plaster and reused in the basement course fills.

Floors. At the southeast corner of Basal Terrace 1, its floor passed beneath Basal Terrace 2. A floor was laid to the base of the second basal and against the first basal at this higher level. Below the cornice was a later floor, that of the terrace supporting the Southeast Court Terrace.

No floor was found at the base of the southeast corner of the Basal Terrace 2; but since Basal Terrace 4 was built on the same level, it seemed certain that the small stones found here must have represented a floor level. Above this, floors were found which had been built against both the second and fourth terraces. At the base of the cornice band, the Southeast Terrace surface floor was again located.

The floor found above the base of the corner may have been carried out level from the base of the Basal Terrace 2 at its junction point with Basal Terrace 1, in an effort to level off the drop from west to east in the foundation line.

At the northeast, where the terrace was broken away, a second floor had been built. This was above the base of the basal terrace, and had been built after the terrace was torn down, covering the lower course of stones, which extended north beneath this later floor.

Few traces of floors were found at the level of the top of the basal, and most of these were attributed to later constructions. The numerous changes were no doubt responsible for the loss of this surface.

Facing. The terrace, like its predecessor, had a plaster-coated vertical wall with an overhanging cornice band. The wall was practically vertical. Considerable plaster, of a deep buff color, remained of the coat which apparently was applied only to cover the joints, since no attempt had been made to bring the plaster to a smooth plane. As with the first terrace, other coats of plaster were not found. The stones and chinks were similar to those in Basal Terrace 1.

At the conjunction point with the round corner of Basal Terrace 1, the second basal stones were cut to allow closer contact and still keep a smooth plane. Spalls and plaster were used to fill the small remaining gap so neatly that the earlier round corner was indiscernible.

The southeast corner of Basal Terrace 2 was also round. It was only three stones high—the cornice and two in the wall. The lower cornerstone extended beyond the curve to the west. The radius of the corner was apparently shorter than that of the corner of Basal Terrace 1, but since neither corner was completely exposed, this was not certain. The earlier corner had a more gentle tangent arc than the later, which turned abruptly from the south plane.

BASAL TERRACE 3

The third stage of the development of the basal terraces was one of the most interesting. The surface of this terrace was higher than that of the second basal terrace, where it overlapped the earlier. The angle formed at their intersection was less than a right angle, the south line of the third terrace distinctly veering to the south from the orientation of the two earlier basals.

In other respects, what remained of this terrace was much like the earlier. The full height of the wall was not exactly determined, and its foundations were not examined. The only rubble that may have belonged to this terrace, that against the east face of Basal Terrace 2, was the same rough, clean, buff-colored stone as found in the two earlier basal terraces.

Floors and Facing. Where visible, the stones of the wall were smaller than those of the earlier terraces, but apparently had been better cut and laid more definitely to courses. Where the wall overlapped Basal Terrace 2, two stone courses occupied the space between the two cornices. The lower portions of the wall were neatly laid against the earlier terraces, and much of the single application of plaster still remained.

The cornice stones varied in length. Here again, the length of the tenon corresponded roughly to the width of the stone. Few spalls were required along the face of either the wall or the cornice, and a generous quantity of good, firm mortar was used in the interstices between the facing stones and their small stone backings.

A floor of plaster was laid on the level of the base of the cornice, and carried north to where it tied in with the south line of a basement. Traces of a second coating to this floor were found; evidently the terrace had stood without a cornice. However, it was possible that these were only construction floors prior to the erection of the cornice parapet. When this had been built, another floor was laid against its north face, extending north to an addition to the basement. The impression here was that the cornice and the basement addition must have been approximately contemporaneous.

These floors stepped down at the west on the line of the west face of the basement, and then continued west beneath the East Wing Basement Addition and above the cornice of Basal Terrace 2. For a short distance at the west, the floor was lower than the top of the terrace wall. When the cornice was built, the same conditions held; even the end of the cornice parapet was not a finished stone line, plaster having been used to carry over the rough edges of the last stones and down to the floor level above the Basal Terrace 2 cornice.

Later, other changes were made; the East Wing Basement Third Addition was built, calling for a higher floor level on the west of the Basal Terrace 3 basement; another addition to the south line of the Basal Terrace 3 basement involved filling in the area between the two basement courses; then the Southeast Annex was constructed, which necessitated demolition of part of the East Wing Basement Addition and a complete covering of the western end of Basal Terrace 3 by Basal Terrace 4.

The cornice was torn out east of the Southeast Annex; the last trace of the terrace was east of the Southeast Annex, where it was then enclosed by the rubble of the first East Terrace.

No reason was found for the increased height of Basal Terrace 3 over that of the earlier basal terraces. Even the basement supported by it must have had its south line at a higher level than its west line. The only logical reason was that it enclosed or abutted an earlier unknown terrace of greater height. This could not have been a terrace to the east, for at its present east end Basal Terrace 3 was on a level with the cornice of Basal Terrace 2; and only extremely indifferent construction would have caused the sloping of the top up to the west rather than continuing level to tie in with the second basal terrace.

It was possible that Platform 4 had by this time been constructed, and that one of the first or second additions to the East Wing Basement had extended south to the south line of Basal Terrace 2, and then west to connect with the increased height of the Basal Terrace 1, along the south side of Platform 4. This would then have permitted Basal Terrace 3 to have been built with its top courses passsing over Basal Terrace 2 to connect with one of the basements.

This, however, would still have left the area behind the terrace wall at a lower level than even the base of its cornice. Then too, neither the first nor the second basement addition was built of the finished ashlar used to raise the south line of Basal Terrace 2. Either one, on the other hand, may have been only construction phases for more finished basements.

Basal Terrace 4

Basal Terrace 4 was probably built for the support of the Southeast Annex, and was the first to be constructed without a cornice or a cornice addition. Where it abutted Basal Terrace 3, its top line was at the level of the top of the cornice of the earlier basal.

50

It carried the south line of Basal Terrace 2 east, and attempted to conceal the round corner of the earlier.

Rubble. The rubble was similar to that of the preceding basal terraces: loose, with few small stones, and buff to light red in color.

Floors. A floor from the base of the Southeast Annex east end plinth apparently tied in with the top of the wall of the basal terrace. A floor covering the Basal Terrace 5 carried this same level on east. No floor was found extending beneath the plinth of the Southeast Annex, and so it seemed safe to assume that the Basal Terrace 4 was built to support the structure.

At the middle of the south wall base a floor, in excellent condition, was found which passed beneath the terrace. This could have been the early floor continuing east from Basal Terrace 1, the one on which Basal Terrace 2 was built, or a floor as late as one belonging to the base of Basal Terrace 3. This floor was not found at the southeast corner of the second terrace.

In this same pit, against the south wall, five other floors were found. A black floor, in poor condition, was supported on a hard mortar of a volcanic gray color. No other example of this type of floor was uncovered in the complex, and no evidence showed that its texture and color were due to a fire on the floor.

The next floor related to the small, round-cornered terrace found there. This and the floor above it were on the same levels as the upper floors found in pits at either end of the south line of Basal Terrace 4. This floor, of light red color, was laid on a level of irregular-sized rubble.

The next floor was built on small, loose rubble resting on the earlier floor. On top of this was a poorly preserved floor, the level of which was at the top of the small terrace. The rubble below the floor was mixed with some lime mortar, probably reused material from a mortar-filled rubble wall.

The top floor, built on loose rubble, was the same as that laid against the cornice bases of the south faces of Basal Terraces 1 and 2.

At the southeast corner of the basal terrace, four floors were found. One was the floor at the base of the terrace. The upper floor was apparently a continuation of the southeast terracing surface; between, two floors were discovered belonging to the battered north-south terrace found here. These two floors were the same as those found against the base of the small terrace to the west.

Facing. At the southeast were five courses of stone, well cut both on the surface and on the joint edges, forming the height of the right-angle corner of the terrace. This was the full height of the basal, there being no missing masonry here or along the east wall. The stones were set horizontally.

The remainder of the terrace was built of more courses of masonry, generally less well cut and set.

At the tie-in with the southeast corner of Basal Terrace 2, an effort was made to conceal the round corner. The effect was not as successful as at the southeast corner of Basal Terrace 1, since the cornice of the second terrace was not continued to the east. The wall leaned out slightly to permit the lower courses to line with the wall of Basal Terrace 2 and also to allow the upper courses to carry the line of the cornice of the earlier terrace. Considerable plaster was used in obtaining a nearly smooth effect.

The stones used in raising the height of Basal Terrace 2 were apparently laid at the time of construction of this terrace. There were two courses on the earlier terrace cornice, one of which had fallen or had been torn out. These stones were set in a firm mortar and were well spalled. It was difficult to understand how these stones could have fallen away, even with weather and root action, and it seemed probable that they had been taken out at some later time for use elsewhere. Several were still lying just off the edge of the terrace on the upper floor level. A floor evidently covered the top course and tied in with the base of the plinth of the south wall of the Southeast Annex.

It was not determined how far west along the top of Basal Terrace 2 the additional courses were carried. Several changes took place in the area where the Southeast Court Basal Terrace partially overlapped and abutted the earlier basal terraces and additions. Probably an addition had been made before Basal Terrace 4 was constructed, and the later terrace overlapped Basal Terrace 2 for only a short distance to where it joined an earlier construction.

Only fragments of the plaster coating remained, principally in the areas about the chinks where the plaster in the joints had given it better bond. Like many of the single or first coats of plaster on the terrace, platform, and structure walls of the complex, the plaster finish here seemed to have been applied as the wall was built, the mortar from the joint being carried over the weather face of the stone. The largest areas of plaster remained where the stones were more irregular; at the southeast corner, the plaster was noticeably lacking on the smooth ashlar.

At the juncture with Basal Terrace 3, the contrast in plaster coatings was marked, that of the earlier terrace being more intact, finer, and more smoothly applied than on the later construction.

BASAL TERRACE 5

Only the southwest corner of Basal Terrace 5, where it abutted the southeast corner of Basal Terrace 4, and several stones of the top course to the east were exposed.

Rubble. The rubble of Basal Terrace 5 was without mortar, and was buff to light red in color. Few small stones were found.

Floors. The floor at the base of the south line of the terrace was not investigated other than in its relation to the southeast corner of Basal Terrace 4. Only two other floors were related to the south line of the terrace. One was that at the top of the battered terrace with its west face near the junction with Basal Terrace 4. The other, only slightly above this, was the floor of the Southeast Terrace. On this upper floor, a set of stairs of four risers had been built against Basal Terraces 4 and 5.

A floor covering Basal Terrace 5 extended north over Basal Terrace 3, passing slightly above the top of the cornice. Along the east line of Basal Terrace 4, the floor was in poor condition; it apparently tied in with the floor coming from the base of the plinth of the Southeast Annex, although probably as an east extension to a floor that had already carried as far east as the edge of the earlier basal terrace.

Facing. The south line of the early basal terraces was continued east by the addition of Basal Terrace 5, the character of the wall being similar to that of Basal Terrace 4. It was of the same height as the earlier terrace, and otherwise similar, except that the ashlar abutting the southeast corner of the earlier terrace was not as large or as well dressed as that of the corner. Nothing of the remainder of the wall was found other than some stones of the top course. These were smaller than the stones used in the top course of Basal Terrace 4.

The junction with the earlier basal terrace was probably at one time a smooth, indiscernible plastered joint; the later terrace had slipped out of line, and no plaster remained except on the stones to either side of the joint.

The base of the terrace probably extended east of the top course of stones remaining in position, but no excavations were undertaken to determine how far. It was possible that this end had been torn out at the same time that the eastern portion of Basal Terrace 3 was removed, and that the southeast corner could never be determined.

MAIN STAIRS TERRACE

Foundations. Indications were that this basal terrace had been built after several alterations to the levels north of the complex. This was apparent from the character of the material found in two pits, one within and the other outside the terrace.

Along the east line, to the north of the stairs, a firm floor was found on which the terrace wall rested. The north half of the west face and part of the north face of the terrace were supported directly on the bedrock, which was considerably higher here than at the center line of the base of the Main Stairs.

Beneath the Main Stairs and the west and north faces of Platforms 3 and 4, the foundations were on rubble fill. In a pit north of the northwest corner of Platform 3, a floor was found tying into the base of the terrace. This floor and the terrace were supported on loose gravel and small stone, beneath which was large, loose, sienna-colored rubble.

The east face of the terrace terminated beneath the north end of the east casing of the Main Stairs. The floor passing beneath the basal terrace was at the northeast corner of the Main Stairs, but south of this it had disappeared. Where the base of the terrace stepped up twice and then continued south toward Platform 3, only mortar-filled rubble was found, but it was certain that there had been a floor, for the one coming from beneath Platform 3 was at this approximate level.

Rubble. The terrace rubble was not mortar-bound except for a short distance backing the outer walls. The stones used in the fill were not of the clean buff color found in such constructions as Basal Terraces 1 through 5, but were of a dirty white, as though coated with lime. The upper interstices were filled with fist-sized stones on which smaller stones and gravel had been spread to give a surface for a floor. Most of the floor was missing, and black earth covered the surface and had filtered down through the rubble.

The loose rubble of the terrace in front of the stairs continued beneath the stairs at a higher level. It rose to the level of the top of the fifth riser, remained at that level for some distance south of the face of that riser, and then stepped down to the level of the top of the third riser. The outer facing of the terrace, found beneath the side walls of the stairs, indicated that it probably maintained that level to the north line of the platforms. There was no indication that the surface north of the stairs had continued beneath them, the rubble there showing no change in character at that level.

Tracing basal
terraces south of
Southeast Annex,
1933

Like the sides of the terrace to the north of the stairs, those beneath the Main Stairs were backed by mortar-bound rubble. The lower five risers of the stairs, those belonging to this terrace, were built in the same manner.

Floors. The floor found at the base of the terrace at the northeast corner of the stairs did not continue north to the corner of the terrace, and was broken away to the south at about the line of the first step-up in this foundation.

There was nothing left from which to ascertain whether it followed the two breaks in the foundation line. No floor was found where the terrace ended. The floor at the base of the terrace, like that at the base of Platform 3, passed beneath it; on the west side, floors were found to abut the terrace.

The only other floor found along the east side was one that carried the level of the top of the terrace to the east, where the late terrace connecting the Northeast Terrace with the Main Stairs Terrace abutted the latter.

West of the stairs, two floors were found. The lower tied in with the base of the terrace; the upper was built after the area to the west had been filled to the height of the Main Stairs Terrace. The lower floor was also found to continue to the west along the base of the terrace, abutting this terrace, which supported Platform 3, but passing beneath Platform 4.

No floors were found to the north, although they had probably existed both at the base of the terrace and at the surface of the later fill. At the northeast corner were traces of what may have been a floor slightly below the present surface level. On the terrace, the only remains of a floor were around the small, plain stone set on the center line at the base of the stairs. The top surface and edges of the stone were well dressed. The south side of the stone slab rested against the bottom of the first riser, and remains of a hard plaster paving were found flush with the surface on the other sides. The stone was on the approximate axis of the platforms. Only loose rubble was found beneath the slab.

Facing. Except for two large stones beneath the south end of the west face of the Main Stairs, the entire construction of this stairs terrace was of small, roughly dressed ashlar with short tenons. The two large stones did not seem to belong to this construction, although they were in the correct position. The tenon length of these was not determined.

The masonry of the vertical wall terrace was well cut. Some stones with larger faces were used in the section near the northeast corner of Platform 3. The larger stones were generally used at the base of the wall, with the smaller along the top. The east line was three courses in height, while on the west and where standing along the north only two courses had been used. Beneath the west side of the Main Stairs, more stone courses were used because of the increased height of the wall.

The joints were small, and few spalls were evident. No plaster remained on the surface.

There were three breaks in the facing of the north wall. These did not fall at sufficiently regular intervals to mark the location for former stairs. The stones had probably given way at the time of the removal of the stairs that must have existed here.

The lower risers of the Main Stairs belonging to the stairs terrace construction were like the terrace facings in their dressing, setting, and short tenons.

Only a few stones of the bottom step were in place, the others having been forced forward; the upper four steps were far out of position or entirely missing. The entire fifth riser was gone, with only evidence of its former position being found. The poor condition of these steps, in contrast to the better-preserved, heavy, long-tenon ones they supported, was striking.

One reused sculptured stone was found at the west end of these lower steps. It appeared to have been incorporated in the construction of the stairs terrace; but since it was a mask fret element of the type used in Platform 5 and was used where repairs may have been made, there was sufficient reason to believe it to be a later alteration.

The sections of the terrace standing beneath the north line of Platform 3 were not fully traced. At the northwest corner of the platform, the highest elevation of the terrace was reached, with five stones of an upper course in situ. There was no evidence that the terrace here was ever higher, and yet no floor was found at this upper line. The corner of Platform 3 was also missing, and so there was no proof that it had rested directly on this course; but since the level of the base of Platform 3, where found beneath Platform 4, was at this elevation, it was most likely at the same level on the north and therefore resting on the present remains.

Just west of the northwest corner of Platform 5, nothing was left of the upper courses of the terrace; but farther west, one stone marked the west end of the top course, with the long-tenon masonry of Platform 4 on the west and above it. This marked the west end of the terrace, and was the point at which the floor abutting the terrace passed beneath the definitely later Platform 4.

The south section of the east face of the Main Stairs Terrace was complicated by the step-ups along its foundation line and its sudden termination at the south with no evidence that it had carried further. Originally it must have extended south to the same line as on the west, that being the north face of Platform 3, and then probably turned east. It was obvious that if this was the case, it had been torn down before the construction of Platform 3.

Northeast Terrace

Foundations. The Northeast Terrace was doubtlessly constructed after the partial destruction of Basal Terraces 1 and 2, and the debris upon which it rested may well have been that of the earlier constructions. Where pits were dug, the bedrock was found to be covered by a level of black earth with some large stones. Above the black earth and stone, a layer of debris had been deposited. This debris contained stone, gravel, soscob, earth, and particles of plaster, some with sections of light red surfacing. The existence of the floor and wall plaster fragments marked the level as debris from an earlier construction. This stratum passed beneath the base of the Northeast Terrace on the approximate north-south center line, and was found south of the north face but not where the bedrock surface was higher.

A layer of red cancob covered the debris; on this was a level of gravel, soscob, and dirt, all forming a russet-colored aggregate. In this level, the terrace foundations were laid, except at the corners where the bedding was in the cancob.

The northeast corner of Basal Terrace 1 had been covered by a thin layer of cancob, and since this was only slightly higher than the same stratum beneath the Northeast Terrace, they must have been the same. This level was also found above the debris south of the terrace north face on the approximate north-south center line. At these two points within the terrace where the cancob was found, only earth, some soscob, and rubble were above it. The rubble was the fill for the terrace.

From the above, it is apparent that the debris level carried north from the remains of Basal Terrace 1 at the approximate level of its base, and that over this a layer of cancob had been placed or had accumulated. The russet level along the face of the Northeast Terrace was probably an accumulation of debris from the construction of the terrace itself. It is conceivable that the builders had leveled the debris from the demolished north lines of Basal Terraces 1 and 2 and had laid on this a stratum of cancob, which provided a firm, red surface as either a temporary floor or a construction level.

The foundations for the east and west ends of the terrace were not examined, but from nearby tests it seemed certain that the rises in base lines at either end were built over rubble fill and with no traces of the plaster debris or cancob.

Rubble. If a floor had been laid on the terrace, no trace of it was found other than the small aggregate on top of the rubble fill. In the absence of a floor, considerable earth had filtered down through the loose rubble. The stones were a dirty white in color, and showed evidence of having been carefully laid.

55

Northwest corner of
Northeast Terrace
and later stairs

Floors. Along the north face there were as many as five floor levels, all complicated in their relationship to the terrace, to the bench built along its face, and to the wall built on the north. On the west, there were also several floor levels, which were similarly complicated.

Of particular importance was the floor extending north from the base of the third addition to the East Wing Basement. This floor was at a level above the Basal Terrace 1 cornice, and extended both east and west of that basal. It was broken off before reaching the northeast corner of Basal Terrace 1, and the same break occurred within a few centimeters of the south end of the east face of the Northeast Terrace. This floor probably belonged to Basal Terrace 2, and its broken edge marked the line of demolition of the two early basals. It had obviously not been used in conjunction with the Northeast Terrace, since it was below that level, the surface of the latter grading up from north to south, reaching the height of the top of the East Wing Basement. This terrace construction covered the remaining traces of the East Wing Basement Additions.

The drain coming from the rear of La Iglesia must have been just below the surface, and its slope to the north demonstrated the terracing at that place. At the east, there was evidently a steady grade from the base of the corner of the terrace to the higher level at the base of La Iglesia, as shown by the drain and the rising foundation line of the terrace. A similar banked effect prevailed at the west, where there were traces of a covering pavement. No indications of floor lines were found to the east.

At the southwest, the terrace also joined an earlier floor, one coming from beneath Platform 3; as at the east, this floor was below the level of the terrace. The floor here could not be carefully defined, and apparently a later floor following along the west side of the terrace had been tied in with the one coming from beneath Platform 3. This floor either stepped down, like the Main Stairs Terrace on its west, or sloped rapidly to the north, following the line of the Northeast Terrace foundation down to the base line of both terraces, below the base of Platform 3. When the area between the two terraces had been filled level with the surface of the Main Stairs Terrace, a floor was laid over that. These were the only two floors on the west.

On the north, a bench had been built against the terrace face. The bench was carefully examined for its relationship to the floors, some five in number, at the northwest corner and some distance from the northeast corner. The findings were extraordinarily contradictory. At the west, four floors had been built, tying into the Northeast Terrace, before the bench and the single floor to its base had been constructed. At the east, only a single, fragmentary floor passed beneath the bench; two floors tied in with its base, and two floors passed above it and joined the terrace wall. All the floors, with the exception of the lower two on the east, were broken away from the wall to the north. Large rubble had been filled into the space against the wall to the level of the upper floor, which had been repaired in a makeshift manner with gravel and soscob, and it too later buried.

Just what happened to the floors between the two tests was problematic. The top floor must have been constructed at the same time at both ends, and somewhere along the terrace it must have either sloped or stepped down. Apparently the bench was not built as a unit, since the east section preceded the west by at least three floor alterations.

The construction of the floors did not help in definitely relating them from the east to the west. The first floor level above the russet-colored gravel and soscob stratum was similar in either case, being a level of packed soscob and lime resting on small rock and gravel without a definite hard plaster line. At the west pit, the second floor was of plaster laid on gravel and soscob base. The third floor was of lime mortar supported by small stone and gravel. The fourth floor was like the third. The top floor, the only one not passing beneath the bench, was of solid lime mortar and gravel for the entire depth. The second floor was the only one rich in color, and apparently had received a renewal coat of deep reddish brown, for much of this was found on the floor but not bound with it.

West of the northwest corner, the fifth floor joined the fourth, having served only to tie the lower floor with the bench that had been built above it. At the east, the second floor met the base of the bench and extended north beneath the wall of the North Building. This floor sloped away from the bench. Small stone with lime concrete supported the hard floor. This floor had two alterations at the north, beneath the wall. Two floors were found above the second floor, the top one meeting with it about midway between bench and wall, and the intermediate being traceable for only a few centimeters south of the wall. Neither of these floors was as firm as the one they covered, nor was their supporting concrete as clean and solid. The upper floor supported the south wall of the North Building.

The third floor was supported by lime concrete with a well-graded aggregate. The floor coating contained considerable gravel, and was not smoothly finished. No color was found on this level; either it had never been applied or it had disappeared. The fourth floor was the first to have buried the bench, and the rubble used to fill the space above the third floor contained some facing stones. On this loose rubble was gravel and then concrete, like that below the third floor. This had been covered with several centimeters of soft lime mortar and topped by a hard surface that was, at the time of excavation, blue-black in color. Loose rubble rested on this floor, and on top of that was concrete with a crude and irregular surface representing floor number five. This floor extended close to the wall, and then only a line of gravel carried it on. The third and fourth floors were broken away from the wall, with large, loose rubble filling the gap.

From this it will be seen that, in spite of the relationship to the bench, the floors retained some traces of connection from west to east. The first floors were alike, while the last floors were similar in their relations to the wall on the north. In each case, the third and fourth floors were alike in their construction, but there was no other structural relationship from east to west. At the

58

west, the floors were laid close to the lower level; for some reason, a rubble fill was used below the upper floors at the east.

Facing. The north face of the terrace was built of roughly dressed stones with short tenons. There were seven irregular courses to the wall, and no effort was made to break joints vertically. Considerable spalling was necessary, and mortar was used. No facing plaster was found other than that remaining about the chinks. The east and west faces were similar except for the variations consequent to the rise in the foundation.

No evidence of stairs was found, and in view of the ramps to east and west, none may have been planned or constructed.

Additions to Northeast and Main Stairs Terraces

The bench along the north face of the Northeast Terrace was of two courses of roughly dressed stone backed by solid rubble. At the east, some earth had deposited on the first floor before the bench was built; at the west, the bench rested on the fourth floor. The bench had a mortar top, but on the face only the plastering incidental to construction. At the west, the bench was broken away some distance from the line of the base of the terrace west face. The plaster marks indicated that it had ended at the west line of the terrace.

The construction of the terrace between the Northeast Terrace and the Main Stairs was similar to that of the Northeast Terrace. The masonry was roughly dressed and laid to irregular courses. Chips of stone were used to fill the chinks, but no sign of mortar was found in any part of the construction.

The terrace rested a few centimeters above the floor from the base of the Northeast Terrace; both terraces were of the same height at the point of juncture. There was no evidence of a floor tying into the base of the later terrace; the floor covering the area to the north after it had been filled to the level of the Main Stairs Terrace was in poor condition. Some concrete had served as the base for this floor, and the loose rubble below contained dirty white stones.

On the east, the top and base of this terrace were of approximately the same level as the Northeast Terrace; but on the west, the base of the latter was lower than the bottom of the Main Stairs Terrace. At this point, the latter reached its upper foundation level, and its existing top line coincided with that of the east-west terrace abutting it. There had doubtlessly been another course on the Main Stairs Terrace, bringing it to the level it reached just to the south. The intermediate terrace was most certainly later than the one supporting the stairs, but it had a lower foundation level. Unfortunately, no floor existed at the base of either terrace.

Beneath the portal to the North Building, the south line of a terrace was found, with the floor at its base on the approximate level of the floor at the base of Basal Terrace 2. This terrace, with a sloping south face, was parallel with the Northeast Terrace rather than at right angles to the east line of Basal Terrace 2, and so probably belonged to the period of the Northeast Terrace. What appeared to be the southeast corner of this terrace was under the east jamb of the portal to the North Building.

ENLARGEMENT OF THE MAIN STAIRS TERRACE

The next construction on the north was probably the enlargement of the Main Stairs Terrace. The east line of this extended north from the northwest corner of the Northeast Terrace. From here it extended several meters west, with the foundation rising close to the surface over loose rubble. No trace of the terrace wall remained between the northwest corner of the Northeast Terrace and the wall on the north. However, the lower section of the wall stopped at the west line of the terrace, and the remaining upper course continued west at the approximate level of the top of the terrace. Apparently the terrace wall had been torn away when the area to the east had been filled in. No trace of the line was found in the lower plaster floor; but since to the north of the wall the floor passed beneath the terrace, this was to have been expected.

The sequence at this point would then have been: first, the Northeast Terrace, with its bench and floors; second, the addition to the Main Stairs Terrace; and, last, the North Building, the rear wall of which, with its alterations, caused the complications here.

The addition to the Main Stairs Terrace had its foundation line on an earlier floor level, except along the north, where its base rose over loose rubble. The west limits of this terrace were not determined. The loose rubble was white, with much dirt and soscob. The east face was vertical and built of roughly dressed stones, and the joints were approximately in line vertically as well as horizontally. The spalls were set in poor plaster, almost a mud. As in most of the constructions, the smaller material was used at the top.

The northeast corner was round. Here a riser with north face extended east, which accounted for the difference in elevation from east to north faces. The point of transition from vertical to sloping wall was not determined, since only the top line of this terrace was traced except at the north and south.

A definite west line for the addition to the Main Stairs Terrace was not found. The bedrock rose considerably on the west, and then dropped away again. This entire area was filled with loose rubble, considerable gravel, soscob, and black earth that had filtered through from above. No floors were found. West of the base of Platform 4, and north of its northwest corner, traces of terracing were found. Here fragments of a floor were slightly above the bedrock, and on that was a crude wall of rubble running north and south. To the east of this wall was loose rubble, and above and to the west were quantities of construction debris of stone, mortar, gravel, and soscob. The wall was nearly a meter high. The floor remains were approximately on the same level as the base of the Main Stairs Terrace and the surface of the rubble-filled area to the west. This terrace line was west of the modern stone cattle wall running north from the corner of Platform 4, and accounted for the slope to the west along this line.

NORTH BUILDING AS A TERRACE

The North Building, in a later stage, formed another addition to the Northeast Terrace. While only part of the north wall of the

59

building was traceable, from a few remaining stones as plaster marks, the south wall was found standing for a considerable distance. As mentioned earlier, the west end terminated against looose rubble on the line of the addition to the Main Stairs Terrace. On the east, loose rubble was also found, but with no probable reason as on the west. The wall may have extended to the east, or there may have been a terrace here facing west. The full length of the wall was not examined to its foundation, and so whether or not it was a unit construction was not proved.

As evident from the discussions of the floors north of the Northeast Terrace, the wall was built sometime after the upper floor. This floor, like those below it, had been removed so that the foundations could be set to a lower—probably firmer—level. It could not be determined how long this wall served as the rear wall of a structure or what the plan of that building may have been; but when that building was demolished or it collapsed, the rear wall was left to approximately its present height and, with the space behind it filled in, served as a northern extension to the Northeast Terrace. Apparently most of the remainder of the building was removed; however, on the east a bench was left, and the east wall also acted as a terrace. The east face of this wall could not be found, leading to the belief that it had been built against the rubble, which was probably of considerable depth. This would agree with the possibility that the east end of the south wall had been built in and against loose rubble. The manner in which it was built to a depth below that of the Northeast Terrace floors further confirmed this assumption.

The east extent of the plaza north of the wall and east of the addition to the Main Stairs Terrace could not be determined, but it must have been as far as the line of the east wall of the North Building; north of this break, it may have continued eastward.

The wall was built both on and below the lower floor belonging to the Northeast Terrace, as already mentioned. This floor also supported the addition to the Main Stairs Terrace, the small terrace between the Main Stairs and the Northeast Terrace, passed beneath the steps on the west and south of the Temple of

60

the Wall Panels, and was doubtless the floor down to which the small stairs on the north and south of that building had led.

Loose rubble was used to fill south of the wall, above the fifth floor, and up to the level where the wall later served as a terrace. No floor was found here; but since it was the final level, it could have been destroyed by the elements. There were traces of a later floor on the north, notably at the southwest corner of the low plaza where stairs had been constructed, the upper floor here being slightly above the other and laid after the stairs was built.

The stairs mentioned above was of four risers. The wall served as the south casing. No trace of a north stairs was found, although there may have been one, since the masonry supporting the stairs projected somewhat beyond it on the north. The stair risers were built of well-cut stones. The top of the terrace they abutted was removed, and the top riser was built on the same line. Mortar was used in the construction, and remained on the treads.

The northern plaza was filled to the level of the Main Stairs Terrace. Only the top row of stones on the north face of the wall, as it then stood, remained. Slightly north, a later row was set, also facing north, and so forming a similar long step. The north row extended west on the surface of the addition to the Main Stairs Terrace, and then turned to the south. Since the top course of the wall was also extended west, it must have had a similar corner. At the time of construction of the north line, the tomb was built; this course of stone formed a small terrace about its top.

The west line of stone probably extended south to the base of the stairs. The lower plinth of the Temple of the Wall Panels was carried to the south, from a point east of its southwest corner, until it tied in with the top course of the east wall of the North Building. It could not be determined whether this was built before or after the tomb, but the next course of stone west of it was later, as shown by the arrangement where it abutted the other at the south.

Traces of floor were found on the upper level of the north plaza, at the base of the plinth to the Temple of the Wall Panels, and beneath the secondary courses of stones on the south and east. The fill below this floor was of loose rubble containing much reused material, including a large metate on the stairs and a stone incense burner with a scultptured face lying in the entrance to the North Building. The stones in the single course steps were probably all reused material, and two were sections of low-relief sculpture. One of these was from an interlacing serpent band similar to, but larger than, those used as end markers in the Ball Court. This stone was above the top of the stairs. The other stone, west of the tomb, was larger, and was like a similar feather motif fragment found in the side walls of the passage through Room 6 of the East Wing.

East Court Terrace

The terrace and structure found beneath the front of the East Building were difficult to relate to Basal Terraces 2 and 3. The west face of this terrace—all that was found—was east of Basal Terrace 2, with its top slightly higher. From the short section exposed, it seemed certain that its face had been parallel with the other, rather than taking the orientation of Basal Terrace 3; its surface level placed it lower, and so was earlier than Basal Terrace 3. The remains of the terrace rounded over from the top, sloped out, and broke away at the bottom with loose rubble beneath and in front of it. If more complete excavations had been undertaken, some portion might have been found in better condition. Where it was broken away, the plaster appeared to have been rounding off as for a floor. The remains of the structure it supported were, by all appearances, integral with the terrace, making it seem likely that it had served more as a basement than as a basal terrace. Had a floor carried west from the broken line of plaster, it could easily have connected with the top of Basal Terrace 2, the slope being so gradual. This would assume that the area east of Basal Terrace 2 had been filled in, sloping off to the east to the level of the bedrock. On this, a building with a basement course and small plinth was built; the remains of these were found just west of the East Building. Further excavations might well have clarified this point.

Clean, buff-colored rubble of uniform size filled the area in front of and beneath the bottom edge of the terrace. The hard, light red plaster finish was rounded over the top corner and onto the plinth and wall of the structure.

East Building Terraces

The East Building and its supporting terraces were among the later constructions of the complex. The two terrace additions to the east were later than the East Building Terraces. Since there was the possibility that the earlier of the two had been constructed along with the Southeast Building Terrace, it followed that that building may have been later than the East Building.

After the area east of Basal Terrace 2 had been filled to the level of the floor of the building remains on the East Court Terrace, additions and structures were built. This set of structures were earlier than the East Wing Basement Addition upon which La Iglesia rested, but, unfortunately, only a few fragmentary traces of the walls remained. Their floor level was higher than the top of the Basal Terrace 2 east cornice, a plinth course aiding the transition. The buildings were later torn down, and the floor covered by debris and surmounted by a firm, dull red floor, this bringing the surface to the level of the top of the East Wing Basement Additions. It was upon this floor level that the plinth along the front or west face of the East Building was built. This floor broke away on the south side, east of the southwest corner of the building, and so from here east the plinth was higher. It became, as it were, a basal terrace. The foundations for the terrace walls and the fill were of loose rubble, with earth and mortar debris in some places.

Only five stones, somewhat dislocated near the southwest corner, remained to mark the line of the west plinth. They rested on the dull red floor. The remainder of the west line was defined only by the break of the floor of the East Building.

On the south, the first stone of the plinth was east of the front of the building and near the building base; the remainder of the plinth to the southwest corner had disappeared. These stones were rough-faced and irregular in line. This single course rested on the dull red floor, and carried east to where the floor broke away east of the west face of the building. Here the wall foundation stepped down and then graded down even more on its southeast corner. No floor was found at the base of this terrace portion of the south line—only debris and rubble.

The ashlar had been roughly dressed on face and edges. Spalls were found in the chinks, but there was no trace of plaster either in the joints or on the surface. The southeast corner was built of two well-dressed stones. The south line was near the southeast corner of the building, and curved slightly outward between there and the west corner.

All the East Building Terrace walls were vertical.

The east line of the terrace began east of the southeast corner of the building, and extended in a nearly straight line north to its northeast corner northeast of the building. The masonry wall was irregular, with some smooth and some rough stones. Traces of a floor connecting with the terrace base were found near the northeast corner, with only fragments of mortar and soscob marking the level.

The north line was exposed at only one point other than at the northeast corner—just east of the northwest corner of the building. The terrace was covered by the floor of the addition to the East Building. Along the north, the terrace apparently remained nearly parallel to the building. No plaster was found to have been used in the construction. Since no floor was found at the base of the northwest portion of the terrace, the position relative to the floor from the west could not be determined, although the base here was lower than that floor and at the level of the floor on the north side of the early building beneath the entrance to the East Building.

To the south and east, later terracing to the level of the floor in front of the building was undertaken; the plinth course carried around these two sides, with the new floor, also a dull red, laid to its base. The plinth angled off to the northeast after passing the north line of the East Building. The loose rubble fill supporting

this plinth and built against the East Building Terrace was probably confined by a terrace wall, no traces of which were found, and possibly a late alteration of Basal Terrace 5. It could have been the first East Terrace, except for the sequence as shown where that tied with the east plinth. There was the ever-present possibility that minor changes had occurred which altered the apparent order of construction.

EAST TERRACES

The round northeast corner of the first of the East Terraces was east and north of the southeast corner of the East Building. This corner was built on a loose rubble foundation which rose rapidly to the west to the level of the base of the outer East Building plinth. Only a single course of stone marked the west part of the north face, and it is possible that the terrace had at some stage been torn away here, this single course being a later, makeshift connection with the plinth. If so, the north line of the terrace may have originally continued west to the east face of the East Building Terrace, and so would have been the terrace upon which the outer south plinth of the East Building was built.

The north line was the only one to be approximately orientated with the complex. The first section at the north end of the east face ran somewhat west of south from the northeast corner; the remainder extended more to the southwest. The foundation line dropped rapidly from the north to south. Complete excavation of this terrace was not undertaken, and so the exact south extent was not determined. It was exposed east of, and on a line with, the south face of the Southeast Annex. At this point, a later vertical wall abutted it.

The terrace was built on a loose rubble foundation, and was filled with similar material. A red floor in fairly good repair extended east from the base of the terrace; on the terrace was the bright red floor of the East Building plinth. No trace of the surfacing floor was found within several meters of the terrace edge, but this was to be expected since even the top course of the terrace had disappeared.

The wall facing was made of approximately square rough-dressed ashlar. Large chinks had been filled with spalls, but no trace of plaster remained either in the joints or on the surface. The face had the appearance of having been constructed with as much regard for vertical as for horizontal jointing.

The second terrace construction of the east series was the line, with south face, extending east from just south of the northeast corner of the first East Terrace. At its east end, it appeared to abut the remains of another terrace of nearly the same orientation, the former rounding somewhat to the north to meet the latter, which may possibly have been an earlier structure. The construction was like that of the first East Terrace. Remains of a floor tied in with its base, although nothing was left of the surface of the terrace. The terrace with which it connected on the east was no more than a rough line of poorly dressed stones.

A stairs of three risers was built into the recess at the junction of the east-west and north-south terraces. The stairs was built against the former, the top of the terrace serving as a fourth riser, with the first East Terrace as a stairs wall on the west. The original east line of the steps could not be determined, nor was there any trace of an east casing. The risers were of rough-dressed ashlar.

The outer East Terrace was the last extension uncovered on the southeast, and there was no evidence of further construction. The terrain sloped to the level of the base of this terrace, and the material found against it was apparently the debris from its missing top courses and fill.

The north end of this terrace was east of the East Building and in front of the earlier East Terrace. Only a single course remained at the north, where it must have abutted the second East Terrace. The foundation dropped to the south, as did that of its predecessor. The original top line must have had some step-down or incline, and at the south may well have been lower than the base at the north.

Somewhere east of the Southeast Annex there must have been a break in the surface. This could be seen from the position of the long line of stairs continuing east from the south line of the early basal terraces and from the wall or terrace built against the southern exposed portion of the first East Terrace. Traces of a floor were found at the base of this wall, but to the north there was no change in the rubble fill against the East Terrace. The entire terrace may have turned west at an unexposed intermediate point and then later have been extended south; or perhaps only a part of the top of the terrace was extended west, while the base continued south. This would then permit, first, the building of the fragmentary terrace found at the south end of the first of the east terraces and, then, the construction of the long, low stairs with a fill to the north of them to the presumed east-west terrace.

The outer East Terrace continued south beyond the excavated area, although, where last exposed, only one course existed. It doubtlessly enclosed the east stairs to the Southeast Building, for the rubble there was definitely that of construction rather than debris.

The face of the terrace at the north was badly preserved and was apparently also of poorer construction than that to the south. At the latter location, the ashlar, though roughly hewn, was fairly uniform in size. Spalls were used freely in the chinks, and traces of plaster were also found.

The fill was of loose rubble, with some reused building stone. At the south, there was evidence of mortar having been used in binding the face to the beginning of the backing. The fill was apparently laid carefully in sections, and strips supported by battered walls of rubble were raised against each other from the buried terraces outward until the last section, needing a finished face with some mortar binder, was laid. The rubble was uniform.

The area east of this terrace was covered with debris of various kinds, most of which was probably from the collapse of the upper courses of the terrace.

SOUTHEAST TERRACE

The area south of the basal terraces and east of the Ball Court was considerably filled in and changed by the construction of a late terrace and its ramifications. The floor level at the base of Basal

Terrace 5, if it had continued on its indicated slope to the east, would have been higher than the foundation of the Southeast Terrace. Apparently an earlier terrace wall had existed, at least in the region southeast of the Southeast Annex. This must have been an extensive terrace, for the floor line was found at many places along the length of the basal terraces. Whether the terrace was continuous or not was not determined, but it extended south under the Ball Court walls. It may well have been buried and was still standing west of the later terrace wall.

The Southeast Terrace was probably built after the first East Terrace, with the area north of the stairs covering the corner, or remains of the corner, of the latter. The terrace wall on the east was slightly higher than the all-over level to its west; at first, only a small east section was filled to this depth, the west limit being east of the southeast corner of the Southeast Annex. Here was a north-south battered terrace. The base of this step was slightly above the earlier floor at the base of Basal Terraces 4 and 5; but since the floor was level to the west compared with the slope of the lower floor, the two converged and met in the vicinity of the southeast corner of Basal Terrace 1. The supporting basement for the Southeast Building was probably built with the Southeast Terrace. It was exposed south of Basal Terrace 4, where it had the same foundation level as the low north-south wall but with its top stood above the full height of the wall.

One other trace of a construction was found on this floor level—a vertical wall with a round corner, probably the west end of some small terrace built against Basal Terrace 4.

Another floor level was laid along the south side of Basal Terraces 2 and 4. The small terrace at the southwest corner of the Southeast Annex was probably built at the same time as the floor, and must have served as a stairs landing, the stairs having led from its east face. No floor was found along the south side of this construction; at its southwest, two courses of the wall were gone. It is possible that the construction was done over sloping loose stone (embutito); then too, during alterations, the floor and even the lower courses of the wall could have been torn out. The fact

64

that the upper courses of the southwest corner were still in position mattered little, for they were above an upper floor level and may have been rebuilt.

Only one other change appeared before the entire area east of the Ball Court was filled to the level set by the east line of the terrace—a floor was found south of the Southeast Annex and against Basal Terrace 4 at the level of the top of the small terrace section there.

This, the fifth floor from below encountered at this location, was in poor condition. It carried south and east from the small terrace. No counterpart was found in any of the other tests.

The bringing of the area east of the Ball Court to the height set by the east wall of the South Terrace was accomplished by the construction of a battered west face and filling behind this with loose rubble topped with a mortar paving. This terrace line was east of the lower east stairs of the Ball Court—which, however, may not have existed at the time this terrace was built.

This west side of the terrace was exposed at only two places—on lines with the north and south ends of the Ball Court Stairs—and was of different character in each test. It is conceivable that the north section had turned east, probably on a line with the south end of the Southeast Building, and that the south section was an extension of this. The north end probably abutted Basal Terrace 1 below the base of the later west stairs to the Southeast Court.

The areas west of this line were not filled in to the Southeast Terrace level until after the construction of the Ball Court.

The order of the construction of the east face of the terrace and its stairs was not determined.

Perhaps the terrace supporting the stairs may have been constructed before the Southeast Building Terrace and the stairs, and that its surface level was at the base of the four steps and the drain opening. If so, it could even have served as the limit for the floors at the base of the basal terraces. The only doubtful point in this assumption was that it was a battered terrace as opposed to the vertical terraces of that period of the complex. Its orientation

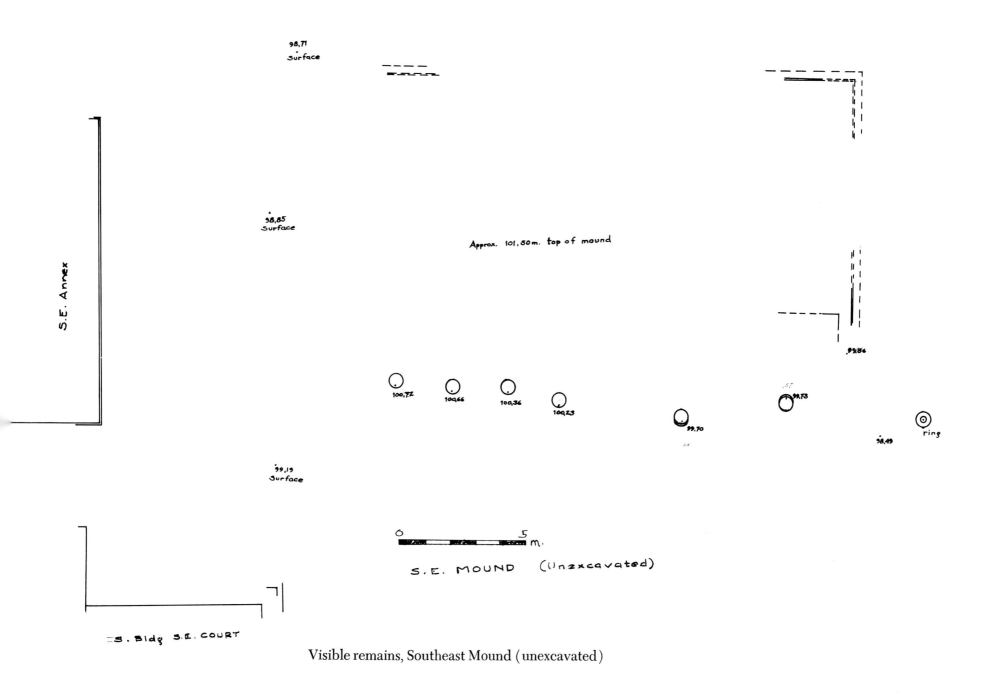

Visible remains, Southeast Mound (unexcavated)

was also at variance with the basal terrace. These two points could of course be disregarded simply because it was an outlying construction to which no architectural or engineering worth was attached, with the simplest of walls sufficing.

This terrace was of crude construction of roughly dressed ashlar. Large chinks were a result of the rough edges of the stones, and these were filled with spalls and mortar. No evidence of a plaster finish was seen.

The terrace was built in courses, and the vertical joints were broken. The heightening of the terrace, if it was a separate undertaking, was built like the lower section except south of the upper stairs. Here it acted as a parapet, and was vertical. The masonry was like the rest. These stones all had short tenons.

The Southeast Building Terrace was built west of the other terrace and, like the stairs abutting it, on a level higher than the foundation line at the southeast corner of the earlier terrace. This fact tended to substantiate the belief that they had been built at different times. Ten courses of wall remained, probably the full height, and the vertical joints were mostly in line, rather than staggered. The masonry was roughly cut and had much spalling for bonding. Except for the greater tendency to align vertical joints, the two constructions were similar.

The stairs was apparently built at the same time as the parapet on the east and the terrace on the west. The floors were in too poor condition for determination of relationships.

Ten risers of the south stairs remained. There may have been another riser, depending on whether it was carried to the full height of the terrace. This stairs was also at 45 degrees, and was built over the first terrace and abutted the second. There was no trace of an east stairs parapet. Either the risers above the seventh had been added when the area south of the northern stairs was built, or the entire stairs replaced an earlier one which had been torn away when it was planned to ascend in one rather than two sets of stairs. The stones for the risers were better cut than was the terrace masonry, and were fairly smooth on end and top edges.

66

Mortar was used in building the steps, but only that in the masonry remained and was in poor condition.

It was obvious that since the Southeast Building Terrace was only three courses in height between the two sets of stairs, it could not have been built before the east construction. Either they had been built at the same time, or the Southeast Building Terrace was the later.

As previously mentioned, the north-south line east of the southeast corner of the Southeast Annex and the north basal terrace of the Southeast Building were probably the early limits of the upper portion of the Southeast Terrace. They both had sloping faces and like the east face, where it passed over the earlier terrace, were three stone courses high. Mortar was used in the construction, and traces of plaster remained on the roughly dressed ashlar, the dull red surfacing carrying over the top, out over the step, and down to the floor. A later, light red floor had been laid above this floor.

The north line of the Southeast Building Terrace was in less good condition; no mortar was present, and the top line had broken off. It was built of roughly dressed ashlar laid in courses.

The remains of the round-cornered terrace south of the Southeast Annex and against Basal Terrace 4 were of a vertical section. This terrace apparently rested on the same level as the Southeast Building terracing, the two light red floors from the base of the step also tying into the base of this terrace. The south line of the terrace was not traced. The construction resembled that of the basal terraces far more than it did the small, rough, square-faced masonry of the later outlying battered terraces. Some plaster remained on its surface. There were remains of a floor passing above it, and so it was possible that it had been higher but had been torn down to below this later floor level.

The small battered terrace south of the southwest corner of the Southeast Annex was built at the time of the upper floor. The southeast corner of this small terrace was covered by the remains of the floor level at the line of the base of Basal Terrace 2 cornice, the floor level of the surface of the Southeast Terrace when completed, while the face and southwest corner rested on this floor. Part of the south top line was represented by a vertical row of stones on this floor, while the west section was apparently homogeneous with, and battered like, the remainder of the terrace. On the east, below the floor line, part of the terrace was missing, with rubble of the terrace filling the void. There had probably been a stairs at this position. Apparently several changes had taken place. The west end must have been removed to floor line and then rebuilt after the upper floor was laid. The east end was probably also built to the new elevation, but was torn out again for an alteration involving the use of the vertical line of stone.

The orientation of the terrace was somewhat different from the line of the basal terraces, its southwest corner being closer to Basal Terrace 2 than was its southeast corner. The masonry was much like that used in the other battered terraces, and was set in course. Mortar was used in the construction; no surface plaster remained, and there was no trace of a top paving. A row of stones facing south was all that remained on the construction, and these had the same top elevation as the southwest corner.

The north section of the final west development before the Ball Court resembled the east terraces. This was a battered wall of poorly dressed ashlar laid in horizontal courses. The south test exposed a stepped terrace, only the lower section of which was battered; it was built of three courses of rather well-dressed ashlar. The upper section was vertical, built of two courses of large, well-dressed stones. Traces of a floor were found on the lower bench tying in with the base of the upper, and there were signs of there having been a floor carrying east from the top of the vertical section.

Where the rubble was exposed, it was without mortar, but no more thorough examination was undertaken, except in the pits along the south line of the basal terraces.

The final floor level of the area was at roughly the level of the bottom of the cornices of the basal terraces, and had been paved. What remained varied from light to dull red in color.

The drain which emptied out through the terrace to the east was traced to where it passed beneath the southeast corner of the Southeast Court Terrace. It was apparently built on the upper of the two floor levels associated with the early phases of the Southeast Terrace, and was a double row of roughly dressed stones set facing one another, capped by small slabs of similarly trimmed stone. No mortar was found in the construction, although lime and mortar debris indicated that it may have been used. How much further west the drain carried could not be determined, but it was too high where last exposed to be of any use in serving the Ball Court north playing area. Its slope was approximately 2 percent, and since it followed a floor line it might be assumed that the builders had also provided for drainage to the surfaces of their terraces by sloping them.

SOUTHEAST COURT TERRACES

For the support of the South Building of the Southeast Court, a terrace was built against the east end of the south line of Basal Terrace 1 and upon the surface of the Southeast Terrace. On the south and east, the plinth for the building was the top course of the battered terrace; on the west, it was slightly away from the building and sloping, as on the south and east.

The surface of the terrace was at the top line of the cornice of Terrace 1 as heightened after the construction of Platform 4, while its foundation was the paving of the Southeast Terrace, which lay along the bottom of the cornice of the basal terrace. At the east, the upper course, which was the building plinth, carried over earlier basal terraces to the first plinth of the East Building. Loose, red-brown rubble was used for the fill. The stones were uniform in size, except toward the top, where a smaller level and then gravel were laid as a foundation for the building and the mortar floor.

The two corners of the terrace were both right-angled, and only one corner of the series of additions was round. The west

67

Stairs and terraces south of Southeast Court

end was vertical, perhaps made so intentionally to emphasize the stairs which was built here. The terrace facings were of three and four courses of rough-dressed stone.

A large X, similar to those used in the East Wing Basement decorative course, was employed as an ordinary building stone in the south face. Some attempt was made to keep in courses, but this was probably more because of the method of laying a first, then a second row, and so on, rather than of a desire for appearance. In this wall, the stones were so varied in size that at the east end of the south face only three were used to attain the same height to which four courses were employed slightly to the west.

All the stones had large chinks, and spalls were used freely. The faces were set in mortar with a solid rubble backing, the depth of which was not determined. No facing plaster remained. The cornerstones were especially cut, fairly well dressed, and generally larger, but no better set, than the wall stones. The top course, on both the southeast and the southwest, was missing.

In the stairs on the west, five vertical risers were used. As usual, the stairs stones were better cut and better set than those of the terrace walls. Only portions of the top three risers were missing. The coping top face was only a few centimeters above the line of the steps. The four stones of the south coping remained, although a little out of position, but only the lower two stones of the north coping were found. These stones were better finished than the terrace, and required no spalls in setting.

A second stairs was built against the south face of the terrace on a line with the south central door of the South Building, and was approximately the same width as the west stairs. No traces of casings were found—they had probably never existed. Unlike the west stairs, the south stairs was built against the terrace rather than as a part of it. The stones were well cut and set in mortar against solid masonry. Several stones of the stairs east end wall remained.

Before further additions at the southwest were made, part of the plinth north of the building had been widened, and then later the level of the courtyard was raised to the height of the plinth, with the west plinth course extending north across the gateway to act as the west barrier for this fill. Only two stones, set vertically on the south line just west of the southwest corner of the original plinth, remained from this addition.

Work then continued at the southwest with a terrace having vertical sides and stairs on the east. The west end of this addition was in line with the west end of the Southeast Court Terrace. Only the top two risers of the stairs on the east remained. These were the width of the addition, and it seemed probable that the construction was intended as a stairs platform giving off to the east. This appeared needless, in view of the other nearby stairs. The construction was of solid masonry faced with rough-dressed ashlar.

The next addition was even more strange—the passage at the west end of the south wall of the building and at the top of the small stairs. The orientation of the passage was askew with the terracing. The remains of the section on the north were built against the South Building, and were of solid masonry with a facing of short-tenon, well-dressed ashlar.

The gateway gave the impression of having been a stairs to the roof of the South Building with a passage left beneath. Only a single course of stones remained in position on the south, and above them were several fallen stones that may have been from upper risers. Such a stairs rising at 45 degrees could have been built leaving ample space for a vaulted passage beneath, but, unfortunately, not enough remained to prove anything. It was almost certain that the boot-shaped arch stones and capstones found in the passage were debris of a vault over the passage and not from the vault of the west room of the South Building.

Another addition was undertaken in the building of a pylon on the south side of the small stairs and against the east face of the south section of the passageway described in the preceding paragraph. The structure was of solid masonry faced with dressed ashlar of irregular size. Only one of the stones of its rounded southeast corner was in position, and its north face, protected by a later fill, was the only one standing to full height.

Following construction of the stair pylon or heavy casing, the stairs was covered by an additional bit of terracing with a vertical south face extending from the northeast corner of the pylon to the southwest corner of the stairs built on the South Building center line. Only one and two courses of this remained, with no trace of the east facing along the stairs. The top of this terrace was at the level of the top riser of the south center-line stairs, and so on the east line of the small stair pylon a single riser was put in to reach the level of the terrace.

At the east end of the terrace, other changes had been made, but with their relationship to the alterations indeterminable. After the small terrace east of the Southeast Court Terrace had been repaired or built up to the level of the heightened Basal Terrace 2, its south line was carried west to abut the Southeast Court Terrace. Only the top two courses of its rough-dressed ashlar face were exposed. It was probably built on the same floor and to the same surface level as the terrace to its west. Loose, clean rubble was used for fill, with apparently some mortar in the facing.

To the south of, and of the same length as, this last construction was a set of stairs. There were two risers on a line with the south face of the Southeast Court Terrace, and north of these were a third riser and traces of a fourth. Remains of a charred area, possibly a fire pit, were found on the landing between the two sets of risers.

The stones used for the risers were fairly well dressed and of riser height. The west end of the explored length of the drain leading to the east lay beneath the lower risers.

STAIRS SOUTHEAST OF SOUTHEAST ANNEX

The stairs leading up from the Southeast Terrace to the Southeast Annex level east of the latter was probably built after the removal of the east addition to that structure. The stairs was of such ample width that only a colonnaded structure or open area would logi-

cally have served at its head. The addition to the Southeast Annex was probably not a colonnade. The top step was at the same level as the remains of the south plinth of the building, and was on the line of Basal Terrace 5. The stairs was constructed on the same floor level as the Southeast Court Terrace and its addition.

Four risers were used to ascend at a gradient of a little less than 45 degrees. The west end of the stairs was on the line of the east end of the Southeast Annex. One broken and three complete stones were in situ in the east coping. The upper third of the length of the coping was missing. These stones were well cut to face and edges, and had rather short tenons. The stone found at the west had a low-relief sculptured panel with the figure of a warrior bearing a shield, two spears lowered forward, and two spears carried horizontally across the shoulder. In size, handling, and direction of march of the figure, the stone was a companion piece to the one found in the northeast room of the South Building of the Southeast Court, where it was used as a section of the south bench. Both these stones were much like the existing east bench in the entrance room of the South Building of the Southeast Court. It seemed almost certain that they were from a similar west bench that had been torn out and replaced without sculpture. If this was true, then the stairs was later than the building from which this casing coping stone was taken.

The stair risers were of well-cut stone. Lime mortar was employed in the construction, but remained only in a disintegrated form.

After the construction of the last East Terrace, the stairs was extended to the east. Only parts of the three risers remained. The top step was missing altogether. The material and workmanship of this series of stairs were similar to those on which they abutted on the west, but their orientation varied, being a compromise between the line of the early basal terraces and that of the east terraces. The stairs was built on the floor of the last East Terrace; as a result, the bottom step was lower at its east end than at its west. This stairs accounted for one change in elevation between north and south in the last East Terrace, although it was not a part

Stairs south and east
of Southeast Annex

of the original construction there, for a floor level was found at its base just north of its center line.

No trace of an east casing was found; nor was there proof of the full length of the stairs, since the terrace had fallen away and may well have taken stairs and casing along. The row of stone north of the east end may have been remains of a step-up construction phase for the East Terrace.

West Terrace

The east face of a terrace was found west of Platform 4. There was probably a stairs location at a break in the terrace. The ends of the terrace wall on either side of this break were well lined but backed only by rubble, the assumption being that the side walls of the stairs fitted against these.

At the north, a vertical wall, apparently a part of the same construction, extended to the east. There it connected with an older terrace, only part of which remained. Formerly this older terrace may have carried further west.

On the east, the terrace face was broken away, though it probably extended along to the south side of the high bedrock outcropping. This terrace was built of poorly dressed stone with no traces of mortar remaining. The later terrace was somewhat better constructed, but with a wide variation of stone work, apparently mostly reused material. Four stones with shallow-relief mosaic decorations with feather treatments were incorporated in the south portion of the east face. These bore traces of red coloring on their backgrounds and faint traces of blues and greens on the feathers. The other stones varied from well-cut building facings to poorly dressed ashlar. The chinks were often large. Mortar was used in setting the facing, and was apparent in the rubble backing.

What may have been the remains of the north line of the terrace was found north and west of its present north end. Here several stones were in an east-west line, having a north face, and with surface and rubble indications that they had continued to the west.

3. BALL COURT

The Ball Court presented a number of sequences, many of which had direct effects on the terracing at the south of the platforms. Insufficient excavation on the east of the court left several important relationships undetermined, but a satisfactory solution would have required almost complete excavation of the Southeast Building and the terraces to the west of it.

The first construction was that of the two side walls, with full-length stairs and playing benches; the walls defined the end zones. The three slabs on the north-south center line probably dated from this first stage. The North Temple terrace was probably the next construction, and then its enlargement. The side walls and benches were then lengthened, and the guilloche end markers were placed or reset. Following this must have come the successive filling operations to the east and west, leading up to the burial of the lower six risers of the east stairs, and then the final demolition of the Ball Court with the filling of the entire area to just above the level of the playing zone benches and North Temple terraces.

FLOORS AND FOUNDATIONS

The floors about the Ball Court were difficult to analyze, but the order as here given is probably correct. A floor, resting on a loose, light sienna-colored, rubble fill, covered the entire area before the Ball Court was built. In places, as below, where the break occurred in the Basal Terrace 1 cornice, the bedrock projected through this level. To the west, the bedrock rose generally, and at the southwest corner of the casing for the west stairs, the floor was much above its normal level, following this slope.

Only along the faces of the benches did the floor fail to carry beneath the walls, and at one such place it was definitely proved that the floor had been removed, the bench facing stone set on or above the exposed rubble, and the floor then repaired up to the face of the stone, with later floors covering this. This same break in the floor assisted in determining the southwest corner of the east bench during the course of the excavation. It was found that only at the decorative panel sections of the benches was the floor certain to have been torn away.

Almost everywhere the second floor was separated from the lower by loose gravel and small stones. Both were firm floors, with mortar-bound gravel penetrating the supporting loose material. Above the second floor, two and three additional floors were found. These floors seemed to have been of similar construction. No definite signs of coloring could be found.

The floors were interesting in their relation to the building sequences. At the south end of the west wall, two floors were found beneath the face of the addition; only one was beneath the original structure, the other tying into the face of the inner wall. Upon this were fragments of another floor; against the addition, a third floor in good condition tied into the wall face. At the south end of the east wall, a similar condition existed, involving only the two lower floors. The second floor tied into the original south end of the wall above the loose gravel on the lower floor, which passed beneath the wall.

Ball Court
east stairs
with burial vault

Ball Court, restoration

At the east, where the base of the stairs was examined, three floors were beneath the lower riser, with only one abutting. In this case, the loose gravel layer was found on the third floor; the fourth or top floor tied in with the base of the riser. Since there were no changes in the rubble of the wall from the bench face to the stairs, the two lower floors probably belonged to constructions of the Southeast Terraces, and were earlier than the first Ball Court floor. They probably terminated beneath the mass of the wall.

Beneath the North Temple Terraces were two floors. The lower floor, on the loose rubble fill, had the north center-line plaque flush with its surface and apparently set at the time the floor was laid. The upper floor was constructed in two sections. One, from the base of Basal Terrace 1 above the lower floor, ended on a line with the center of the plaque, where its edge was rounded; the other carried this level south, overlapping the rounded edge of the north section.

In the northeast corner of the north playing zone were two floors. The lower belonged to the base of Basal Terrace 1, and extended east under the end zone wall; the upper floor dated later than the end zone east wall. The lower floor was built upon the loose rubble and bedrock, the latter rising to above floor level to the west and to the north under Basal Terrace 1. The loose rubble was laid to an approximate level on the bedrock, and then small stone and gravel were used to bring it to a suitable construction level for the basal terrace and its floor. Above this firm lower pavement was gravel, with some dirt, and on this the lime concrete for the upper floor was placed.

At the south, no floor was found beneath the end wall, the loose rubble of the wall appearing integral with the rubble of the fill below it. The wall and pavement were in such poor repair that little could be ascertained.

WALLS

The walls and the benches both had undergone alteration, but apparently no changes had been made in the stairs.

Both the west and the east walls had sloping base zones at the ends. No beveled-edged stones were found in the debris belonging to a molding at the top of the base zone, as had occurred on other buildings with sloping bases. The sides of the wall were vertical, with the remains insufficient to determine whether a molding from the top of the end batter had carried along them.

The wall facings rested a few centimeters above the first floor, with one or two floors tying in immediately above. Nothing remained of the extended south end of the east wall, and there were only the bench enlargements to prove that the wall had also been increased in length to the south. The remains of the west wall addition ends showed that they had been sloping, as had the original ends.

PLAYING BENCHES

The benches were somewhat shorter on their faces than against the wall. The benches had been lengthened with the wall, and the new ends bore the same relation to the wall ends as did the originals. The ends of the benches at both stages had the same relation to the floors as did the ends of the walls; along the face, obvious alterations had been made in the floors. It was also certain that the entire facing had been removed at the time of alteration, and it was possible that the sculptured panels had later undergone several changes. The center-line panels certainly did not appear in their original situations.

The height and slope of the face of the bench were determined from the two cornerstones of the west bench. The north corner had fallen next to its original site; the south was discovered on the surface of the south slope of the small mound west of the Ball Court, some distance west of its position in the bench. Both east bench corners were missing. The north cornerstone of the west bench was in good condition, except for a missing fragment bearing the face of the sculptured figure.

Where a trench had been cut through the east bench on the south, a level of gravel debris was found near the present surface, but only within the area of the bench. Because this debris was also sloping from east to west, it was assumed to be the remains of the bench top surface.

The bench, except for the corners, was built up of probably three courses of stone, of which only the lower course generally remained in situ. At no point was the face found at full height, and none of the sculptured panels had a second course of stone left. The debris in the court contained much of the plain and sculptured material, but some was found outside the complex. The number of sculptured fragments belonging to the bench and found in the debris where the southwest corner of Platform 4 had fallen away gave a good indication of the relationship of the two destructions. Many beveled-faced stones, both plain and sculptured, forming the top obtuse angle of the bench were found.

STAIRS

Except for remains of the end walls, no trace of the west stairs could be found, but there was sufficient remains to prove its former existence and that it had not been lengthened, as had the walls. Of the east stairs, six risers remained, as did the end walls to a corresponding height. This stairs had been covered by the extension of the Southeast Terrace to the west, and so had been excellently preserved, except for some root action on the upper risers and the insertion of the small tomblike chambers near either end.

The stairs had been built with the first wall of the Ball Court, and had never been altered. Considerable plaster bonding and finishing remained. The stair stones were well cut and laid in very good alignment. The level of the top edge and the verticality of the face were the prime factors in setting, and all irregularities in height were adjusted at the base of the stone. The tenon lengths were approximately the same as the stone heights, while the stone faces were generally much longer.

No coping was used to cap the end walls, the stairs carrying through the full length. The end risers were square in section, and finished on the end face.

RUBBLE

The rubble within the two parallel masses was loose and of irregular, rough stone. Since no floor had covered the remains, much humus and earth had filtered through to the floor beneath. Below the small section thought to be the bench surface, the stone was russet-colored.

END WALLS

Terrace 1 served as the north end wall for the Ball Court. Walls were built to close the east and west ends of the north end zone, and another wall enclosed the south end zone. Access had been at pavement level to the east and west sides of each end zone, but these had been eliminated when alterations were made, stairs apparently having been provided when the terraces to east and west were higher than the Ball Court pavement.

The long south wall was at considerable distance from the original south end of the east playing wall and from the first west playing wall. At either end, approximately in line with the lower risers of the stairs, the wall was continued north to close the ends of the end zone. The west wall left a wide opening between its north end and the end of the stairs. The east wall left a gap at its north end. The south and west walls were in poor condition, and no traces of their outer faces were found. The outer face of the east wall was traced for some distance. Four courses of roughly dressed masonry were used; the top row was somewhat smooth, indicating that this may have been the full height of the wall. Spalls had been freely used, and there was sufficient plaster debris to indicate that the wall facing had been set in mortar and probably plastered over. Loose rubble was used for the core. The south and west walls were probably of similar width, height, and construction.

The west boundary wall for the north end zone was built in two parts and on a line with its south counterpart.

The east wall of the north end zone was not thoroughly examined, but was found to be of similar construction. No excavations were made to determine whether this might have been a freestanding wall, but it seemed safe to assume that it had been, rather than a terrace built against the west line of the southeast terracing. The area between the two was probably one of the first alterations to the end walls, and a continuation to the east of the south line of the wall was built to hold this fill.

The end zone walls, like the playing walls and benches, were built upon an earlier floor level, with a later floor laid after their construction.

Many additions had been made to the end walls, chiefly in filling in the areas on the east and west to their present level. The filling of the lower east stairs to make a level approach from the Southeast Terrace had been one of the first undertakings. The end walls of this construction followed the lines of the north and south ends of the stairs, and were of roughly dressed ashlar with a loose rubble fill between the walls.

The first change noted in the south end zone was the blocking of the passage to the east. This had been done with a wall face in line with, and similar to, the west face of the east wall of that zone. The area behind this facing had been filled with loose rubble. Later, several small constructions had been built on this fill, but only traces of these remained. In the angle formed against the end of the stairs, a small step was built. The sides of this were of face stone surfaced with mortar. Its function could not be determined; nor was there evidence of additional stairs above serving as an entry to the Ball Court playing level.

At the east end of the north zone, somewhat similar additions had been made; in either two or three stages, the earlier terracing had been carried out to the line of the west face of the east end wall. The first of these was the fill behind the wall itself; the second, a rough-faced wall west of the Southeast Terrace west face; the final section continued the east end wall south to join the terracing east from the stairs. Rough-dressed ashlar was used with considerable chinking and possibly with mortar; loose rubble was used for fill. Remains of a platform built against the south

end of the west face of the east wall of the north end zone were found; this probably represented the location of a set of stairs down to the court level.

The first change about the west end of the north zone had involved the addition of a small terrace on the west side of the end wall. There was no evidence of its function.

When the area west of the north end zone had been filled, a wall face was built connecting the east faces of the two sections of the west wall. To accommodate the runoff, a drainage canal was built of evenly dressed stone with the pavement as the bottom surface. This drain carried to the northeast, where it apparently entered a small sump. This sump seemed to have been inadequate for the runoff from even a small portion of the north end zone, although the entire north half of the Ball Court sloped in that direction. What was found to represent the sump was a silt-filled depression at the end of the drain. It is possible that there may have been an unexposed large crevice or cave in the bedrock of sufficient size to handle the runoff from the court.

NORTH TEMPLE TERRACES

Only the south line of the first platform at the north end of the court remained. As in both constructions, there was no trace of a surfacing floor. Four courses of moderately well-dressed, square-faced, short-tenon ashlar were used at this point, which may represent the full height of the original terrace.

Only a few stones of the side walls of the stairs remained. The stairs casing seemed to indicate it did not have a coping course. The face of the terrace did not carry through behind the stairs. Mortar and spalls had been used in the construction of the stairs and terrace facing, with a backing of loose rubble. No traces of an east or west line to the terrace were found.

The second terrace was more complete, and its ground plan was intact except on the southeast corner and the side walls to the end stairs. None of the top-course stones remained in position; on the east and west faces, no more than two courses were left. The joints were fairly well cut and chinked, as on the first terrace. One reused bit of low-relief sculpture of unknown origin was found in the east face.

The copings of the south stairs were not complete, with probably one of the well-cut stones gone from the west and two from the east coping. The stairs stones were well faced on the riser surface, and were evenly cut along top and edges. Like the other material of these terraces, they had short tenons.

The end stairs was in poor condition. Three stones remained of the bottom riser of the east stairs. The southernmost of these marked the south line of the stairs.

The west stairs, like the one on the east, had no trace of a casing. The lower riser and most of the second riser were in situ. Several stones marked the south casing, which lined in with the width of the terrace break. No plaster marks were left on the face of the terrace to indicate the location of the remaining stairs or the height of the terrace floor. Traces of mortar remained on the faces of the stairs as well as in their joints and backing. It seemed evident that the entire structure had had an overall rough coat of plaster.

On the terrace center line, stones were missing from the heightened section of the Terrace 1 cornice. In the gap, several boveda stones were found resting on the original top surface of the basal terrace cornice with their faces in line with the edge of the cornice. What may have been the intent of the builders at this place could not be determined.

PLAQUES

Three well-cut flat slabs were found on the north-south center line of the Ball Court. One came to light beneath the first North Temple Terrace, set in the lowest floor. It had been covered by the two later floors, which overlapped along its center line before the terraces had been built. The other two slabs were equidistant from the center of the playing area. Like the north plaque, these were flush with the earlier floor, but were not covered by later floor levels. Since the fill above was loose, they had received the same discoloration as had the floor; their original color could not be determined. The north plaque apparently had the same wash coat of red plaster that had been given to the floor. All three plaques were examined, but were found to be only plain slabs set on the loose rubble foundation for the Ball Court floor.

There may have been other similar markers in the Ball Court, and possibly one at the south end, but only one trench was dug other than those following wall lines. Thus the greater part of the playing and end-zone floor areas was never exposed.

END MARKERS

Two bands of stone extended from bench to bench at the ends of the playing area. Upon each of these had been carved a low-relief serpent guilloche. The end stone, rather than depicting a head and tail of a serpent, had simply a loop closing the two lines of the motif. These end markers for the playing area were set flush with the upper pavement level of the court, and evidently had been used to mark the original shorter length of the playing area, for on that line, just in front of the former southeast corner of the west bench, a break was found in the second floor, from which the band had probably been removed. Below this break was a groove in the lower floor. This groove may have served as the first end marker, although it is possible that it represented only the bedding mark for the base of the stone band when it had been in the second floor.

SCULPTURED PANELS

Of the eight panels which had adorned the face of the playing benches, only seven were found, and of these only the lowermost of the probable three courses of stone. The remaining sculptures had been removed; some were found in the Ball Court fill, in the

Platform 4 southwest corner debris, and scattered about the surface of the south and west. To endeavor to restore even one panel would have necessitated careful handling of all the fill in the Ball Court playing area, end zones, and the Platform 4 west end debris.

The end panels all had the central motif with three narrow bands or feathers falling from a top depression toward the side of the panel nearest the end of the bench. The north-quarter panels each had a circular disk at the center. The panel on the east bench was carved with a death's head facing south. One of the long central panels had two plain stones at its center; the other had two sculptured stones, the pattern on neither of which could be discerned. Each of the short panels had one kneeling figure next to the center. In the end panels, the kneeling figures were on the far side of the central motif from the end of the bench; in both quarter panels, the kneeling figure was at the right of the center disk. The short panels had eight figures; four on either side of the center. In the long panels, there were six standing figures in each half panel, except in the south half of the west bench, where there were only five figures. In all the panels, the figures faced toward the center of the panel.

In general, the sculpture of the west bench was in a better state of preservation than that of the east bench, perhaps because it had been cut slightly deeper than that on the east bench.

The sculptures had certainly been carved before being placed in their present positions. Although the irregularities led to the belief they had been carved prior to being set up, the variations might be attributable to errors of alignment and spacing of the stones when moved. From the plaster lines and floor levels, it was certain that changes had been made.

The only full figures remaining were those on the two end blocks of the west bench; the southernmost of these was badly weathered. The latter stone was found on the southeast slope of the small Southwest Mound and, because of its proximity to the south end of the west bench, was assumed to have been there originally rather than at the north end of the east bench. The

80

north stone of the west bench was found fallen forward northeast of its original position.

The north stone of the south panel of the west bench had no border for the panels; the next stone was plain.

When found in situ, many of the sculptures had been buried by later floors halfway to the knees of the small figures. Generally the sculptures had been set with the bottom of the panel even with the second floor and with the succeeding floors overlapping some of the sculptures. In some cases, the base of the stone was set below the level of the lower floor, with the bottom of the panel level with the floor.

RINGS

Three fragments of rings for the Ball Court were found. One was on the north-south center line of the court south of the north guilloche marking band, in the fill above the Ball Court pavement.

The other two fragments were found near the west bench, opposite the south figures of the north quarter panel. These last two pieces were apparently from the same ring; the other fragment belonged to the other ring.

Most of the color and plaster washes on the sculpture had weathered. What was left gave a general indication of the original and subsequent color schemes. The background varied from a light to a deep blood red. The north quarter-point panel of the east bench had a consistently deep red background; the north panel of the west bench varied in values and tones of red through the entire range of lights to darks. These variations may have occurred with time. In some places, the red was found to be covering a dull chrome yellow, which appeared as something of a stain and may not have been a definite applied color. It also occurred under the body colors. The reliefs were in general a dark blue-green color. Where the plaster line of the later floors overlapped the sculptures, there were traces of a light turquoise blue. In some places, later colors were found over the red backgrounds. These colors were all dull, heavy dark greens and blues. On the north cornerstone of the west bench, a gray and then a gray-green color appeared over the red of the background; the later floor plaster line had turquoise blue on top of the other three.

Small figures attired like those of the decorative panels were used as decoration on the sides of the rings, and feathered serpent designs were on the peripheries.

It is possible that fragments of the rings might have been found anywhere about the court, but evidence led to the belief that the rings had occupied positions in the walls near where they were found. This assumption would place them behind the north quarter panels; their location there would also help justify these extra panels. In this respect, the court differed from the arrangement of the principal Ball Court of Chichén Itzá.

4. PLATFORMS

PLATFORM 1

Not much of this platform was exposed. When excavation began, only a few meters of the cornice of the north face and a small section of the top of the south cornice were showing. These had been exposed by the collapse of the northwest casing of Platform 3 and the subsequent removal of some of the loose rubble fill of that construction. Only by excavating could the full height of the platform and its probable length be determined.

Foundations. Loose rubble was found beneath the walls and fill of the construction, and there was no evidence that any of this had been covered by a pavement prior to the erection of the platform. Whether or not the platform rested on Terrace 1 was not determined. The rubble of the platform was uniform down to the top of the construction level found beneath its center, and that was assumed to be the surface of the terrace construction. Under the south face, no change in the rubble was noted below the base of the platform; under the northwest corner, only dry rubble was found.

The small stone and gravel layer found above the construction wall beneath the center of the platform was lower than the base line of the platform, as determined by a mean of the two exposed base points, but there was no change or line in the platform rubble at the upper level. Perhaps a basement, similar to the East Wing Basement in height, supported and was built with the platform, causing the discrepancies found between its base level and the apparent surface line of Terrace 1. It was also possible that a basal terrace, earlier and smaller than Terrace 1, had been built; yet that would fail to account for the lower level of the working layer beneath the center of the platform.

The east line of the platform was not exposed at any point, but was assumed to bear the same position relative to Platform 2 as on the west. The top surface sloped down from north to south. The exposed section of the north cornice was level, indicating that the entire top surface was flat from east to west but pitched to the south.

Facing. The cornice and cornerstones were generally large and well cut, and the facing material was well-dressed smaller stones. The faces were apparently laid in irregular courses, but so little was exposed that these could not be definitely ascertained. The cornerstones were well cut to the curve and edges; spalls had been used in setting them.

The plaster of the wall carried beneath the cornice, as did that on the walls of rooms, apparently for the purpose of arriving at a level line and permitting the wall to set before adding the cornice. Because of this construction, a recess was left back from the face of the wall and between its top and the base of the cornice. This plaster line did not carry across the platform.

A heavily scratched surface coat of plaster covered the sides of the platform, tending to obscure the jointing of the stone. There was apparently only one coat, integral with the jointing plaster. Where the stones were irregular, the protruding areas of the surface had only a thin coat, which in places had disappeared. At

82

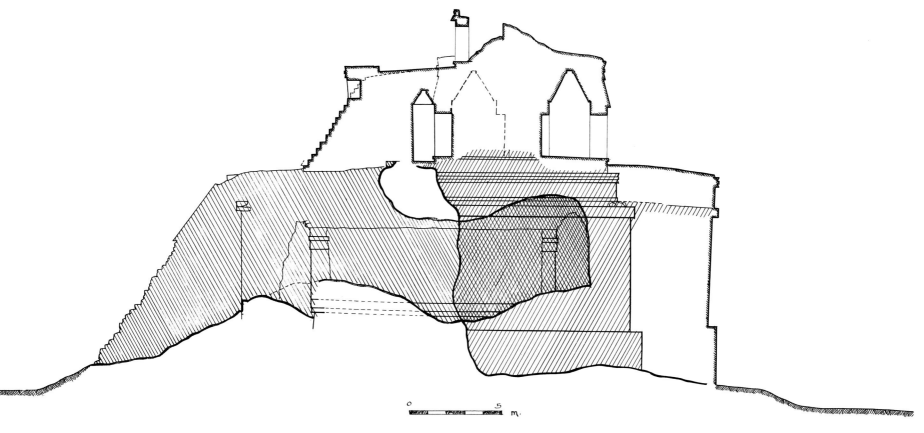

North-south section through "Cave," 1932

the south, it was impossible to determine the number of stone courses, since they were covered by a hard layer and were also well protected by the Platform 3 fill. The wall plaster, in addition to carrying over the top, rounded off at the base to form the floor. At the rear, this wall plaster rounded off in a curve and disappeared in the plaster and gravel debris marking the floor line.

The cornice was also covered by a single firm coat of plaster that left the jointing nearly indiscernible. The plaster had been smoothed with a fiber tool or cloth in long sweeps of the arm which followed the surface irregularities and pulled away from the wall at the end. This resulted in a series of long, scratched patches. Beneath the cornice members, in the reentrant angles, the plaster had been applied by hand, and the grooves left by the fingers were plainly visible. These patches were in arm-length strokes, and the hand had swept away from the wall at the ends of the strokes. The faces of the cornices were finished like the walls beneath. The plaster of the cornice did not carry beneath Platform 2, and was apparently the same as that carrying over the latter construction. This would indicate that Platform 2 was contemplated before Platform 1 was completed, and that when

83

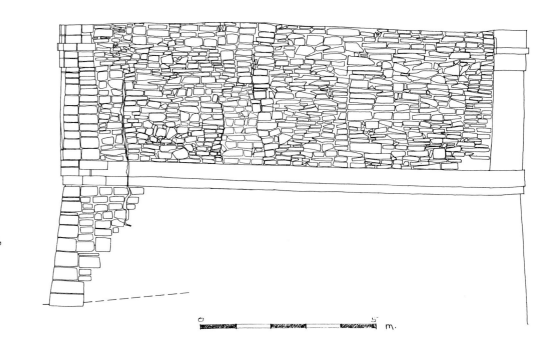

West elevation,
Platforms 1 and 2 (top),
and north elevation,
Platforms 1 and 2

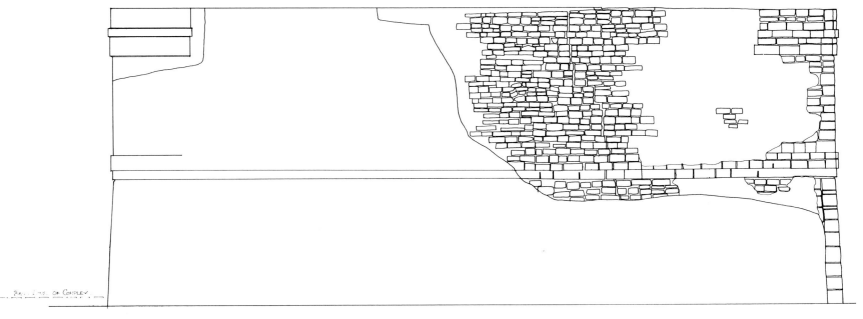

the cornice had seen set, Platform 2 was begun. A small section of graffito was found just south of the northwest corner above the base.

Floors. The powdery condition of the floor level on the south seemed to indicate that it had never been given a hard plaster coat. There were some small stones on the rough rubble of the foundation. At the northwest corner, similar traces of a floor line were found; on the west of the platform, this sloped up to the south; on the north, it sloped down away from the platform. Floors were often broken up when another platform was to be superimposed; this may have occurred with the floors of Platform 1 when Platform 3 was planned.

Rubble. Although no definite break was found between the fill of the first and second platforms, there was a level of some black, fist-size stone mixed with loose rubble which may have been the rough top surface of Platform 1. Resting on this level was a north-south construction section wall of the Platform 2 rubble; below was the top of an east-west section in the Platform 1 rubble. This construction wall rested on what were apparently successive layers of flat, large and small stones. There may have been a regular pattern to the sections of rubble, but if so it was too large to be seen in the small shaft. The stones for the walls were undressed but regular in size.

The dry rubble fill of the platform was contained by the mortar-bound shell. The thickness of this shell was not determined, but probably closely approximated that of Platform 2.

PLATFORM 2

Platform 2 was set back from the cornice of the lower platform, except along the rougher portion of the north face, where its irregular surface was flush with the upper cornice of Platform 1. The greatest variation in height was along the west.

Facing. The finished south face carried around onto the west face, with the north corners extending around to the east and west faces.

The masonry of the south elevation and of the corners was of well-cut stone of uniform size, with the cornerstones well rounded and somewhat larger than the others. The corners appeared to have been built before the areas on the three rough sides; the south face retained too much plaster for analysis by surface examination. The west face was rough in surface alignment, and the construction did not have regular horizontal ranges. Several definite vertical sections could be seen, between which the stonework was among the most varied and irregular of the complex. Generally the stones were laid horizontally; many had irregular faces, with many small stones used as fillers. The chinks were often as large as the stones, and so the line between spalls and facing stones was difficult to distinguish.

Only part of the east face could be seen. The area between the cornice breaks was found to be much rougher than on the west, and had not been smoothed over with plaster, as had the west end. So it is possible that when the West Wing was not built as intended, the builders smoothed off the rough face against which they had intended to build.

The north face, between cornice breaks, was built flush with the edge of Platform 1, and was much more regular in stonework and alignment than was the east elevation. The stones were laid to courses, were covered by a rough coat of plaster, and were little smaller than those of the exposed areas. Several lines of vertical cleavage may have been construction phases, but certainly did not compare with the work of the east facade. A definite effort had been made to keep in horizontal courses.

The faced surfaces had been covered with a single firm coat similar to that applied to the cornice of Platform 1. On the west, no effort had been made to cover the stone faces, although the spaces had been filled flush with the stone surfaces and smoothed off. The plaster of the cornices and rough walls rounded over the

Platform 1 restoration (top) and Platforms 1 and 2 with East and West Wings restoration

top edge of the platform; the plaster of the lower zone carried over beneath the first projection of the cornice. This occurred only on the surfaces with the cornice, tending to indicate that these sections—at least the corners—had been erected first.

In the area exposed, two deep red vertical bands were painted on the south face, and were the only signs of color found on the otherwise plain, dull buff-colored plaster surfaces of the platforms and basal terraces.

Rubble. Like Platform 1, the upper platform was of the shell type of construction. The solid masonry casing was probably built up as the fill was laid, for it was found to thicken from bottom to top, indicating probable simultaneous erection with the dry rubble. There was no other attempt to effect a tie-in.

The penetration of the platform was from the west. Thus the nature of the backing for the south and north facings could not be determined. The masonry of the shell was of large slabs laid horizontally and so close together vertically that the mortar between the layers occupied only the irregularities in the stone surfaces. There were larger horizontal gaps that were filled with small stone and mortar. The mortar of this work was the firmest found in the complex—the same mortar that covered the exterior and was so hard and well preserved that it made definition of stones difficult.

Only one construction wall was found in Platform 2, a north-south rough, dry partition near the center of the platform. This had the same appearance as the one in Platform 1, and had some spalls of fist-size black stones similar to those used at the top levels of both the platforms. The wall carried from the level of Platform 1 up to nearly the top of Platform 2. Above, there was loose rubble of reddish-brown, irregular stones with no apparent coursing similar to that found west of the wall. No definite floor was found on top of the rubble.

Large vertical cracks were found on the west and north faces, extending down through Platform 1, and were probably the result of a weakness of the northwest corner foundation.

These cracks could have been prevented by effectual breaking of the vertical jointing.

Two fragments of metates were found in the platform rubble near the center line.

PLATFORM 3

Platform 3 completely encased the first two platforms, and shortened the length of the East Wing by one tier of rooms. As a result, its foundations and rubble were largely buried.

Foundations. The southwest and southeast corners of the platform were found to be directly supported by Basal Terrace 1. On the southwest, the floor was traceable from the edge of the terrace cornice to the base of the platform, and along its west face to the first step-up; it could not be traced beneath the platform, where it probably extended. On the southeast, the low plinth course found under the Southeast Court had evidently been torn out so that the platform foundation would be at the terrace surface level as established at the base of the basement to the East Wing, from which a floor extended only a few centimeters south and certainly passed beneath the platform.

The northeast corner rested upon the floor at the level of the north base of the East Wing Basement, which was here slightly higher than at the south. This floor extended west and passed below the base of the east casing of the Main Stairs, sloping down from the northeast corner of Platform 3 to the stairs. It was traced for some distance beneath the stairs and beneath the edge of the platform.

West of the Main Stairs, the platform rested on the veneer-faced west extension of the Main Stairs Terrace. In this section, the breach in the platform shell occurred. The base of the platform itself was probably higher here than east of the stairs, where it rested on the floor. Nothing was left in situ of this section except portions of the supporting terrace, but it had probably been built at the same level as the stairs casing upon the Main Stairs Terrace. Even the northwest corner had fallen away.

87

Platform 3 with East Wing restoration

The west tier of rooms of the East Wing had been torn down before the construction of Platform 3, but the north-south walls on the east were left standing, probably to the vault line. The platform foundation stepped up over the basement and then up to the East Wing floor line; but at the face, it passed over standing short sections of the East Wing walls. Between these outer walls, the face of the platform set back to the west side of the standing north-south partitions.

The west base line had the same breaks as those in the south half of the east facade, where the foundation rose first to the top of the basement, carried over to the building, and then, at the west, rose to the level of the building floor. The position and height of these steps were so identical that there was little doubt

that some work had been accomplished on the construction of a West Wing before Platform 3 was built. Except for the break at the west end of Platform 2 and the foundation steps in Platform 3, no other evidence of this construction was found.

After reaching the level of the floor of this West Wing, the foundation extended north over a dry rubble fill to the northwest corner, which was supported by the Main Stairs Terrace extension at approximately the same level. Whatever caused the collapse of the northwest section of Platform 4 also was responsible for the failure of the footing for several meters of the north half of the west face of Platform 3, leaving the lower face of the platform out of position.

In the interior, the dry rubble was built against the faces of

88

Platform 3 and
Second Story from
southwest before
excavation and
repair, 1932

Platforms 1 and 2 and upon the remains of the floor about the base of the former. The solid masonry top of the platform was built on the surface of Platform 2.

Facings. The facings were in two stages, the lower being approximately one-third of the total height. The lower offset had a definite outward tilt, or negative batter, while the upper plane sloped inward. The upper wall differed from that on the north in that it bulged out slightly at about its one-third point and then sloped inward. The lower wall of the southeast corner and the east facade were nearly vertical; the upper east wall leaned inward.

The corners had long radii that had required rounding of the stones to either side of the special corner blocks. The corners were of the best material. The tenons were cut in V shapes; the edges were well dressed, requiring far less chinking than the other facing stones. The stones next to the corners were not so round on the face, were generally smaller than the cornerstones, and were less well cut.

The shell was of solid masonry. A firm concrete, with high gravel content, and large spalls were used to bind the tenons of the face stones with long, rough, flat-laid masonry behind them. The rounded irregular face edges of the exterior stones left large chinks, which had been well spalled.

The cornice was of two courses of stone except for the single corner blocks. The lower course was of larger stone than the upper and was well dressed, especially on face and lower line. The distance to which the east-end north facade cornice extended beneath the east casing of the stairs was not determined. The wall surface continued to the top of the platform in the interval.

Except on the east end of the north facade, where three thin wash coats were found, only one coat of plaster had been used. This coat carried over the setback and also filled in cracks in the floor caused by the extreme weight imposed upon it. At the north end of the west facade, the plaster was in such good repair that a

careful examination showed that the mortar from the joint had been used to flush off the irregularities of the stone face and that it overlapped the already dry mortar of the joint beneath. The effect was a smooth surface entirely covered by the dull cream-colored plaster coat. In the exposed cross section, the building-up process was in evidence.

The plaster finish on the east was carried over onto the face of the East Wing walls. Traces of scratch lines similar to those on Platforms 1 and 2 were found. An incised line on the plaster of the platform was found west of the east face of the stairs. These may have been a construction guideline for an earlier stairs, but did not coincide with the cornice break on the west.

Rubble. The core of the platform, surrounding the two earlier structures, was of loose, large stones with the interstices filled with nut- to fist-size rocks. The large, deep sienna-colored stones were laid horizontally in rough strata one to two stones deep with an application of the small material to fill the gaps. The hearting was laid up simultaneously with the shell, and the stones adjacent to the solid masonry were often tied in with the concrete of the latter. Where the setback in the shell occurred, nearly half of the upper face rested on the dry masonry of the fill. The fill was carried to the height of the top of Platform 2, above which was solid masonry of similar aggregate and a firm lime concrete.

In a construction level in this concrete below the cornice line, two weep holes were found.

Floor. The floor surface rested on a layer of lime concrete having aggregate of up to small fist-size stones. This concrete was flushed off on the surface to give the hard, smooth floor of Platform 3.

PLATFORM 4

Foundations. Before the erection of this platform, the remaining three central rooms of the East Wing had been filled and the doorways leading into them had been walled in and plastered over.

When Platform 4 was built, the vaults were again removed and the outer walls torn down about their doorways; the inner walls, with their encased fill, were left standing.

Except for these filled Rooms 6 and 9, the east foundations of Platform 4 were similar to those of Platform 3. The low plinth course under the Southeast Court was torn out near the face of the platform; south of this, the floor of Basal Terrace 1 was found to pass beneath the platform. The foundation rose over the East Wing Basement, floor level, and walls that were left standing. The face of the lower section of the platform was slightly east of the west ends of Rooms 5 and 7. Since the walls of these rooms had been left standing, the platform facing was built in front of them. Room 6, like Room 9, had been filled from above, and so the foundation line was carried over it. The only demolition found below the vault line was of the doorways to Rooms 8 and 10 and of some of the exterior facing where the south portion of the east facade of the platform abutted the East Wing.

The northeast corner and north wall east of Platform 3 rested on the same floor, as did the earlier platform. The entire south wall rested on Terrace 1; but in the construction of Platform 4, the Basal Terrace 1 cornice was slightly heightened for the length of the south line of the platform, and the lower wall face was set back from this.

Only a small section of the west end of the platform remained, with the missing portion comprising parts of the west and south facades. The remaining northwest corner stood on a pavement and the western end of the extension to the Main Stairs Terrace. Only a few of the basal terrace short-tenon facing stones remained, and even the lower wall of this platform had collapsed when the poor foundation offered by the earlier terrace had failed. The floor upon which the platform rested was lower than the top of the standing section of the terrace, and was the same floor that abutted the base of the north face of that terrace. This would indicate that the terrace must have ended near here, and that possibly only its corner was missing. At least part of Platform 4 was built on the same basal terrace that supported the northwest corner of Platform 3, and that was probably responsible for the latter's failure.

No trace remained of the southwest corner or of the foundation between it and where the northwest section had broken away. Basal Terrace 1 at that time terminated at the approximate west line of Platform 4. As a result of its destruction, there was little hope of finding traces of the platform it supported. Within the limits of Platform 4, a deposit of face stones and fragments of sculptures from the Ball Court panels was found above the terrace floor level and, where the floor disappeared to the west, above a rubble of rough stone containing many small stones and considerable gravel and soscob. The absence of Platform 4 rubble upon the pavement about the southwest corner of Platform 3 made it apparent that after the collapse or destruction of the southwest section of Platform 4, the remains had been removed down to their foundations.

The Ball Court debris found here was separated from the top of Basal Terrace 1 by black earth containing potsherds; above the face stones, a layer of rubble was found. This latter may have been from the more recent collapse of the two broken ends of Platform 4 masonry which had been constantly eroded by rain and foliage. The large facing stones of the platform were not found, although fragments of mask motifs that may have come from the simultaneously destroyed section of Platform 5 turned up in excavations in the Ball Court.

The failure of the platform may have been caused by a settling of the edge of the basal terrace. Apparently that had happened to the remaining south wall, which, at the top, had separated from the west end of the south face of Platform 3.

Facing. The facades of Platform 4 were similar to those of Platform 3, except that the offset between the upper and lower sections was higher in the second of the two constructions. Where the north elevation of Platform 3 had been incorporated into that of Platform 4, a single course of dressed stones had been placed on the offset of the earlier platform, bringing its level up to the same as that of the later structure. Along the south, the addition to the top of the Basal Terrace 1 cornice in effect shortened the height of the lower face of the platform, as compared with the greater height on the north and west. Since Platform 4 had the same cornice and top floor as Platform 3, the upper wall faces had been shortened by the increased height of the offset.

The setback of Platform 4 was at the level of the base of the lower cornice of the East Wing, which may have been the determining factor for the new height. It certainly gave a better corner than it had when at the lower level. Only one stone remained in situ in the top course at the northeast, and that was held in place by the East Wing cornice. Similarly, only one stone remained to mark the top of the lower wall of the northwest section. The south face was in good condition, with only a few missing stones.

The cornice was similar to that of Platform 3, with generally two courses to make the total height. The cornice corners were single stones; along the south, three stones of full cornice height were set at the approximate quarter points as though by design rather than by coincidence. Their positions and their relationship in size of 1:2:3 from west to east may have had some significance.

The lower walls were slightly forward of plumb at the top; the upper walls leaned inward, as did the Platform 3 sections. The masonry was generally larger than that of Platform 3. The corners were only twelve stones high, compared with the seventeen used in Platform 3, where the height was only slightly greater. The variation was less marked on the wall surfaces. The cutting of the stone for Platform 4 was probably less well done than on its predecessor, and larger chinks were left, the spalling of which, on Platform 4, was principally confined to the horizontal joints. The stones were laid in rough horizontal courses, which, on the south face, were marked by occasional lines of vertical joints that may well have been construction sections.

The two north corners of Platform 3 were concealed by the tenons of the Platform 4 stones, which had been cut to fit over the round corners. The earlier cornice corners had been removed, and the later cornice tied in with the earlier.

The corners were in no way tied in with the facing stones on either side, although they must have been built at the same time as the walls and rubble were.

Only one coat of plaster surfacing was found—the finishing coat following the irregularities of the masonry surface. A plaster line above the setback and just west of the northeast corner may represent the top level of a small structure built against the platform, as the South Addition had been against the East Wing. In this case, it must have been a timber-roofed construction. A break in the floor level just east of the northeast corner of Platform 3 may have been a wall line. The existence of remains of such constructions west of the Main Stairs justified this hypothesis.

Rubble. Platform 4 was built of solid masonry. Large, irregular material was used, with many small stones to fill the voids, and a firm concrete with considerable gravel filled the remaining interstices. The hearting was placed at the time the wall was built, and bound in with the wall tenons. No regular series of construction blocks or levels were observed, although several horizontal strata may have represented daily or periodic construction phases. Where large, flat stones were used, these were placed roughly horizontal, but there were no other indications of horizontal stratigraphy in the construction of the core.

A large cavity had formed in the northwest section of the platform, the face of Platform 3 forming a part of one side of the large opening. There was a small south opening through which a person could crawl, and some cleaning about the northwest corner of Platform 3 disclosed an opening on the north which led beneath the corner of that platform and then southwesterly to the cavity. There was considerable earth debris in this north tunnel, but it may have been washed in by rain. However, there may have been an earth fill, on which Platform 4 rested. In this cavity, a section of the lower zone of Platform 3 had fallen. As in the north entrance, there was no foundation left beneath the wall,

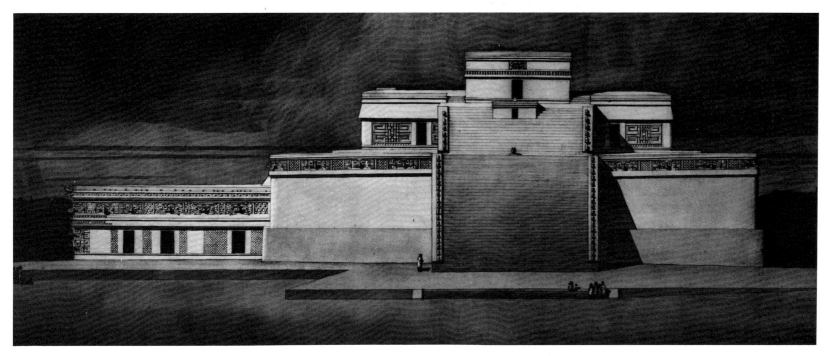

Platforms 4 and 5 with East Wing restoration

and the same absence of a foundation probably led to the formation of the cavity in Platform 4.

On the floor of the cavity was a pile of debris of Platform 4
rubble; above this was a somewhat dome-shaped space. The
collapse seems to have occurred beneath the platforms, either in
the material behind the western end of the Main Stairs Terrace or
beneath that in the bedrock. There were many natural caves in
the limestone, and it is possible that the roof of one of these had
broken through at this spot after Platform 4 had been built.

No drains or vents were found in the Platform 4 rubble. The
two found leading north in Platform 3 indicated that others in
that structure must have led out beneath the cornices of the other
faces and probably continued through the later platform.

Floors. The Platform 4 floor had been overlaid by one extending
out from the base of the Second Story Basement and by fragments
of floors found beneath the basement.

PLATFORM 5

Within the Second Story Basement were remains of a structure
that had been built, or at least commenced, either upon Platform
3 or Platform 4. The basement belonged to the period of Platform
4, and the Second Story may have stood, without its present vault
zone, at that time. Platform 5 had been built around the Second
Story Basement, having as its limits the cornice line of Platform 4.
It had also included the five top risers of the Main Stairs. This
entire stairs may have been erected at the time of Platform 5,

Platform 5, east elevation, from roof of East Wing, 1934   (Photograph by Raul Cámara)

the original stairs to Platform 3 and Platform 4 having been removed, under this assumption, to make way for this alteration.

Facing. Platform 5 was the decorative mask course and three-member molding above the cornice of Platform 4. The faces were well cut but were not uniform in height, and many spalls were necessary to bring the edges to line.

The stairs occupied a large area of the north face. At the base line of Platform 5, the lower riser of this upper section was forward of the Platform 3 cornice. These upper five risers, their end copings, and the masonry back of them had definitely been parts of the Platform 5 construction. The risers were approximately of the same height; these had been set on the same stairs angle as those below, and employed similar material. It was possible that when Platform 5 was projected, a new stairs was planned, and that it was built up to the level of Platform 3, a plaster leveling off done, as was customary, and then the upper stairs had been built when the facing of the platform was completed. The top riser seemed to be in proper relation to the platform, which led to the belief that the construction had been for Platform 5 rather than for the lower level.

The masks were bordered by stiles, and the panels so formed were separated by lattice areas composed of X motifs. The X-motif stones varied in workmanship and design. All but one stone of those remaining about the northwest corner had overlapping bars; in the panels east of the corner, all but three stones in one top course were crossed in the reverse of those in the single remaining panel to the south of the corner. Elsewhere, the overlapping bar was the exception rather than the rule, and even where they did occur in multiple, no attempt had been made to develop a symmetrical pattern.

Rubble. Platform 5 was like Platforms 1, 2, and 3 in that a shell of solid masonry backed the platform facing and confined the dry rubble core. The shell was built up of flat stones laid horizontally, with many small stones to fill the interstices. The loose rubble was irregular in shape, size, and setting. The area was capped with a level of small stone and gravel that had probably supported the floor, now missing. North of the northwest corner of the Second Story, the loose rubble filled an area north of the basement; between this and the shell was a heavy deposit of small stone and soscob, above which was more of the regular dry rubble. This particular deposit looked like debris from a building from which the large stones had been removed. It was possible that a change in the Second Story had been in progress, and that the refuse had been used here as part of the Platform 5 fill.

As first built, the platform surface was in line with the top of the Second Story Basement cornice. Later, a row of face stones was laid around the Second Story, and the enclosed area was filled, bringing the level of that portion of the terrace about halfway up on the plinth of the building. This step was not built until after the erection of the stairs to the Third Story.

The north-south center line weep hole opening beneath the cornice of the Second Story Basement was continued south through the Platform 5 masonry, and ended beneath the platform cornice in the top of a mask panel. The line of this vent was direct from the face of the basement. With most of this weep hole in dry rubble, it was obviously for draining water, and must have been used also to facilitate the circulation of air through the masonry.

No other weeps were found. The western vent in the Second Story Basement was probably continued through, as was the one exposed on the south.

Several large stone blocks lying on the top of Platform 5 near its southeast corner may have been remains of a parapet wall around the edge of the platform. There was no other evidence of such a construction.

MAIN STAIRS

The front stairs of the building was built in three phases to a height of thirty-nine steps. The bottom four risers were the small short-tenon stones of the Main Stairs Terrace, and these were

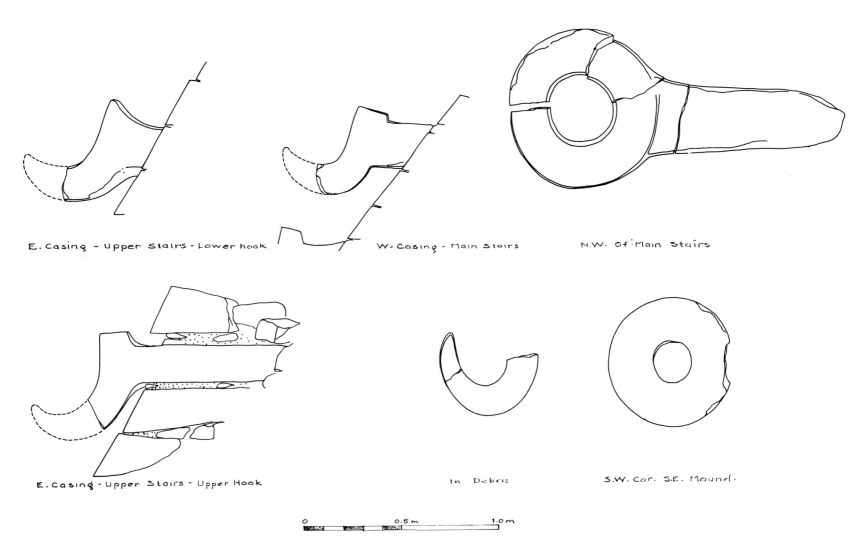

E. Casing - Upper Stairs - Lower hook

W. Casing - Main Stairs

N.W. Of Main Stairs

E. Casing - Upper Stairs - Upper Hook

In Debris

S.W. Cor. S.E. Mound.

0   0.5 m   1.0 m

Stairs parapet ornaments and rings from Southeast Mound

96

topped with a somewhat larger fifth course. The central section comprised the next twenty-nine risers to the level of Platforms 3 and 4. The top section comprised the five steps incorporated in Platform 5.

Copings. Nothing remained in situ of the east coping, or stairs parapet, and only a short section of the upper part of the west coping was left. Photographs taken before the turn of the century show more of the copings in position. Only a small percentage of the stones that had fallen were left about the stairs. The coping was built of well-cut, bevel-edged stones. Some of these stones were the full width of the coping. The facing and edges were well cut and were laid with narrow joints; considerable chinking had been necessary about the rough tenons. If the face of the coping had continued down at the angle of this section, the lower portions would have been beneath the plane of the outer edges of the steps. What adjustment had been made for this situation could not be determined.

Just inside the center line of the copings, hooklike stones projected from every third course. Three of these and the butt of a fourth remained. While none was in complete repair, only the lower section or points were missing. Enough remained to determine that their forward projection had been on the line of the base of the tenon.

The stairs copings had been built at the same time as, and integral with, the stairs in the upper two sections. The bottom riser, in the lower section, extended beyond the coping line to east and west, and doubtlessly carried through to the ends of the casing. None of the other steps did this, and it was possible that the copings had ended at the top of the bottom step, as they did in the upper stairs. In order to have done this, the top four steps of the Main Stairs Terrace small, short-tenon, stairs would have had to have been altered at their ends, since there was no reason to believe that they had had a similar coping.

In the absence of vestiges of either stairs or coping, there were several possibilities. The coping may have stopped at the top of the fifth riser, as happened above the lower riser of the upper stairs. Or the one remaining piece of low-relief sculpture found in the construction—the mask element at the north end of the west casing—was so situated that it may have been part of a full corner stairs mask somewhat similar to those at Uxmal. Such a mask panel would have been compact had the elements been similar to those of Platform 5, as the one fragment indicated, although the central features could have been placed in the width of the coping. This mask would have occupied a position similar to that of the serpent heads in such later structures as El Castillo and the High Priest's Grave. The hooks on the coping seemed to have been derived from the nose element of the masks, and may have been used as an extreme modification of the Uxmal stairs motif, where a series of mask panels formed the stairs coping.

Steps. The lower four steps were of small, well-cut face stones. The fifth row, which was missing, had probably been represented by the longer-tenon stones now forming the fourth in-situ course in the east half of the stairs. These were in contrast with the stairs above, where the stones were well cut but had rounding top corners and tenons generally longer than the face length. The thinner stones required spalls to bring the top surface to the tread level. The stones were fitted tightly end to end. The top course of stones at the level of Platform 3 was well marked. These top steps required less chinking than those below.

Some plaster remained on the steps, but, rather than sharpening the edges and recesses of the rounding stair stones, it emphasized them, giving a washboard effect.

The lower courses had fallen out of position, causing the collapse of many rows above. The action of plants and the failure of the foundations on either side were responsible for other damages to the stairs. At no place was there a continuous series from top to bottom. The east half of the stairs was pointed up with concrete in the position in which they had been found. On the west, the lower five risers were rebuilt and the steps above raised into position. The fourth and perhaps fifth risers of the Main Stairs Terrace series were missing on the east.

97

Main Stairs, west end,
after foundation failure,
1933

Main Stairs and platforms before excavation and repairs, 1932

Main Stairs and Platforms 1 and 2, excavation, 1933

near the north end, where it could be more or less directly attributable to the weakness of the lower construction.

The west wall was similar to that on the east, but had generally slightly smaller stones, resulting in more rows and less conformity to courses. The face had a slight bulge at the center, but was otherwise vertical. Some of the south base of this face had collapsed along with Platform 3.

A single coat of plaster, from the joints, had covered both faces; some of this plaster remained.

Unlike the east elevation, all the Main Stairs Terrace remained beneath the west casing, but had settled under the load, allowing a section of the west end of the stairs to slip down and away from the main mass.

Rubble. The rubble behind the lower five risers was the loose, rough stone of the Main Stairs Terrace, with only the stairs and a few stones behind them bound in mortar. In contrast, the upper sections were of solid masonry whose foundations were the surface of the lower terrace, which dropped down to about the level of the third step. The masonry of the main body of the stairs was not sufficiently exposed to determine if there had been any levels or sections in its construction. This could not be seen where the steps were removed for repair; nor did it show up in the tunnel at the south end of the east casing. The large rubble was firmly bound with lime concrete, and contained many small stones that helped to fill the irregularities. The masonry of the Platform 5 section was similar, resembling the dry fill of the platform with the addition of mortar. The floor of the level of Platforms 3 and 4 separated this upper masonry from that beneath.

The stairs structure had slightly separated from Platform 3 at the top on the west, and the mortar of the fill appeared as a wall face from having been poured against the smooth face of the platform. A large crack had developed near the west face of the stairs, and the exposed surfaces of the masonry were badly disintegrated. These surfaces were removed and repaired during the general work on the west end of the stairs.

The east wall was nearly vertical. It bulged somewhat one-third of the way down from the top, recessed slightly from this point at the level of the platform setback, and at the base was in approximately the same plane as at the top. The wall had been laid in regular courses. Thirty-four rows remained next to the platform, which they abutted, leaving only slight chinks. Although nothing remained of the facing of the Main Stairs Terrace beneath the south part of this casing, the only failure had been

Main Stairs, east face and
Platform 3 (Photograph
by Raul Cámara)

Main Stairs, repair

It was possible that earlier stairs had served Platforms 3 and 4, and that this was narrower than the present structure. Although no definite positions for such earlier constructions could be given, several clues pointed to their possible widths. The vertical line inscribed in the plaster facing of Platform 3 west of the east face of the present casing corresponded to the failure line of the west casing, which developed at a similar distance from that edge. The lower step of such a stairs may have been somewhere near the offset in the surface of the stairs terrace south of the face of the fifth riser.

The cornice break on the north face of Platform 3 was in slightly from the west face of the present stairs casing. The corresponding east break was not uncovered, but the symmetry common to the platforms should place it within approximately the same distance from the east face of the stairs.

Between the ends of the cornice, the platform wall carried up flush to the top of the platform. The stairs construction could be assumed to have been approximately the same width as this break in the cornice. Had a stairs of lesser width been erected, the provision for the cornice would not have been sufficient. There was of course the ever-present possibility that the cornice might have been remodeled. A construction level found within the platform corroborated this possibility.

The antithesis was that the present construction was the only one that had ever served Platforms 3 and 4. The crack on the west could then be attributed to the failure of the foundation, and its position to a possible construction phase or task within the masonry. The position of the cornice break might have been influenced by remains of the stairs to Platform 2, which, as shown by the cornice break on that structure, was in this approximate line; or the builders may simply have carried the cornice a sufficient distance to insure an end within the stairs construction. The line groove in the plaster face of Platform 3 would then remain unaccounted for.

5. BASEMENTS

EAST WING BASEMENT

Tests had been made about the East Wing, so that when the major work of the complex was undertaken, several meters of the north and east face of the East Wing Basement were already exposed. In the course of the excavations, most of the details and relationships of the construction were determined, with the exception of the important question of its connection with Platform 1. This could not be determined at the west end of that platform where a possible West Wing Basement might be expected; tunneling through the loose rubble of Platform 3 to reach the east base of Platform 1 was not safe with the facilities at hand.

Foundation. The base of this construction lay on the line of the top of Basal Terrace 1. At the east and south, the floor surfacing of this basal was found to pass under the edge of the basement. Pits dug within the area of the basement failed to unearth any change or level in the loose rubble which would tend to show that a floor had completely covered the basal terrace before the basement had been built. This condition tended to confirm the supposition that the builders often removed floors before erecting structures upon them. At the east, the cornice of Basal Terrace 1 was missing, but a nearby floor rested on the level of the cornice top and continued beneath the East Wing Basement. The base of the basement was slightly above this level, and a floor extended east from it and rounded down onto the terrace surface. Neither of these floors was hard, smooth, or colored, and perhaps they were only construction phases that had been covered by a better floor

that was lost when the long-tenon stones of the basal terrace cornice were removed. A construction level on the otherwise loose rubble would have given a smooth line to aid in the erection of the facing, and may have accounted for these floors.

At the south, the condition was much the same. Here, the plinth beneath the Southeast Court confused conditions. The firm, red floor from this plinth was covered by the floor from the base of the basement. Nowhere was this lower floor found close to the face of the basement, although every indication from its broken edge was that it went on north rather than rounding up onto the basement.

The plinth for a building beneath the present Southeast Court was apparently earlier than the basement. Its floor tied in with the basal terrace cornice on the south. Along with the remains of buildings north of the East Wing, it was surely one of the earlier structures on Basal Terrace 1. The East Wing and its supporting basement might have been built after the basal terrace had been extended to the east.

Facings. The three courses making up the basement were of well-faced stones with sharp corners, set with tight joints, and in excellent alignment. The plain top band, or cornice, generally projected beyond the plane of the smooth lower band, or plinth; the face of the decorative middle zone was vertical and set back from the base.

The decoration was in a series of colonnettes with either lattice or frets. At the two corners were large colonnettes, with a

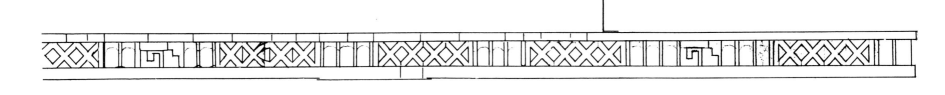

East Wing Bench, north (lower) and south (top) elevations

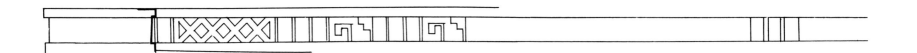

single normal colonnette on either side. The remainder of the colonnettes were in groups of three, with lattices or frets between the groups.

Only a single thin coat of plaster was on the basement course, and this appeared to be a continuation of the plaster used in the jointing and background. No trace of color remained anywhere, although there were several places in which it might have been preserved if there had ever been such additional ornamentation. The lattice and colonnettes of the south and the fret and colonnettes of the north face where exposed beneath Platform 4 were in much the same condition as those east of the platforms.

The facing stones of the basement all had relatively long tenons, which were held in by concrete binding into the solid shell of the construction.

Rubble. The fill of the East Wing Basement could not be distinguished from that of the basal terrace supporting it or of the plinth of the East Wing above it, although there was considerable but gradual change from the top of the latter to that of the terrace. The large, rough rubble contained considerable small stone. There was also some dirt and ash toward the top, which must have filtered down from a level below that of the East Wing floor. This dry masonry was held in place by the shell or casing of concrete-bound masonry. On the north and south, the outer walls of the East Wing were supported by the dry rubble just inside the line of the solid shell.

Except for a firm floor from the base of the building plinth to the edge of the basement cornice and the strip around the base of the basement, no other floors were found tied in with the construction. Later floors passed above its top line.

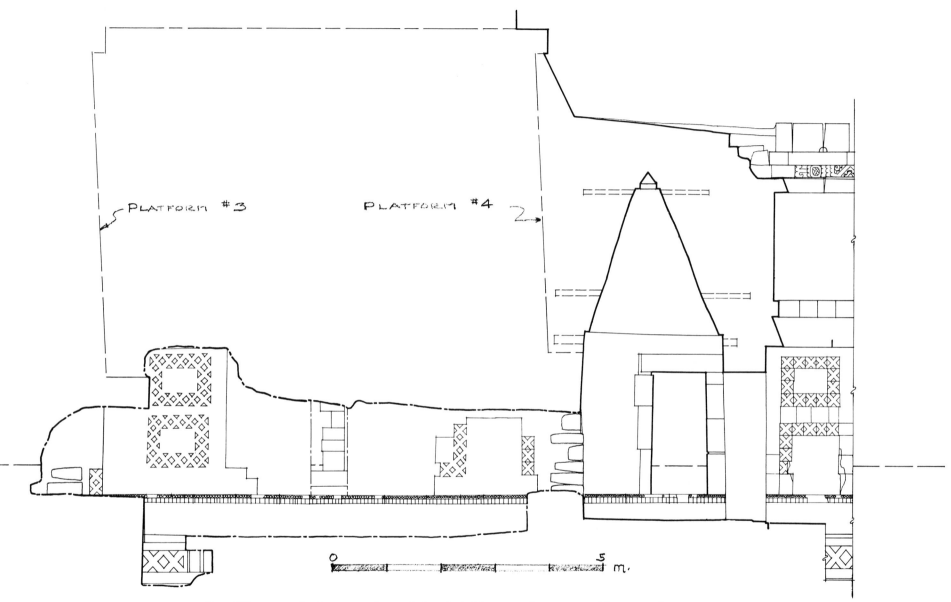

PLATFORM #3   PLATFORM #4

East Wing, south elevation through South Addition and as exposed by tunnels

FIRST ADDITION TO THE EAST WING BASEMENT

Earlier tests had destroyed the section of the first east extension of the East Wing Basement where it joined with the northeast corner of the latter. There were traces in the floor plaster showing that the wall had turned west on a line north of the north line of the East Wing Basement. This was sufficient evidence to assume a direct connection of the rough plaster of the extension with the corner of the first construction.

Foundation. The first basement addition had been built on the surface of Basal Terrace 2, except on the west, where it overlapped, but was above the cornice line of, Basal Terrace 1. Within the confines of the addition, no floor was found on Basal Terrace 2, although there was a stratum of small stone and gravel covering the large, dry rubble of the terrace.

Facing. The addition had been faced with undressed stones set in, but not backed by, mortar. The plaster was carried over the faces of the stone, rounded over the top edge in a large, rough radius, and similarly sloped off at the base to form the floor. About three courses of stone had been used to erect the wall. The wall gave more the appearance of an irregular mud construction than one of masonry. No color was discernible.

Rubble. The hearting stones were similar to the facing in size and irregularity. These had been dry-set, but contained much lime debris that may either have been from the floor above or have resulted from their being reused material. In only a few places—near the East Building of the Southeast Court and La Iglesia—there were signs of a surfacing floor, which could have been that of the second addition.

SECOND ADDITION TO THE EAST WING BASEMENT

The next extension to the east was much of a repetition of the first. Only its north and east lines were known. The east line was

106

traceable to beneath the Southeast Annex, but it may have continued south to the edge of Basal Terrace 2 and then west. The traces of floor found along the east base of the basement indicated that these were part of the floor from the west line of Basal Terrace 3, upon which the more finished face of the third basement addition rested. Its alignment was a compromise between the orientation of Basal Terraces 2 and 3. It would be difficult to determine whether the orientation of Basal Terrace 3 influenced the departure of the East Wing Basement Third Addition from the orientation of its predecessors, or whether the poor alignment of the latter affected the former. The first hypothesis seemed the more probable, and tended to be confirmed by the scanty floor remains.

Foundation and Rubble. This addition had the same foundation and rubble as did the First Addition. The floor around the First Addition had been largely destroyed, and all that remained were some small stone and gravel marking the level and the change from basement to basal terrace rubble. This again confirmed the impression that floors had often been removed before other fills were placed above them.

Facing. Less plaster remained on the rough facades than on the inner basement. This was attributable to the use of mud instead of lime mortar in setting the basement faces; the plaster coating had crumbled with the disintegration of the mud. The stone work was as irregular as in the First Addition; the floors both in front of and on the basement were only fragmentary. No color was found.

THIRD ADDITION TO THE EAST WING BASEMENT

The best-preserved of the expansions to the East Wing Basement had been built after the basal terracing had been extended east of Basal Terrace 2. At its northwest corner, this addition supported La Iglesia; its south end either was never completed or was re-

East Wing excavation

moved when the Southeast Annex was erected and the end of the basement north of it was built. When the existing plain south end was built, it was necessary to remove part of the Second Addition.

Foundation and Rubble. In some places, two floors were found beneath the face of the basement. Within these limits, the floor from the base of the Second Addition was missing or only fragmentary, and the construction had been allowed to rest directly on the small stone and gravel surfaces of the Basal Terraces 1 and 2. Along the east, the floor—or floors—from Basal Terrace 3 supported the facing, both where it was above Basal Terrace 2 and where it rested on Basal Terrace 3.

The rubble contained much small stone, gravel, and earth that had fallen through from the surface. Where exposed beneath La Iglesia, this rubble, and that of the First and Second Additions, was relatively free from debris.

Facing. This addition had the profile of the East Wing Basement, with which it tied in west of the northeast corner, but it had no decoration on its medial band. On the west of La Iglesia, a later floor rose against the base at its south end.

The south end of the east face stopped at the line of the inner face of the Basal Terrace 3 cornice parapet. There were several possibilities as to what may have happened here, and they all hinged on the unsolved problem of what took place at the plastered-over west end of the cornice parapet. This addition had been built after Basal Terrace 3 and the plinth course facing the addition, but it had not necessarily been built after the cornice parapet to that terrace.

Had this addition continued to the south, some distance vertically and horizontally would have separated it from the cornice of Basal Terrace 2, presupposing a lateral and vertical addition to the east of the terrace. Yet Basal Terrace 4 could not have existed, for its surface was that of the top of the cornice of Basal Terrace 3 at about the mid-height of this East Wing Base-

ment addition. In view of this, it seemed safe to assume that this addition had been constructed only as it stood and that at its south end it tied in with some phase of Basal Terrace 3.

A plain course of face stone carried west from this corner, with the floor from the base of the Southeast Annex meeting it on the west and on the east below its surface. When this floor was laid, a row of stones facing north connected the south end of this addition with the blunt end of the cornice parapet, continuing the inner line of the latter to the face of the basement and forming a north line for the floor from the Southeast Annex.

Following the erection of the Southeast Annex, several changes had been made in the space between this addition and the plinth courses on Basal Terrace 3, with a gradual filling and eventual covering of the whole when a row of stones facing south was placed on the inner line of the north door of the Southeast Annex and the entire area to the north was smoothed to the level of this and the surface of this addition.

FOURTH ADDITION TO THE EAST WING BASEMENT

The Fourth Addition covered the building remains west of La Iglesia and filled in front of the Third Addition there. It was similar to the Third Addition in facing and rubble, but was either less well set or had been exposed longer, for it had weathered considerably. Only part of this basement remained, from the East Wing Basement north. Since it broke away near the destroyed north line of Basal Terrace 1, its north line had probably been removed, like that of Basal Terraces 1 and 2. Because of the subsequent erection of the Northeast Terrace and other changes on the north and east, the original limits of this addition could probably never be determined.

FIFTH ADDITION TO THE EAST WING BASEMENT

Before the Fifth Addition was erected, stairs had been built against, and continued west along, the East Wing Basement. A floor, above that of the basement and its Fourth Addition, tied into the base of these steps.

This last addition, of which a facing remained, was the plain vertical basement continuing the line of the north face of Platform 4 east to the Fourth Addition. This wall was higher at the east than at the west. A floor tied in with the base of this wall, making the third floor of that area. The top floor rested on a hard surface of light-colored gravel and stone, this being the floor from the base of the steps against the East Wing Basement and the Fourth Addition. The lower floor was not so firm, and was covered by a thin deposit of black earth. This floor contained more lime and soscob than did the others. Below was small stone that capped the large, loose rubble of Basal Terrace 1.

Second Story Basement

This basement had been buried by the erection of Platform 5, but was later exposed at the west end by the collapse of Platforms 4 and 5. The fissure in the west end on the Second Story and Platform 3 had facilitated decay of the mortar in a small section of the west end of the basement, where a number of stones had fallen from position. The remaining facades, well protected by Platform 5, were in excellent condition.

From the remains found within the basement, there was little doubt that another construction had been planned or built upon either Platform 3 or 4. Two sections of smooth paving extended north and south, with the north section overlapping the turned-down edge of the south. Their surfaces were slightly above that on which the basement had been built above the top of Platform 3. On the north, four large stones were faced on two sides, as though for corner use. On the south was only a firm construction level, which was probably made preliminary to the erection of the present basement.

The exploration of the remains within this basement was limited to tunnel work and not on a very extensive scale. The four-faced blocks were south of the north face of the basement. In line with these blocks, a hard mass of lime concrete lay on the approximate north-south center line of the basement.

The two smoothly worked faces of each block formed angles of greater than ninety degrees with one another. The other two faces receded from the right-angle planes as though they had been so cut to facilitate bringing the edges together while permitting mortar to fill the joint back from the edges. Only the westernmost of these four blocks appeared to have been bedded into a final position, with its finished faces to the north and west.

Foundation. The foundation was the above-mentioned construction level and pavement slightly above the surface of Platform 3. Large stones set in concrete formed this stratum beneath the edge of the basement. Outside the basement, a floor covered this layer, and was tapered off to the surface of Platform 4; on the south, the two floors converged near the cornice of the platform.

Facing. The basement was in three sections. The vertical base was plain, with the floor covering a small area at the bottom. The wall was nearly vertical, and was set back slightly from the face of the base course. The cornice was composed of three members. The lower apron and upper inverted apron members had their edges in the same vertical plane just forward of the wall face.

The medial band face was only slightly back of this line, with the beveled edges of the aprons joining near its face. The wall section was of two nearly equal courses. The joints were tight, with only a little mortar for bedding purposes, and thin spalls where needed. The stones all tailed into a tightly spalled, solid masonry backing. The wall face had tenons of medium length.

The stones were uniformly the best-worked and -set in the complex. These seemed to have been dressed with a hammer. Many of the stones had slightly accentuated edges projecting knifelike beyond the general surface line. A thin, hard coat of plaster covered the facing, and rendered the small, trim joints almost indiscernible. The facing was backed by firm masonry; the basement filling, though solid, was less well bound. This thick, solid backing was not found between the quoins within the construction and the north face, although the firm masonry on the west may have been part of the face construction.

Two weep holes opened in the facing just beneath the cornice. One was on the west center line; the other, on the south. There may have been more. The openings were at the joint line and top edges of two stones.

No trace of color was found at any exposed portion of the basement; nor were there vestiges of stairs.

Rubble. The solid filling was bound together with a dark mortar that seemed to contain only a little lime and crumbled easily. The rocks used were rough and of many sizes. No apparent effort had been made to lay the stones roughly horizontal, and the weak mortar, rather than small aggregate, was all that separated much of the material. A traceable construction surface overlaid the basement, but was in no sense a definite pavement. This rough level was also noted beneath the outer face of the Second Story plinth.

The weep holes opening on the west and south center lines carried through the filling in a fairly direct line. They were rough openings in the masonry through which light could be seen for several meters. A rough, flat stone was laid over an opening in which no attempt had been made at smoothing or lining.

Floors. The only pavements were those about the base of the construction and fragments of a floor from the base of the Second Story plinth to the edge of the basement cornice. At the northeast, the Platform 4 floor was missing, and the floor from the basement base course was overlaid by a second floor on the east. These floors were not traced, but probably both met at the cornice of Platform 4. The surfacing to the rubble masonry was the only semblance of a floor covering the basement, but a hard floor could scarcely have been expected in an area where a building was to be erected.

6. BUILDINGS

EARLY REMAINS

Two buildings that had apparently been built on Basal Terrace 1 before the oldest standing structure—the East Wing—could be traced only by their scant remains. Beneath the level of the Southeast Court was the south edge of a building plinth. The west end of this plinth was not known, but it had extended beneath Platform 4; traces of what were probably the plaster marks at the base of its north edge were found at the east face of Platform 3. Thus, the building was definitely a long one. No remains were found upon the plinth to give any indication of the type of structure it supported. A dull, light-red plaster was broken away just back of the top edge of the face, but carried out to all sides below as the pavement on Basal Terrace 1. On the south, this floor was continuous from the edge of the basal terrace to the plinth, rounding up onto the plinth in a short radius and completely covering the stone faces with a firm coat. On the north, the red floor was broken away along the line of the East Wing Basement, and was covered by a stratum of plaster belonging to the basement. The filling of the plinth was similar to that of Basal Terrace 1, there being no change in the large, sienna-colored, loose rubble from the surface downward into the basal terrace.

The building remains north of the East Wing were definitely earlier than the Third Addition to the East Wing Basement, which was supported by the floor from their plinth. Other floor ties were not satisfactorily traced, and were in poor condition. Further, there was no floor beneath the building. The floor carrying east from the plinth was apparently the surfacing to Basal Terrace 1. That would date the building as of the same period as the plinth beneath the Southeast Court. Unlike La Iglesia, this building was oriented with Basal Terrace 1, the plinth being parallel to the east edge of the basal terrace. Evidence of two rooms was uncovered, but the total extent of the building was not determined.

No remains of a plinth were found for a west line. The east face was in situ for only a short distance. Roughly faced stones were used. The red floor from beneath the Third Addition to the East Wing Basement rounded up onto the face slightly below the top. No floor was found at the bottom of the plinth. The wall set back around from the face of the plinth. Some remains were found of the west wall and of an east-west partition wall, both of which were of the same width and construction as the east wall. The room so formed was wide and had thin walls, and therefore probably had some form of timber roof. Traces of floor were found between the walls, but no definite doorway could be determined. The doorways were assumed to have been on the west. On that side, the Fourth Addition to the East Wing Basement seemed responsible for whatever removal may have occurred.

EAST WING

The relationships of platforms and basements established the East Wing as certainly the first structure of the complex about which a more or less definite date could be determined. The structure had, however, undergone so many changes that, although the walls appeared to have been the originals, there was

111

East Wing, east elevation, 1933 (Photograph by Raul Cámara)

East Wing, east elevation, after restoration

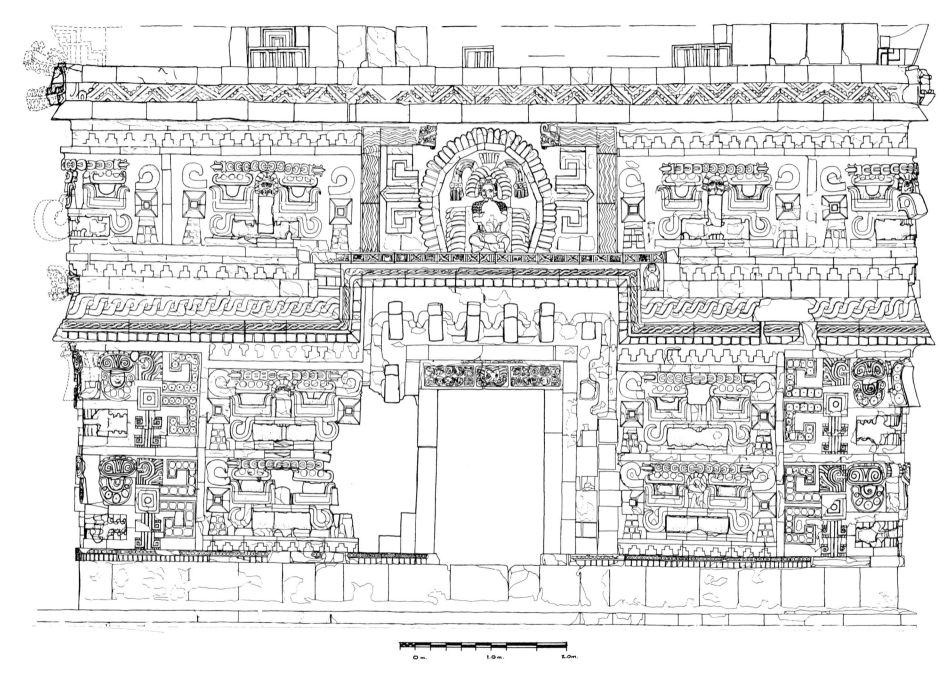

East Wing, east elevation

little reason to attribute the upper zones, or vault area, to the earlier period. The walls, in which several minor changes had taken place, continued beneath Platforms 3 and 4. The vault zone, although it had several types of decoration, was, as far as could be ascertained, without a structural break; and it certainly abutted Platform 4.

Plinth. The building floor line was above the basement, supported by a high plinth. Like the East Wing Basement, no part of the East Wing was followed more than three meters west of the east face of Platform 3, and so nothing other than the rough east end of Platform 2 indicated the west end of the constructions. The northeast and southeast corners of the plinth, like the building, were round.

A single-stone-course plain vertical zone, topped by a decorative band, faced the plinth. No floor surfacing the basement, other than traces of a construction level, was found to pass beneath the plinth; nor was there a floor surfacing the plinth prior to the erection of the walls above. The plain face stones were well cut on the faces and edges and set with good alignment and tight joints. The decoration of the cornice band was a series of disks or buttons above overlapping feathers or shingles, and was reminiscent of the ends of the plumes on the headdress of the figure over the east doorway. The disks were enclosed by two horizontal reglets. Each of the irregularly formed disks had a small hole at its center. The stones may have been carved in a quarry, but were not carefully placed in position.

The later floor, which had met the plinth slightly above its base, preserved the original thin coat of plaster below that level. Some of this remained above and, on the upper band, softened the lines of the carving. In the tunnels beneath Platform 4, horizontal fiber strokes, similar to those on Platforms 1 and 2, were distinguishable in this thin coating of plaster. No color was found on the plinth.

The construction of the plinth was similar to that of the basement. The facings were backed by solid masonry confining the fill of loose stone. The rubble was similar to, and integral with, that of Basal Terrace 1 and the basement, but with more stone topped by a layer of gravel and small rock. A layer of ash and charcoal was found below the floor in the east end of Room 4, and considerable earth was above this. Here, however, the floor of the room was gone. Whether or not the fill for the plinth provided for the increased height of the central chambers was not determined.

There were no plaster or stone indications of stairs up to any of the doorways.

Walls. Beneath the medial cornice, there was no point along the outer walls that could be said to show a change or repair of the original structure, with the exception of the hole in the south end of the east room and a possible revamping of the east facade between the two vertical bands defining the corner masks. The partition walls showed several alterations, but the original plan was readily distinguished. The hole or passage in the south end of Room 1 was cut through at a relatively late time. Although it was not finished off on its sides, an extension to the floor of the room was carried through the opening and above the break in the plaster marking the outer base line of the removed wall section. This small bit of floor rounded up onto the sides of the opening and abutted the broken edge of the room floor.

The possibility that the east facade had been altered could be documented by stylistic changes in the masks, and by the fact that the so-called cord holders at either side of the inner face of the door were different from those found in the other rooms of this structure. The pair of masks on each side of the door were like the four in the vault zone above, but those at the corners were unlike any found elsewhere in the complex.

The north and south facades bore somewhat similar designs, making use of lattice panels composed of X-shaped stones. At the east end of each wall was the pair of corner mask panels. The incomplete extent of the excavations along the faces of the walls left several phases in the arrangement uncertain, but a restoration according to information at hand and a reliance on symmetry of pattern produced a pleasing architectural design for both elevations.

North Elevation. This wall had been buried successively by Platforms 3 and 4, and was not exposed at any point within the former. It had been torn down about the area of the door to Room 10, but was standing to full height at the face of Platform 3. It had probably met the same fate as the other walls traced within the platform. Further excavations might have proved of little help in the final determination of the entire wall treatment.

The base of the wall rested upon the cornice band of the plinth in line with the vertical section below and leaned out at the top. There was no entrance to Room 1 from the north. Room 4 had two doors; the only other room standing had a single doorway. There was little doubt that Room 10, within Platform 4, had only one door, or that Room 11, which had been equal in length to Rooms 5 and 10 and had been buried by Platform 3, had only a single entrance. The doors were generally a little narrower at the top than at the bottom.

The lattice panels were balanced about the two doors of Room 4. Between the doors there was a panel of four X-shaped stones. This panel must have been of the same width as that on the east, but it was then covered by the lower zone of Platform 4.

The door to Room 10 was missing, but on both sides of the opening were remains of lattice panels at least three motifs wide. Because of its central location along the facade, the door of Room 5 must have been more fully emphasized by the increased exterior wall decoration.

The west door of Room 4 was not at right angles to the wall face, but a stone had been cut with an allowance for the angle, as had the correspondingly large stone of the west jamb.

A single stone had been used for each lintel, and it filled the space from the top of the door to the top of the wall.

The lintel for the door to Room 5 was similar to the other in section. It had a large natural hole through it from face to soffit

116

which had been filled with plaster and spalls. The soffit of this lintel was convex.

There were single small windows in the north walls of Rooms 1, 4, and 10. These were placed at the top of the wall, so that the lower cornice of the vault zone formed the lintel of the window.

West of the west door of Room 4 and above the plinth was a cord holder. This was a U-shaped groove cut in the bottom edge of the stone, with the open end of the letter at the face.

In places on the wall surfaces and in the recesses of the lattice panels, two firm coats of colorless plaster remained. The first layer was the all-over finishing coat covering and filling the joints. Beneath Platform 4 and carrying over the top of the wall, only the preliminary plaster, with its scratch-finish surface, was found. In the recesses of the X-stone lattice, as many as four and five thin layers of soft plaster could be traced, with the second of these often light red in color. These thin coatings could be found only in the recesses that had been well protected, but probably had once covered the entire surface. This red wash may have been all over or had been applied only to the lattice recesses. This was the earliest phase of the complex on which color had been applied other than on floors and in the stripes on the south face of Platform 2. It could not be found beneath Platform 4, and so it may be dated at any time later than that construction.

The hearting of the wall was solid masonry, built up with the facings and rough rocks. Firm concrete and many spalls were used for binder. In places, the facing had fallen away, exposing the wall core, which in turn did not suffer particularly from weathering.

South Elevation. The south wall was more fully exposed by excavation than the north, and offered a variation in the lattice patterns. There were little differences in the wall width, height, and construction from those of the north wall, and the doorways and windows occupied roughly similar positions. Like the north doors, those on the south were capped by a single stone lintel, with the first plaster coat covering the irregularities in the jambs and lin-

East Wing, north elevation, 1934 (Photograph by Raul Cámara)

East Wing, Room 2,
facing east

tels and rounding over the top of the wall. The lintel over the east door was larger than any on the north or south facades.

The stones making up the lattice panels were the same as those on the north, although some had been trimmed on the edges to offset errors in alignment.

Between the door of Room 7 and the west door of Room 2 were four panels set in two vertical groups. A similar group of four panels decorated the wall between the doors of Rooms 7 and 8.

The plaster on the south elevation was much the same as that on the north. Beneath Platform 4, only a thin construction coating covered the facing and the recesses of the lattice panels. This coat, or a wash coat over it, was so fluid when applied that there were vertical streaks with bubbles at the bottom where the wash had run. In Room 14 and along the present exposed wall, there were remains of two firm coats. It was not possible to determine if the second coat had been applied before the erection of the structure containing Rooms 14 and 15. On both the interior and exterior walls of Room 14 were two coats, the outer of which tied in with the second coat on the East Wing.

On the jamb of the door to Room 7 and slightly to the west were several series of small holes in rows in the outer plaster, some of which had been cut through to the undercoat. Whether they had been functional or a part of some graffiti design could not be ascertained. Beneath the cornice west of the west door to Room 2 and on the South Addition were traces of line paintings on the second firm coat of plaster. Also on the east jamb of the east door to Room 2 were traces of similar paintings on the second layer. Represented here were traces of a headdress and guilloche pattern. Traces of deep-red paint, with touches of light blue, were on the lintels of the other south elevation doors.

Beneath the cornices and in the recesses of the lattice panels were vestiges of three thin wash coats. In two instances, these included colors—a light green between the two upper panels between Rooms 2 and 7, and a bordering faint red stripe on the plain plaque within the westernmost of these panels. Because the wash coats covered the line paintings on the South Addition as well, it was obvious that the thin coats were later than that building.

Interior Walls. The floor of the central east-west range of rooms was built at the same time of the walls, for the inner faces of the walls of these rooms did not go below this floor to the level of the base of the wall in the outer ranges. The plan of the East Wing originally provided entry to the inner rooms from, alternatively, the north and the south, and the walls in which doors were placed were set back at the level of the upper floor and were thinner than the other partitions. The west wall of Room 1, having two doors and the offset at the base, was in the same group with the other interior walls with doors. The sides of this wall in Rooms 2 and 4 were also offset at the same level. Considerable chinking had been used in setting the walls, both in facing and in hearting, the construction being similar to that of the inner faces of the outer walls. The longitudinal and transverse walls had been erected at the same time, and no attempt had been made to interlock the interior corners other than where some stones extended slightly beyond the face of the abutting wall.

The east-west partitions were not in true alignment with each other. The exposed transverse partitions were not at exact right angles to the lengthwise walls; nor were they in line with one another. This of course did not apply to the back wall of Room 1, which was a through wall on one face and at right angles to the length of the structure.

The only section of interior wall exposed beneath Platform 3 was part of the base of an offset wall and the plaster line of the wall that had rested on this base. Beneath Platform 4, the north and south walls to Room 9 were found standing to full height, as was the north end of the west wall and its continuation between Rooms 10 and 11, against which a rough facing for Platform 3 had been constructed. The wall between Rooms 5 and 10 was stand-

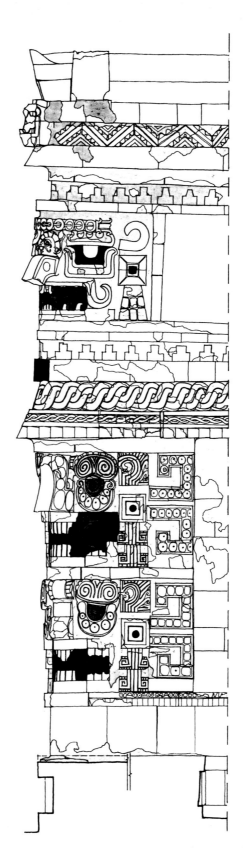

East Wing, northeast corner (left)
and southeast corner

120

ing to full height, protected by the facing of Platform 4, which had been built slightly east of it. The east face of the continuation of this wall between Rooms 6 and 9 was partially uncovered.

Two coats of plaster were on the walls; the first was the filler coat, and passed over the top of the wall section; the second was the finish coat, which was not applied until after the vaults had been erected.

Upper or Vault Zone. With three styles of mask panels employed for the decoration of the upper portion of the East Wing, it was assumed that several structural changes had occurred. No definite evidences of such alterations were visible. There seemed little doubt that the South Addition to the East Wing had been built after this upper zone, and yet the only indication of this was found on the facing where the cornices and wall area were all abutted by the extensions to the south. Some of the facing had been removed down to the top of the wall, but the skillful repair and even the replacing of the tail motif for the upper cornice serpent pattern hid these alterations. If it was correct to assume that the South Addition was a later construction than the East Wing vaults, then it was possible that changes could have been made in the facing of the upper zone without any breaks being discernible other than in the variation of decorative patterns.

The lower cornice was decorated only at the east end of the north and south facades and on the east elevation. The upper cornice had the same serpent feature throughout. The first full mask panel at the east end of the north and south elevations was, with the addition of the side frets, like those on the east facade, other than the four corner masks of the wall zone. The three westernmost mask panels of the north facade were alike, and were separated from the easternmost masks by a third type. Such variations were common, and it was difficult to analyze these as attributable either to the reuse of decorative motifs from other constructions, to different craftsmen, or to symbolism.

The East Wing vaults were probably separated from their outer facings, although the excellent preservation of the structure made other than surface investigation of this feature impossible without excavation. The Southeast Annex had this type of vault exposed. With such a construction, any portion of the decoration above the lower cornice could have been removed without affecting the vaults, and so it was impossible to determine any structural date for the north facade masks, other than to observe their obvious relation to Platform 4 and the vaults they were built against. Even so, these could have been reused material from an earlier edifice.

The east facade presented a different problem, for here the same mask panels occurred above and below the cornice, and alterations of the lower zone would have been more difficult. It would seem in this case that at least the central portion of the lower zone and the upper zone, including the vault of the east room, had been built at one time. This vault was built after the central rooms had been filled and after the east end walls had been built in Rooms 2 and 4, and so it could not have been the original East Wing vaulting.

Since the type of mask on the east facade was carried a full panel onto both north and south facades, to the line of the east end of the vaults of Rooms 2 and 4; since there were no other panels to the west on the south elevation, it was within reason to assume that, when first built, the north facade had likewise been without the full complement of mask panels it later acquired.

The vaults usually overran their end walls by several centimeters, and so it appeared that the vaults had been built after the end walls. This was notably true of the east ends of Rooms 2 and 4, where the vault end walls, above the built-in wall, were parts of the vault construction over Room 1. It would have been possible to alter the vaulting as well as the facing along this line. In view of this, both the vault and exterior facing of the east room— Room 1—could have been earlier than Platform 4, but probably not earlier than Platform 3, since the vault was probably built after the central chambers had been filled in.

It was doubtful that there was ever more decoration on the lower cornice than was found. The upper cornice, with its dentate

121

serpent motif, could be ascribed to any of the periods of the development of the East Wing. Complete removal or partial alteration was easily effected without disturbing the building beneath.

Facings. Supporting the facing, and in places projecting to within the rooms just below the spring of the vaults, was the large lower row of stones of the apron of the medial cornice—the bottom cornice of the vault zone. The cornices and the T-shaped frets above and below the masks, in contrast to the masks, had square east corners.

North Facade. The lower cornice was in two parts—an apron, with an overhanging vertical band above. Two courses of stone made up this member, the lower range being the large stones mentioned above. The upper course was covered by the plaster, protected by the projection of the band, and so was not examined. On the south facade, it was of two rows of small face stone, cut to the angle of the apron. The recess at the top of the apron was approximately in line with the face of the wall beneath.

The vertical wall area containing the mask panels was set back slightly from the fascia of the lower cornice. Below the mask panels, an area of vertical wall was almost completely covered with plaster. The lower mouth motif, with its serpent in the three west panels, was flush with this wall section. A band extended above the masks, and similar bands or stiles separated all but two of the panels.

On the sides of, and separating, the three west panels, Masks 30, 31, and 32, were lattice panels of carved stones which were cut similarly to those of the serpent pattern in the cornice above and on the end panels of the Second Story, but were smaller here.

The upper cornice was a variation of the Maya tripartite molding; in this case, the lower apron was cut in half, and the upper section was a decorative vertical band.

This band terminated at the east in a serpent head projecting from the corner of the building; at the west, separated from

122

Platform 4 by a plain stone, was a motif representing a serpent tail with rattles.

The upper cornice fascia was similar to that in the lower cornice, and was in approximately the same plane.

Much of the upper inverted apron was missing, only two stones definitely being in their original positions. With few exceptions, two courses of stone had been used to build the member. The upper stones were all missing. The small holes left by notching the lower corners of a number of adjoining stones may have been vents, drains, or possibly intended for the placing of small poles from which to hang banners or other decorations.

On the east end of the lower cornice and on the intermediate wall section, decorative features carried around from the east facade. Part of the lower course of the bottom apron had an overlapping feather or shingle motif banded together along the top by parallel fillets separated by two interlacing lines. Part of the upper half of the apron had been decorated with the modified S-shaped guilloche motif of the east facade.

The T frets above and below the masks of the east facade were continued above and below on the upper face of the north elevation. The upper pattern stopped at the west end of the first full mask panel, as on the south elevation. In both cases, the narrow top band of the motif turned down to form the end of the pattern.

Other decorative features were at the northeast corner of the fascia of the lower cornice and in the upper splay of the top cornice. These had belonged to the east facade decoration, but had disappeared. The butt of the lower—perhaps a serpent's head—and part of the east face of the upper geometric pattern remained in place.

The plaster was much the same as on the wall below.

South Facade. There were few variations between the north and south faces of the East Wing upper zone other than in the shorter length and fewer mask panels on the south facade. The east facade decorations carried around onto this elevation about the

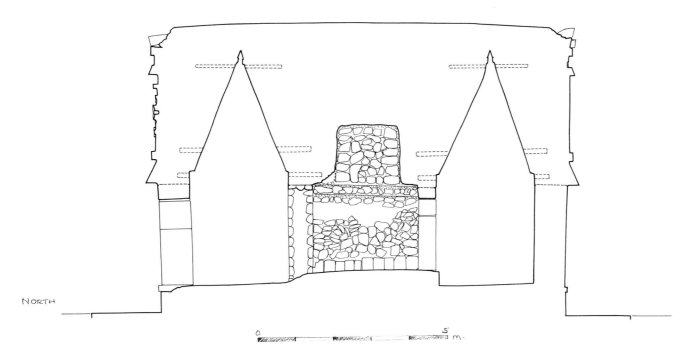

NORTH

East Wing, north-south section

same distances as on the north. The upper-cornice serpent-tail motif was somewhat shorter than on the north.

There were more full-height boot-shaped stones in the upper inverted apron than on the north facade, but fewer of these had their lower corners notched. Fragments of two gargoyles remained in this course. The westernmost of these was not definitely in situ as was the eastern one, the latter being above the space between the two doors of Room 2. Both had been broken off at the cornice line. Since the upper line of the top apron was apparently higher than the level of the roof, it was possible that a gutter had carried along just back of the edge and the water allowed to flow out where the spouts were placed between door-ways. All but the north part of the roof sloped toward the south, and would, in a tropical rain storm, provide considerable watershed.

East Facade. Except around the doorway, the arrangement of cornices and wall areas on the east was the same as that on the north and south elevations. This facade was one of the most ornamental conceived by the Maya, and had apparently been a development of the design in which a large mask was used around a doorway. In this example, most of the elements of the mask had been modified, with small mask panels occupying positions of the eyes and other lateral elements.

123

Many stones were missing on this elevation, some of them leaving gaps that could be filled only by imagination and comparison. The projecting teeth or hooks about the door originally carried down to the floor line; on the north door, their remaining tenons could be seen. A meander pattern about these teeth—the individual stones of which were strongly reminiscent of the mouth scrolls of the mask panels on this facade—did not follow down on the north of the door where the wall appeared intact. It was found that the single vertical range of stones between the tenons of the hooks and the mask panel to the east had been set in mud mortar in what was obviously an attempt to patch the facade where the original meander and vertical band had been. There was no way of determining when this was done; the face stones bore no traces of having been covered by plaster, and these stones had been in position in the earliest photographs of the elevation.

None of the masks was complete in every detail. The terminations of their noses could only be conjectured from what remained.

The upper-cornice serpent heads were partially destroyed; only the tenons remained of whatever might have occupied the corner positions of the vertical band of the lower cornice.

The door into Room 1 was slightly wider at the bottom than at the top. The cornice of the plinth, on which the floor was laid, was broken away between the door jambs. Two well-faced stones formed each jamb; there were two lintels, the upper being smaller and functioning also as part of the projecting band about the door. Both lintels were cracked. The wall face, as represented by the door, had an outward lean. The outer face of the large lintel had three panels, the central one carved with a stylized head projecting from the lintel. Each of the other two had ten glyph blocks. The inner end of each side panel was apparently the top of the hieroglyphic panel, the hieroglyphs being placed on their sides with their bases away from the projecting head of the lintel.

Above and to the sides of the door-encircling band was the flat wall surface in which were spaced the hooks which probably represented teeth and about which was the meander pattern.

Each of these sections was reminiscent of the mask mouth and, if the hooks were considered as teeth, might well have been adapted from it. The hooks were somewhat similar to those of the stairs, with the tenon carved as an adjunct rather than as a part of the design, as in the mask noses.

The stiles separating the door motif from the mask panels were in the same plane as were the bars between masks. The lower ends of both stiles were missing; the plain ashlar set in mud mortar occupied the area formerly embellished with the north one of the two strips.

The mask panels flanking the center were set off top and bottom with T frets.

The lower section of the splay of the medial cornice contained one of the most interesting handlings of design and sculpture in the entire complex. The central part of the cornice was raised in emphasizing the door feature, and the overlapping and guilloche treatments on its sloping face were continued unbroken around the right-angle turns. The upper section of the splay, containing a triple meander formed with central grooved S stones, was discontinued where the lower section stepped up.

The lower vertical projection of the lower section of the apron was composed of overlapping flaps; the remainder was of two interlacing bands in a panel bordered by reglets. The upper edge was back of the projecting sharp base. Large blocks were used for the cornerstones, and the design was carried unbroken over the arris. Two stones supported the vertical section about the door, and their tenons carried through to the inner wall face. The reentrant angle of the splay was cut in the door end of each of these blocks. These corners were also cut, so that the vertical splay receded at the top. This was necessary because of the recess in the plane of the section of cornice over the door, a difference due to the abandonment of the upper, or S-guilloche, section of the apron. In order to accomplish this slope in the vertical section and still have both splays meet in a common reverse arris, the top of the horizontal splay had been rounded inward toward the corner. In executing these difficult problems while still retaining the line and shade of good architecture, the builders had displayed their skill in design and knowledge of stereotomy.

The upper corners were cut from smaller stones. In these, the guilloche was again well handled while passing over an arris at the same time as turning a right angle. Between the upper and lower corners were single stones which continued the design and were set with their upper ends sloping in, taking up the difference in planes between the horizontal sections of the cornice which was not fully accounted for in the lower-corner cutting.

The stones making up the splay had been carved before being set in their present position, with each stone made for the place it was to occupy. The reglets sometimes varied slightly in width at the joints, but the guilloche fitted remarkably well, as did the fringe hanging from this band. Had the carving been done in situ, the reglets would have been equal in width on adjacent stones. The sculptors were obviously conscious of the desirability of having the guilloche in a continuous, unbroken pattern, but apparently did not mind slight variations in the narrow confining bands. Their knowledge that plaster would disguise minute errors might have had more to do with their seeming carelessness than did an inability properly to execute the task.

The general effect on the north part of the elevation was that of three intertwining bands. On the south, the stones had been too vertically set to determine what was intended. Had the effect desired been that of two bands, the individual stones would have been expected to be more fully S-formed.

Other than a small horseshoe-shaped motif, at the north end of the south section, there was no terminating element to the guilloche. This small stone was similar to three found at the ends of the serpent band in the upper cornice, two of which occurred at either end on the east elevation, and one next to the tail on the south facade.

Since the raised section of the apron interfered, the fascia of the medial cornice had been omitted for some distance at the center. At the end of this gap, between the end of the fascia and the vertical section of the splay, was a small figure on a pedestal.

The corners of the fascia had had projecting ornaments, of which only the tenons remained. The nature of this corner element was not known, but might well have been a small serpent head, in this case belonging to the S guilloche. The fragments of the butts did not belong to simple cornerstones, for two obvious reasons. The plain fascia corners elsewhere were always large blocks, with both faces at least as long as other stones in the same course. Had small cornerstones been used, contrary to custom, heavy, well-placed blows would have been necessary to break them off, and there was no reason for presupposing intentional disfiguration of plain surfaces. On the other hand, a projecting motif such as a serpent head would have provided an object for vandalism, and the additional leverage of its own length would have facilitated its destruction.

A constellation band occupied the center of the facade in the level of the top of the T frets above the medial cornice. Its ends overlapped the plain stones terminating the frets; the remainder was supported by the statuettes and the top of the cornice apron over the doorway. It overhung the top of the splay; above, in the center, was a shelf on which the large figure was seated.

The south end of the band was mutilated, but probably had held two blocks. If these had been similar to the other stones, there would have been one cross motif and one glyph panel missing. Reglets formed the horizontal borders of the sunken reliefs, and each block had its own pair of vertical end reglets. There were eleven glyph blocks and eleven cross blocks, and an additional one of each was assumed to have been at the south end.

Since even the north end of the strip had been broken off, it was impossible to determine whether the constellation was of full length or was merely a borrowed section from another structure. The central stone and the ill-fitting stones next to each end pointed toward this possibility of borrowing, but it would have been counter to the general feeling of the entire facade, in which everything seemed carved for the position it occupied.

In the area between the constellation band and the upper cornice was a feature adding emphasis to the door. In the center, a life-size seated figure had a feather headdress and was flanked by feather panels. A large, horseshoe-shaped frame surrounded this figure of a diety; and on each side of that were lateral frets like those of Masks 34 and 39, the masks next to the corner on the north and south facades. The sides of the panel consisted of serpent patterns, which terminated at the top in serpent heads.

A conventional feather treatment was on each side of the figure, whose headdress was formed of other conventionalized plumes.

The figure had suffered considerable wear and damage. It was seated, with its legs and probably its arms crossed. A shawl covered the shoulders, and there were traces of garments about the waist and thighs. The mouth, eyes, and ears had been treated stylistically, like those in the mask panels of this facade. The hair was in a checkered pattern; two projections from the forehead had broken off.

Considerable plaster remained on the facade, but, in the absence of plain wall surfaces, no distinction was noted between the construction plaster and the finishing coats. It seemed possible that the first finishing coat was the one that also covered the sculpture, and that the construction plaster was the finish for the backgrounds, covering the joints and spalls. In places, there were two and three coats on the sculptured surfaces, generally in their recesses, and on these were traces of color. The facade had probably been treated like the north and south elevations with several later color washes.

Most of the remaining color was on the central motif over the door. Probably it was given color treatments when the masks and other decorations were kept more subdued. The first color was applied to the finish plaster coat, perhaps when first built. The serpents on either side of the panel and the lateral frets had only one color coat; the figure and its appurtenances had had two changes. Red was the predominating color, with yellow, blue, green, and orange also in evidence. The serpent heads were red, and their bodies yellow chrome. The lateral frets and surrounding surfaces were light red. The plumes about the horseshoe-shaped

126

niche were alternately red, yellow, and green, except toward the base, where red predominated. Later changes increased the red on the side plumes. The figure was only red, but its flanking feathers had been changed from orange to red. The long plumes from the headdress had been changed from blue, to orange-red, to red; the tassels, at the ends, had remained red. The small plumes above the headdress were originally bright yellow, but were later painted red. The background of the niche had two layers of different shades of red and then a layer of cerulean blue.

On the mask elements, one and two coats of color were found, not as much as on the central motif over the door. Changes in color were noted when a second wash was found, but no color was consistent for all examples of any one element. The plaster itself had often changed the motif on which it was applied as well as had softened the contours and hidden irregularities of the jointing. Notable were the lateral frets of the lower wall northeast corner masks, where central dots were left in the plaster which had been left out in the stone carving, and vice versa.

Vaulting. All the standing vaults of the East Wing had been built after the center range of rooms were filled. The vaults of Rooms 1, 2, and 4 had been constructed after the additional walls were built in the east ends of Rooms 2 and 4. The vaults all had peaked capstones, rather than flat slabs, laid above the vertical offset band at the top. The spring line of the vault was at the top of the large stone course forming the bottom of the exterior medial-cornice apron. This was one stone course above the plaster top of the wall. The lower edge of the vaults and their end walls overhung the walls, the greatest variation being in Room 1, where the east wall angled east toward the door while the vault was built nearly straight from north to south. The paired capstones were in somewhat the same plane as the wall faces. In each room, the central pair of peaked capstones had been plastered and painted with a design and inscription before having been set in place.

Two rows of beam holes had been left in the vault, with one row just below the spring. The beams were smaller from top to bottom, but were more abundant above. Traces of wood grain on the plaster in the holes and the outward flare of the room plaster about the holes proved that the beams had been put into place during the construction of the vaults and were still there when the final plaster coat was applied.

In the east-west rooms, the beams above the vault spring were more concentrated toward the ends, a condition that would tend to refute the possibility of their use for support during erection. At the ends of the rooms, if support was needed, the end walls would have been sufficient, while the beams would be used toward the center. The upper row of small holes was just below the molding. Had the vaults been successfully erected to this height, capstones, rather than beams, would have been the logical way to complete the task so as to insure against collapse. The beams, to be effective, would have needed masonry built about them, especially above, and any mass applied there without placing the capstones would have been an additional overturning force on the overhanging vault faces. Some support must have been given the vaults during construction, but it was doubtful that the beams alone, through supposed sound end bonding, were sufficient in the case of the East Wing.

Rooms. The builders were apparently acquainted with the fact that the outer walls would be subjected to overturning moments in addition to the simple bearing loads as supported by the interior walls. This difference in types of loads on the walls might account in part for the attempt of the builders to erect wider central rooms on thinner walls than they provided for the outside of the building.

The rooms varied in length, with Room 1 the longest, Rooms 2, 3, and 4 the next in size and the remaining rooms all shorter but roughly of equal length.

The beam holes were regular for each size of room. In every room with vaults, there were four roughly equidistant beams in the stone course between the vault spring and the plaster cap of the wall.

With the single exception of those around the east door of Room 1, the cord holders had the U grooves cut in the side of the wall stones with the open ends at the faces.

Fragments of a single layer of hard plaster floor were found in Room 1. Both Rooms 2 and 7 had excellently preserved dark-buff floors that had been laid after the walls had been erected. In Rooms 4 and 5, no traces of floor surfacing were found other than rough construction levels at the bases of the walls. The filled and buried rooms had only firmly packed construction levels, with no evidence of finished flooring.

Interior Decoration. Notable features of applied designs were the pair of painted capstones in each room. Those in Room 2 were removed and accurately copied before being replaced. In Room 1, the stones were badly weathered, probably owing to infiltration of moisture from above, but there were still traces of glyphs. The Room 4 capstones were in much the same condition as those in Room 1, while those in Rooms 5 and 7 had only slight traces of pattern left. Those in Room 2 showed more before having been removed than those in the other rooms, and careful cleaning almost doubled the number of distinguishable lines. Similar handling of the other capstones of the complex would certainly have yielded additional glyph blocks, but there was little hope of finding an intelligible inscription.

Nothing could be determined from the areas of graffiti in Rooms 1 and 4. The west wall of the former was covered with lines, most of which were undoubtedly the graffiti of recent years in the moss and soft surface of the plaster on this wall. On the other hand, definite patterns in firm plaster at more inaccessible points could be ascribed only to earlier efforts.

SOUTH ADDITION TO THE EAST WING

The building containing Rooms 14 and 15 had not necessarily been built before the other standing structures of the Southeast Court complex. Its position simply indicated that it followed the East Wing and Platform 4, and had been erected after the East

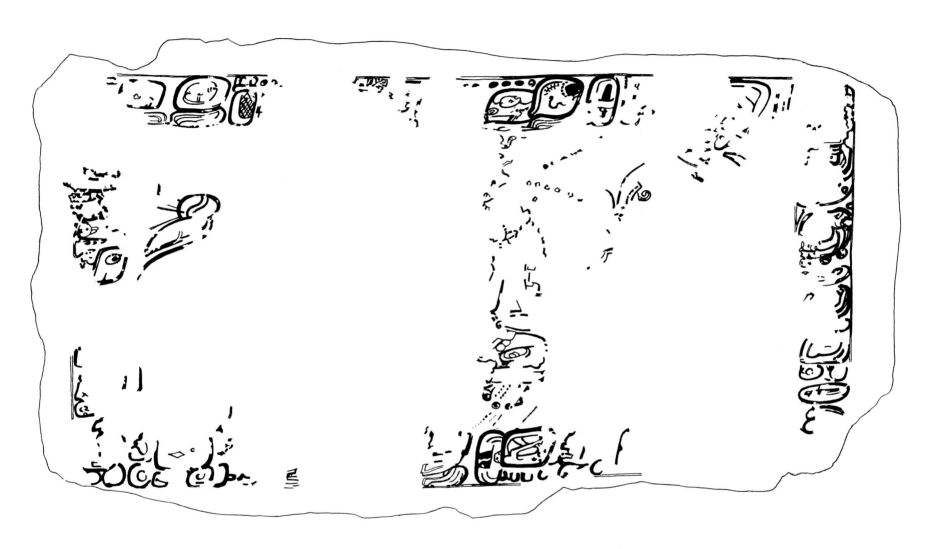

East Wing Room 2, south capstone

East Wing Room 2, north capstone

Graffiti, East Wing Room 1

0 _____ 5 cm.

East Wing Room 4, graffiti on vault

131

Wing Basement was filled against, and extended south to the line of, Basal Terrace 1. Its construction was similar to that of the East Wing, and so it probably preceded the erection of the East and South Buildings of the Southeast Court, which belonged to the later group, distinguishable by their wooden lintels and columned entrances.

There had at first been only two doors to the edifice, one to each room, but two additional doorways were later cut into Room 15, one on either side of the original. Only the bottoms of the jambs of the late doors remained, but the other two doors were intact.

There was the possibility that Room 15 had been a free-standing structure and was later tied in with the East Wing. The walls definitely gave this impression, even though the partition wall was thinner than the south wall. The south jamb of the door to Room 14 was strikingly similar to the southeast corner of the building, and so might have been a freestanding corner, with the top stone removed to provide a footing for the lintel. There was nothing in the upper-zone construction to prove or disprove this assumption.

Elevations. A small window had occupied the space over each of the destroyed doors, while there were similar windows in both the north and south walls at the top and on the center line. These windows were left as channels in the top of the wall, with the cornice stones forming their lintels. Only traces of the two east windows remained. Their location over doorways was unusual, although probably they had been in situ before the doors.

The upper cornice varied from that in the East Wing in that the upper portion of the lower apron was made up of series of colonnettes spaced by plain vertical areas.

The butt of a water spout remained in situ on the center line of the south facade. It was similar to those on the East Wing, and rested on the top of the medial band of the upper cornice.

The construction coat of plaster was so thin on the stone surfacing as to be scarcely discernible. A second firm coat, com-

Southeast Annex, graffiti on interior door jamb

cm

South Addition to East Wing, east elevation

South Addition to East Wing,
south elevation (Photograph
by Raul Cámara)

ing from the earlier building, remained in large sections. Beneath the cornice at the north, there were two wash coats similar to those that had also been applied to the East Wing. Beneath these washes, on the firm plaster, were traces of line drawings, one of which was an easily distinguishable side view of a face. It was one of the finest examples of competent handling of the brush found in the complex.

Vaults. The offset of Platform 4 remained constant relative to the floor, but the outer wall varied. A single course of stones was used for the peak course, and at the center of each room was a pair of painted capstones.

These capstones were not removed for careful study, and were not in good repair. As in many other cases, the bases of the paired stones were set back slightly from the face of the vertical band. The two coats of plaster on the vaults were not carried across these stones, only onto their edges. This slight setback from the line of the other stones aided in locating the pair to be examined, and also tended to prove their existence in other edifices, such as in the inner annular chambers at El Caracol, where nothing of the painting remained.

Rooms. There were two coats of plaster on the walls and the vaults, the second coat having been applied to both the Platform 4 and East Wing surfaces within the rooms. In each case, these were apparently the only layers on those walls over the working coat. In Room 15, the rear wall—Platform 4—had red and green areas, but with no definite design visible. Black lines defined the colors. On this surface, a third coat of thin plaster seemed to have been applied, and this too bore traces of coloring.

Both the inverted U type and the ring type of cord holders remain. In Room 15, only one of the U type was visible, north of the central door and below the level of the lintel soffit. Others of this type may have existed about this door, but remained filled with mortar. In Room 14, there were this type on both sides of the door.

In each end of Room 15 were two rough holes large enough for the tails of rings or for spools. In Room 14, stubs of two rings remained, set horizontally, in the south wall. Those in Room 15 must have been the same, but their purpose could not be determined. Although about the same distance apart as those on the east wall of Room 15, they were at different levels. Any of these could have been placed after the walls were built.

In Room 14 were the stubs of two rings set vertically with holes north of the door in the east wall. There were no traces of corresponding rings for either; since they were set facing one another, they doubtlessly functioned as a pair, as did the horizontal sets in the end walls of each room.

Room 15, with two windows on the east and one each on the north and on the south, was more plentifully supplied than other rooms of the complex.

Graffiti. Two small areas of graffiti remained, but both were illegible. On the south jamb of the standing door of Room 15 were traces on the plaster. The rest of the plaster was gone. Beneath the medial cornice on the south elevation were traces, but here too the plaster had broken away. In Room 14, there was the series of holes described under the East Wing. There were traces of graffiti about these perforations.

SECOND STORY

This building represented two distinct building operations and a number of secondary alterations. From the surface of the basement to the vault line represented one period, in which the eight-room structure had been erected as a unit. The basement, which may have been complete with vaults and even a roof comb, probably belonged to this period.

The second stage of the building included the fill of the north central chamber (Room 18), the existing vaults, and the Third Story with the stairs leading to it.

The upper stairs was not built until after the erection of Platform 5. Since it was built in two distinct stages, there was the

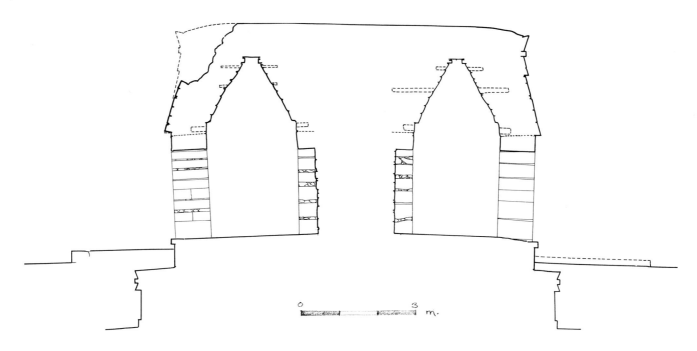

Second Story, north-south section

possibility that it had served a third story other than that now standing, or as the probably earlier roof of the Second Story. The distinctions in masonry between the two stages of the stairs were as marked as those of the Second Story walls and vaults. The present vaults and the upper section of the stairs had certainly been built at one time.

The Third Story may have been built along with the present upper zone.

The low plinth about the building had been built after the stairs. The small, single-stone-height dais at the east end of the Second Story roof could not have been defined as belonging to, or as being later than, the roof.

Facing. The vertical wall of the plinth was of only one stone course. These blocks of masonry were almost identical with those used in the East Wing plinth, being large, finely cut, and surfaced. Like the East Wing Basement, the plinth had well-formed, round corners cut in single blocks. Any slight variations in the stone heights had been taken up in the bedding of each, so that the top line was straight. The edges of the stones were so well cut that almost no chinking was necessary.

As in the basement, the only plaster was that in the joints of the plinth, which was washed over the surface and fairly well concealed the clean edges of the blocks. The ashlar in each case was so well cut that application of a finishing plaster coat had

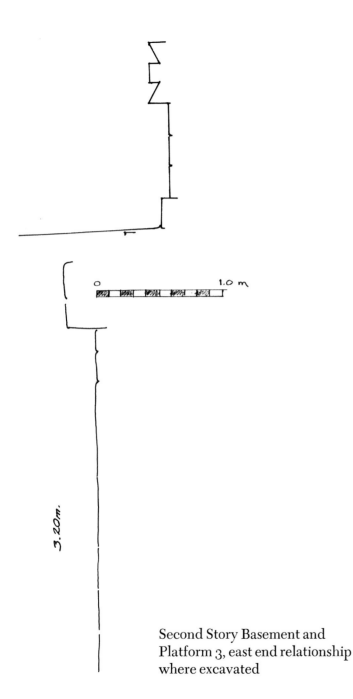

0   1.0 m

3.20 m.

Second Story Basement and
Platform 3, east end relationship
where excavated

not been necessary. The builders may even have been so well
pleased with their accomplishments that they intentionally
omitted the final coat that was so commonly applied. The fact
that the remains of the East Wing beneath the platforms had only
a single plaster layer, and on well-executed masonry, might also
be so explained. The workmanship of the East Wing and Second
Story plinth courses was sufficiently alike to have been executed
by the same masons, but at least Platforms 3 and 4 had been built
in the interim.

Only the lintels of the south range doors had been left un-
adorned, the others bearing hieroglyphic inscriptions on their
soffits and outer faces.

The decorative panels were of two kinds, each bordered top
and bottom by a band of T frets. Above the panels, the T's were
inverted. The north and south elevations each had six panels, in
which a central area of colonnettes, banded spools, and rosettes
was flanked by pairs of frets similar to, but larger than, those on
each side of the mask panels of the complex. The decorative
panels of the end facades consisted of lattice designs in which the
dentated stones, similar to those of the East Wing upper-cornice
serpent, had been used for the diagonals.

Three patterns of sculptured stone were used in the mosaic
lattice panels: the dentates used for the diagonals, the triangular
fillers around the edges of the panels, and the square fillers set
diagonally in the spaces between the lattice. One stone in the
south panel of the east facade had a groove along its center line,
as was common with the East Wing dentated stones. The ends
were double-beveled so as to joint with the other stones.

Usually little plaster remained on the wall. The construction
plaster, which bedded in the spalls used both for backing and for
fillers in the decoration and about the door jambs, was apparently
carried over the facings, while a second coat was traceable. The
construction layer was firm over the top of the wall. The only
signs of color were bits of brick red on the second and third panels
from the east of the south elevation. The color in each of these
panels was on the upper frets, with the addition of some on the top

central rosette. It was strange that on these two panels, the east one of which had suffered more from weathering than had any others, there should remain traces of color, while no sign of it could be found elsewhere.

The only sections of the upper zone standing to full height were two parts of the north elevation and two parts of the south. The rest of the zone was missing from no more than the upper splay of the molding to the entire section over Room 23.

Vaults. The Second Story vaults were the only ones standing in the complex that had flat capstones. This type was used in the later outlying structures grouped about the east end.

All the rooms had a row of beam holes in the course below the vault. Only Room 20 was without beams in the level just below the upper molding; all the rooms had a row of beam holes about mid-height of the vault. The top row of holes was generally the smaller and had the shortest beam lengths. The lengths of the beams used in the middle row varied greatly from as short as those above to longer than those below.

Rooms. The rooms could be classified into three groups, according to size and location: the end rooms were the narrowest; the central ones of the north and south range, the longest; the four other ones of the north and south range, the shortest.

A number of pieces of reused, low-relief stones in the vaults could not be identified with any phase of Las Monjas. In addition, a number of stones had counterparts only in the upper portion of the Second Story stairs and in the Third Story.

The second coat of plaster was apparently without paintings, except in Room 17, where it was covered from floor to capstones. In no room was there a complete wall surface finished, and the rule was that only patches of plaster remained. In Room 21, there was a small area of what either may have been all that remained of a third plaster surface or was simply a repair job. Room 23 had traces of two smooth coats over the construction finish, but with no color. Room 22, the long south chamber, had the first two

normal applications with a third heavy layer on which the murals had been painted. On the north vault face of this room, in the third plaster finish, was a large scene presumably representing the besieging of a walled city.

On the face of the pier between the central and south niches in Room 16 were six red hands on the stonework. The impressions had been made by dipping the hand in color and then applying it to the wall. This example may have been modern, for no plaster overlapped them. However, they did occur in other Maya edifices and in places where they were thought to be contemporary with the building.

No painted capstones were found. In Room 22, the entire length of the capstones had been covered with plaster and painted with what appeared, from the remains, to have been a plumed serpent design.

Room 16 had been repaired in recent years to be used as a sleeping room for expeditions. In the course of these repairs, the walls and vaults had been painted and a cement floor laid.

The plaster remained in many of the holes in Room 22, and the inference was that the beams had been roughly dressed or had only the bark removed, for there were few tool marks; the general profile was that of a cleaned timber. The plaster on the vaults rounded out onto the beams, showing that they had remained in situ even after the heavy overall frescoes were applied. There was no relation between the great irregularities of the vault and the arrangement of beams, and it was significant that between the center and west doors, where the vault had the greatest spread at the cap, there were no beams in the vault itself. If the beams were placed to offset the overturning moment of the vaults during construction, the capstone span would have been expected to be less where such support was lacking.

A variation of each of the four types of cord holders found in the complex was found in the rooms of the Second Story. Beside the inner jambs of each door having cord holders, there were two —one pair in the approximate line of the lintel soffit, and the other near the floor. In a number of cases, only the hole remained where

Second Story, Room 22,
facing west (Photograph
by Raul Cámara)

Second Story, south elevation, from southeast

Second Story, east elevation, 1934

Second Story, west elevation, and Platform 3

the stone had been, but the size of the hole and the nearby holders made the type reasonably certain in each case.

The room floors were in varying stages of preservation. That of Room 18, protected by the fill, was in almost perfect repair. It consisted of a firm, smooth plaster rounding up slightly onto the base of the walls and carrying out into the doorway. It was light red in color. A crack, caused by foundation settlement, ran from beneath the west jamb of the west doorway and southeast across the room.

As in Room 18, only a small section of the floor in Room 23 was exposed, but it too was in good condition, protected by the debris of the fallen vault. It had a smooth finish, and was bright, light red in color. About half of the floor in Room 21 remained, and was in better condition than in the other open rooms. It was a light buff-red in color, and had a firm, smooth finish which rounded up onto the walls. The other rooms, except Room 16, where there was then a cement floor, had traces of floors, more particularly in the less-used and better-protected niches and corners. The color was always red of some shade, degree of intensity, and brightness.

Stairs. The approach to the roof of the Second Story had been built in two stages. As in the building itself, there were marked differences in the quality of the masonry employed. The lower stage, which extended to the tops of the building walls, had been built of large, clean-cut material, and with no signs of reused stone. The upper stage, which was within the plane of the building vaults, has been built of many reused sculptured stones and of generally inferior and smaller masonry.

The stairs were on the level of Platform 5 and the Second Story Basement. The stairs had a slightly steeper gradient than the Main Stairs.

The first of the hooks in the parapets may have been in the second course, the level of the third stairs riser. Nothing remained of either, other than the condition of the coping, which had been crudely repaired. In the west coping, three hooks remained, in various stages of repair, and were in every third stone course. Above the fourth course of stone in the east coping, two courses were missing. Above this gap, there were three hooks, one in every third row, the uppermost being on the level of the twelfth stair riser. Only one stone remained above this top hook; since it was the upper stone of the first stage of the stairs, nothing was left of the second construction. The west parapet was not standing above the eleventh riser. The completed stairs may or may not have had an upward continuation of the side treatment of the lower section.

Both casings were repaired in the course of our work, the west one having been removed and rebuilt on a new foundation. As it now stands, each stone is as close as possible to the position in which it was found.

The original surface of the stairs platform was at the approximate level of the central band of the three-member molding. Remains of this floor were traceable. The stones on the south of the dais above the niche had been set before the floor had run. Since some slope was apparent, there was little reason to believe that more than five risers were ever used above the twelfth.

Vault. The passageway between the Second Story and the stairs structure was covered by a vault stopped at the ends and center by walls supported on lintels, and so divided into two sections of approximately equal lengths.

Rubble. The masonry of both sections of the stairs was set in well-chinked mortar. The vault over the passageway had been set in mortar, and must have been backed by some solid masonry.

Plaster. A smooth coat of plaster had been applied to the vaults. What remained indicated that it was carried down only to the supporting walls below. The surfaces of the stairs, end walls, and the niche platform all had remains of firm plaster in places.

143

Third Story before excavation, 1932

Third Story after excavation and repair (Photograph by John H. Jennings)

Plinth Course. The single course around the Second Story had been built after the stairs to the Third Story.

THIRD STORY

The top structure of the central mass of the complex was a building of a single room with a single doorway. Its floor level was in line with the medial band of the three-member molding of the Second Story. The rear wall of the structure was above the central core of the building below; the end and north walls were supported by the fill of Room 18. The floor level was close to where the top of the Room 18 vault would have been. The vault would probably have supported this load, except that little space would have been left for construction of the plinth of this small structure about the tenons of the vault stones. Had the building been erected only slightly forward, there would have been no danger to the room below. The builders had either made other plans for their superstructure or were unaware of the load that the vault could have supported.

Many reused sculptured stones were found in both sections of the plinth and building.

The remaining stones of the walls, interior and exterior, were smaller and irregular in size and shape. The reused sculptured material of the north elevation consisted of three S stones, four-banded double X's, half an ear motif, and a feather treatment.

No definite plaster level on the top of the wall remained. Above were only vestiges of three courses of a medial molding; on the interior, only two stones remained above the spring line. The molding consisted of a high splay or apron, a row of spools or banded colonnettes, and fascia. The spools were set flush with the top of the apron, while the only two remaining stones of the fascia were, according to plaster marks, set in approximately this same plane.

The interior faces of the walls contained many reused sculptured stones, but a complete investigation could not be undertaken, since the west end of the room was not excavated. Ap-

145

Third Story Stairs

Third Story Stairs from
northeast

Third Story, niche and stairs, 1934

parently the reused sculpture was all covered and so invisible in the completed structure.

Fragments of blue and black plaster were found about and within the dais. Within the dais, four face stones appeared to have formed the south and east sides of a cist. The small fresco fragments were found within this section, along with black earth, small, sharp stones, and possibly ash.

Debris. The debris about the Third Story contained quantities of sculpture, much of which had doubtlessly been used only as building blocks. Some evidence pointed to the possibility that masks may have decorated the upper zone. A dozen fragments of roof frets or adornos were found, all appearing to belong to the G type found in El Mercado and El Castillo of Chichén Itzá.

At the east end of the Second Story Roof was a dais, the ends of which had broken away. The length was determined from remaining stones in situ. The center of this altar or dais was on the line through the centers of the south doors of El Castillo and El Caracol, this line being approximately N 14°30′ E. From the map of Chichén Itzá, this line was found to center on the important pyramidal edifice, #5B21, in the Southwest Group, the so-called Temple of the Atlantean Figures. Most of the building and groupings had approximately the same angle of repose relative to the meridian.

LA IGLESIA

The structure known as La Iglesia rested on a low plinth. The building walls were set back from the plinth; both walls and plinth were without decoration. No pavement was found on the basement beneath the plinth, and the room floor was obliterated, making a clear definition of basement and plinth rubbles impossible.

The east face of the plinth had been protected by debris, and was in good condition. The well-cut stones had been set with tight joints, and their upper surfaces had been kept even. The west face of the plinth, as well as the wall above, was exposed,

and appeared to have suffered from fires as well as other disintegrating agents.

Walls. The south and west walls were nearly vertical on the exterior, but leaned in toward the room.

The corners were of four to six well-cut blocks with small joints. Each of the door jambs had four courses, the second of which was two stones wide. The lintel was a single block that had been dressed on the three exposed surfaces. The remaining masonry had been unevenly dressed, and was of broken range ashlar in nine to twelve courses.

There were seven windows in the single chamber. Six of these had been placed with the cornice stones serving as their lintel. There was one window in each end, one on either side of the entrance door, and three in the east or rear wall.

The east and west facades had cord holders. Two U-type holders were on the east exterior wall. Only one U-type remained on the west, south of the door and on the level of the lintel soffit. This may have had a counterpart at the same distance north of the door where the stone joint had been broken away.

On the west wall were the butts of four ring-type cord holders. Four sockets in the wall masonry north of the door had probably been intended for some type of cord holder. The lower holes were too narrow to have held spool-type holders; the upper set appeared too wide for the stubs of rings. A fragment of a tenon in the upper south socket may have been that of a ring.

Two coats of plaster had covered the lower exterior walls. The first, being the construction layer, had carried over the top of the wall; the second had been the smooth finish coat applied after the upper zone had been built. Most of the plaster was missing, but at the southeast corner, where protected beneath the cornice, was in good condition. Traces of several later wash coats were found on the finish plaster.

Upper Zone. From the top of the wall to the roof, two cornices bordered a band containing mask panels. On the west facade,

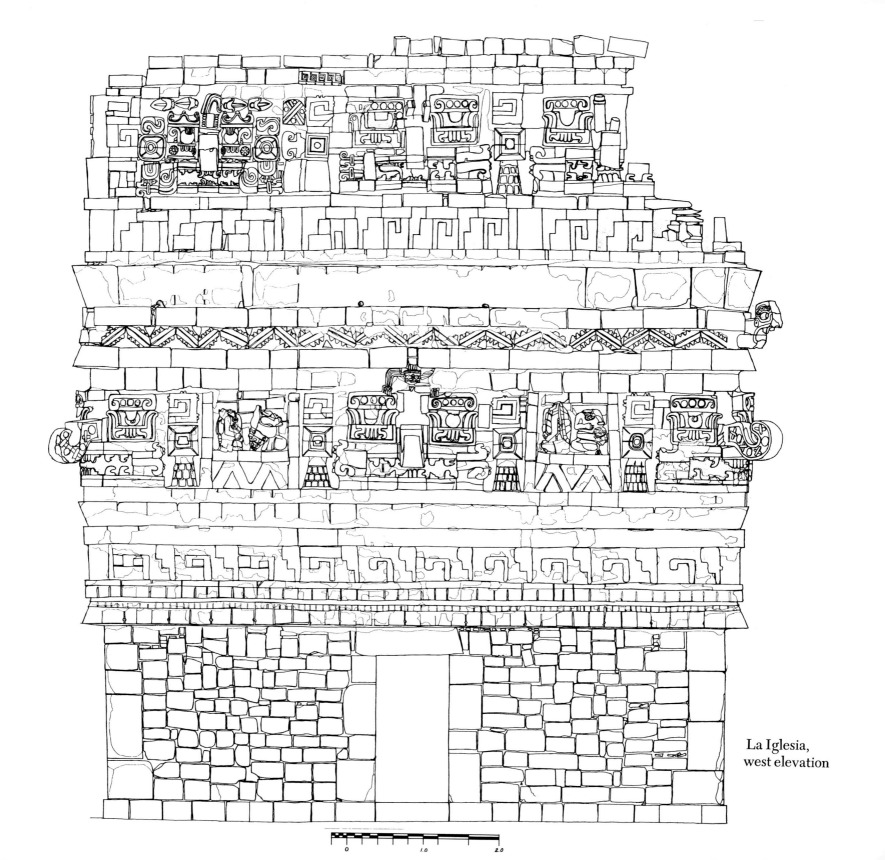

La Iglesia,
west elevation

0   1.0   2.0

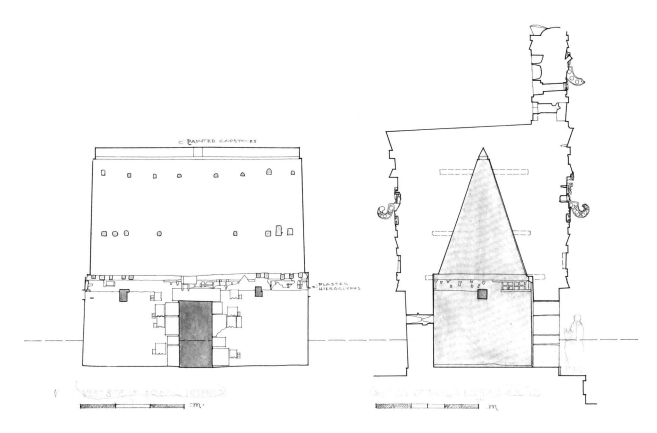

PLASTER
HIEROGLYPHS

WEST SIDE OF IGLESIA INTERIOR

m.

m.

La Iglesia, sections

each of two niches contained two zoomorphic figures. The upper cornice was like that of the East Wing—a three-member molding with a sawtooth serpent design occupying the upper half of the lower apron and with serpent heads projecting from the corners. The lower cornice, the medial molding or cornice of the building, was composed of five members, and was a variation of the three-member molding in which the fascia had been broadened and

decorated. The false facade surmounting the west elevation was evidently a later addition.

The lower apron or splay of the medial molding consisted of blocks that rested entirely on the wall. The cornice overhung the wall. Grooves had been cut in the joint edges of nearly every stone, forming small, round holes through the arris of the apron. These holes curved from face to base of the apron. Each cornerstone had a similar hole drilled through it at the right of the corner. This series of holes, which somewhat resembled the U-shaped cord holders, must have been used for the hanging of draperies or festoons.

The face of the lower splay was decorated in three horizontal bands. The lower band consisted of a fringe motif, with individual sections. Some of these sections had been cut so to appear overlapping, as on the similar member of the East Wing; the others were separated by narrow grooves which extended from the arris up toward, and sometimes into, the upper bands of the apron. The middle band of the lower splay projected beyond the lower motif. It functioned much like the guilloche and disk bands above the East Wing fringe designs, but in this case was simply a series of nearly square rectangles formed by cutting vertical grooves in the band. The upper, plain band projected beyond the middle one, as that one did beyond the lower. All three bands had approximately the same slope.

The middle band of the cornice was composed of an upper and lower fascia and a high-step fret course. The lower fascia overhung the top of the apron. The lower fascia was divided into an upper plain fillet and a fringe motif below formed by vertical grooves, with their tops rounded in beneath the fillet. The upper fascia was plain, and had apparently been constructed of stones similar in length to those used in the lower fascia.

The step fret band was continuous about the building, except at the corners, where blocks terminated each face. These blocks were in the same plane as the frets. The step side of each fret was at the right. Like the East Wing Basement pattern, three forms made up the motif; but in this building, both the horizontal top member and the short-legged U were often built up of several stones.

La Iglesia, north elevation

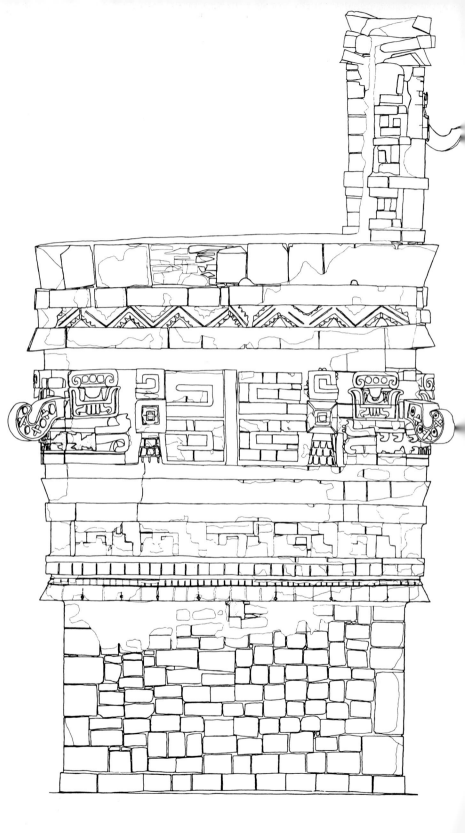

La Iglesia, north elevation, 1934 (Photograph by Raul Cámara)

153

Set back from the upper splay arris of the medial molding was the vertical band supporting the mask panels. The plane of this section was slightly out from that of the two fascias of the medial molding.

Above the mask frieze was another plain area. Both of these narrow wall areas had round corners conforming to the masks they framed. The upper section was in reality only a continuation of the background of the mask elements, thus accounting for the irregularity in the sizes of the stones. A space was necessary in design for the shadow of the cornice above, and provided an opportunity structurally to bring the wall to a level again before adding the next motif.

The corner masks, with their lateral frets, made up the full length of the ends of the building. On the east was a full mask, which, with its lateral frets and those of the corner masks, filled the frieze. No stiles separated the mask panels of the east facade, as they did on the ends and the west. The lateral frets had been omitted on the west elevation, and in their stead were shallow niches containing zoomorphic figures in three-quarter round. Stiles had been used to border and to separate the niches from the central and corner mask panels. The central mask of the west facade differed from the others in that a seated statuette with an elaborate headdress took the place of the usual supernasal motif. The headdress had been built with tenons in the surface above the mask and with a vertical projection into the lower apron of the upper cornice. The figure had fallen from its seat on the tenon of the mask nose, but was replaced during the repair of the building.

The figure was in such poor condition that it could not be fully described. The head, arms, and legs were missing, except for those portions which were integral parts of the torso. The figure wore what probably represented a beaded necklace, and appeared to have had an ornamental disk on the chest. A crown was part of the remaining headdress, and had been cupped out to fit on the head of the figure. A central band of disks surrounded the crown; the front disk was carved to represent a human face.

154

Above and below the disk were rows of small dots with projecting fringes. At the sides of the top of the crown were stylized plumes which extended out and then downward, overhanging the inner corners of the superorbital motifs of the mask. There were remains of a section of vertical plumage above the crown, with a tenon in the apron of the upper cornice.

The hands, on which the seated figures in the two niches rested, were flush with the stiles forming the sides of the recesses.

The heads were missing from all four figures. They had been cut in the full round, so that well-placed blows had been required to remove them. The bodies, with their tenons into the masonry, remained. The shoulders had also been carved in the full round; below that, the figures were in three-quarter relief. When complete, they must have nearly filled the height of the niches. The north figure was not clear, but apparently the design on its back was that of a winged insect such as a wasp, a fly, or a mosquito. This figure wore a corded necklace with an oval pendant. The other figure in the north niche was definitely a zoomorphic conch shell. One figure of the south niche had the attributes of a turtle, with both back and breast plates; the other figure could not be identified, but appeared to have had a cross section of a conch shell at its left side.

Serpent heads, each cut from two stones, projected from the corners of the upper cornice. The tenon of the lower jaw piece rested on the lower splay, in line with the meander; the upper stone tailed into the fascia. The lower section of the serpent head in the southeast corner was complete except for the broken teeth, of which there had been three sets.

Holes were formed by notches cut from the lower corners of the inverted apron stones, the plaster giving the final form to the opening. Similar openings in the base of the upper apron remained on the north and east elevations.

Two normal coats of plaster were found on the building, with traces of later wash coats in protected areas, notably beneath the medial cornice on the east wall. The dentate meander of the upper cornice had been painted with red lines over the buff color

La Iglesia, east elevation, 1933 (Photograph by Raul Cámara)

of the plaster, the red apparently having been used in the grooves and possibly as a background. The best-preserved section of this color was on the north elevation.

Roof. The roof of the building had probably been completed prior to the erection of the flying facade on the west elevation. A few traces of a plaster level passed beneath this upper addition. These may have been remnants of a normal construction level, but the workmanship of the superconstruction was so markedly different from that below that there seemed no doubt it was a secondary phase. The plaster and flatstone and mortar indicated that the roof had sloped to the edges of the upper inverted apron. There was no evidence of gutters or drip provisions other than that the roof had a marked slope to the east away from the entrance facade.

False Facade. The false, or flying, facade above the west elevation consisted of a series of step frets resting on a plinth, a mask frieze, and a three-member cornice. At the rear, or east, face of this wall the masks had been replaced by a bold lattice pattern.

The lattice was stopped at the top by a band in the same plane as the lattice stones. The band was similar to that used over the masks, and formed a plane for the cornice. The ends of the roof structure were broken away, so that no definite determination of the lattice end motifs could be made.

Room and Vault. Only a few fragments of floor remained in the interior of this building, and neither number nor color of floors could be ascertained.

There were three rows of beam holes in the room: two in the

La Iglesia, east face of roof facade

La Iglesia, west elevation
(Bernie Tun, *captain*, in
doorway), 1933
(Photograph by Raul
Cámara)

vault, and one just below the spring of the vault. Stubs of beams remained in the three northernmost holes of the south group in the west wall. The wood was in an excellent state of preservation, and each stub was firmly embedded in the wall. The tops of these beam holes were flush with the spring line of the vault. The stub of one beam of the middle row remained in the west side vault in the third hole from the south. This stub was firmly embedded in the vault, and was in excellent condition. The beam appeared to have been cut with an ax or machete. Enough remained to demonstrate that it had never been more than a barked timber.

As usual, the upper beams projected farther into the masonry than did the lower ones. In this room, it was obvious that the beams had been set in place when the vault was under construction and were left in place during occupancy, since the finished plaster coat rounded out onto the beam. This was also observed in several other rooms in the complex. The general arrangement of the beams did not indicate their use structurally or for forming. The concentration toward the ends, where they would be least needed structurally, and the general pattern of their arrangements supported the belief that they served some decorative scheme.

There was an abundance of cord holders in the chamber of La Iglesia. About the door were both the U-groove and the ring type. With the exception of the stone on line with the door soffit, the four U-groove holders on each side of the door had the cord holders in the lower edges of the squared face stones from which they had been cut.

The walls were well covered with a filler or construction coat of plaster; in the vaults, it was rough and sparse. The outer or second coat was thick, and contained considerable fine gravel, which was uncommon, and followed the general irregularities in the construction.

The vaults were covered with a thin, dark moss through which could be seen traces of dark lines. Every attempt to remove the moss resulted in simultaneous removal of the lines. In places, the lines seemed to take on features of a design; in others, they

appeared to be no more than impressions in the moss made by running long sticks against the vault faces. This hypothesis might account for the ease with which the lines were removed.

Below the vault spring was the top of a band modeled in plaster in relief. The borders were painted blue. Between the borders, on a red background, was a double row of hieroglyphic blocks. The band had been interrupted by windows and by the projecting tenon of the cornice member over the doorway. The modeling of the band had been done and applied after the second coat of plaster on the wall, and so did not have sufficient adhesion to withstand the ravages of time and man. The date 1888 had been painted in bold letters where formerly a decorative frieze had encircled the room.

As with other painted capstones in this complex, the plaster coats on the walls were carried up to, but not over, the face of the pair of decorative stones in the center of the vault apex.

SOUTHEAST ANNEX

This two-room building rested upon Basal Terrace 4. The continuation of the well-trimmed extension to the East Wing plinth, which supported La Iglesia at its northwest, was abruptly terminated slightly north of the Southeast Annex; at this point, the floor at the base of the Southeast Annex (which was probably the surface of Basal Terrace 4) lay at about two-thirds of the height of the plinth. The floor carrying north from the base of the building was traced out over the cornice of Basal Terrace 3.

Walls. The masonry of the walls was found to be tied in—the cross walls with the side walls; the plaster cap was continuous over all the walls. The masonry differed only in that the north and east elevations were faced with well-cut, square-edged stones; the interior walls and the south and west facades were of a roughly cut masonry with large spalls. On all faces, the stones were too irregular in size to lie in definite courses.

The four corners of the building and the door jambs had been built of smoothly cut stones. Each of the doors had three large

Southeast Annex, from southeast, 1933

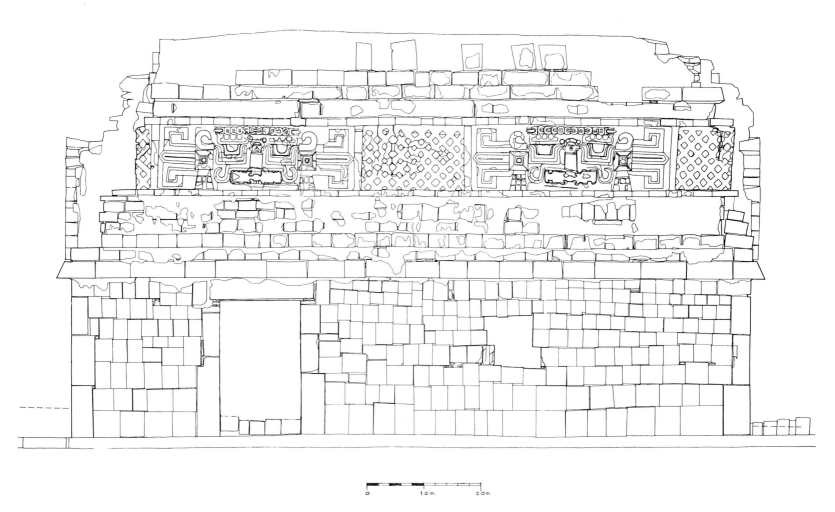

Southeast Annex, north elevation

Southeast Annex, north elevation

Southeast Annex, from southwest, 1933

stones forming each jamb, with faced spalls filling up to the lintel. The faces of these jambs were nearly plane, and had sharp right-angle edges. Some type of hammer must have been used in dressing these, for the small pockmarks of the tool showed on the surface of the stones.

There were seven windows in the building, set into the top course of the wall, with the construction plaster of the wall top forming their side and bottom facings. One of these windows was in the west-end center line; the others were divided between the north and south facades. Two of the south windows opened into the west room; two of the north ones, into the east room. In addition, there was a window over the interior door and one over the east door; the sill of each of these rested on the top of the lintel over the door.

Only the two normal coats of plaster were found on the interior walls; on the exterior were traces of several wash coats.

Both the north and south walls had suffered some damage. A large hole as high as the cornice carried through the south wall opposite the north door. There remained no evidence of trim to mark this as a later door arrangement. The north elevation had lost some facing stones. There were signs of fire on this section of wall, and perhaps calcination had taken place. Except for the corners and door jambs, more than half of the facing stones were missing from the east elevation.

Upper Zone. The vault of the upper zone had been constructed before the exterior facing was added. The apron of the medial cornice was first laid upon the wall, and the vault carried up from this with a shell construction less than a meter in thickness. Only a single flat, rough capstone above the pointed crest was incorporated within the plaster covering this shell. There were traces of a possible second phase of this construction, the fascia at the base of the masks being the plane for the base of a section of rough rubble with a plaster facing. The mask panels and other facing above this level were then added to complete the building.

Such a type of construction made alterations to the facades a relatively simple process.

No evidence of more than the two usual coats of plaster was found on the vaults. Little plaster remained in the east room, but considerable was found in the west room. The only signs of painting were on the paired capstones in each room, which were not covered by the room plaster. The south stone in the west room retained considerable color at the center of its decorative panel.

The north and south facades had lower cornices composed of an apron and fascia and upper cornices of the typical three-member type. The general profile was similar to that of the East Wing. The south facade was plain; the north facade contained a frieze with two masks spaced by lattice panels.

It was the lower apron stones that afforded the clue to the building's original unit length above the wall level. The cornerstones were faced both ways, and were set with their tenons well bedded on an angle of forty-five degrees with the corner. Above this level, the present facades appeared to have continued over onto the now demolished additions.

The vault ends were similar to those in the room in both type of masonry and size and form and position of the vault. There was no apparent break or division in the masonry to indicate that these vault ends were not constructed at the same time as those for the existing room vaults. From this it was obvious that the upper zone, with the exception of the lower course of the medial cornice apron, was constructed at the time of the east and west additions to the building.

The upper sections of both north and south elevations retained a large amount of the original plaster. On the north, the coloring in the mask and lattice panels was clearly defined.

Rooms. Both rooms had contained benches. The floors of the rooms were apparently at different levels. Traces of a rough floor level were found in the west room at the level of the east room floor, with no signs of there having been a finished floor below the present level. In the east doorway to the building, there were two floor levels, the upper being the present floor level, which had been laid during or after the period of the East Addition. The lower floor tied in with the building plinth; the upper floor was level with the floor of the addition. The East Addition floor turned up at the east line of the door, as though the doorway had been filled at one time during the period of the East Addition.

In the north doorway were remains of three floor levels, all with finished surface coatings.

The only cord holders in situ were on the west face of the partition wall. There were six holes, three on each side of the door. Two of these holes retained their spool-like cord holders. Each of the two outer doors to the building had a similar series of holes on the sides of the room. None of these outer-door cord-holder sockets contained their special type of holder.

The beam holes in the two rooms of the Southeast Annex were in three rows, with a similar spacing arrangement in each room.

The pattern or arrangement of beams was symmetrical, with the beams in each row divided into three groups, one at each end and one on the center line. In the lower and upper rows, there were two beams in each grouping; in the second, there were three.

The doors had undergone several changes. As noted earlier, the east doorway may have been filled during the period of the East Addition. A course of stones in the doorway, with their well-cut faces up, served no apparent function, and did not relate to any phase of the building. There were remains of two coats of plaster on the east door jambs, with traces of graffiti on the inner coat.

Southeast Annex, west elevation

164

Southeast Annex, east elevation

There was also a row of stones in the north door, with their faces on the line of the inner face of the building. Traces of plaster on the west jamb of this doorway indicated that there had been a floor at the top line of these stones. These may possibly have formed the south face of a high threshhold. The plaster remaining from this floor and on the jamb was deep red. The east jamb had traces of graffiti on the first coat of plaster.

The inter-room doorway presented the only graffiti of the complex having discernible designs, on what appeared to have been a reused jamb stone. The south jamb retained most of its original finished coat of plaster, which had been scratched with designs along its full height. The surface had, however, weathered to such an extent that the essence of the design was lost. A firm plaster coat was noted on the top stone of the south jamb, under the coat described above, and this was found to cover nearly the entire face of the stone, having broken away toward the edges of the face. Where broken away, the later finish coat of plaster filled the gaps and covered the graffiti on the remains of the hard surface. The freedom of the design and the roundness of the shallow groove indicated that the drawing had been done while the plaster was still soft.

East and West Additions to the Southeast Annex

The East Addition to the Southeast Annex had more definite remains than did the west structure. The north plinth remained for some distance east of the building, veering a bit south from the line of the plinth of the elemental structure. There was also a section of the south plinth for the East Addition. The East Addition had been built, so far as could be ascertained, on the east extension to Basal Terrace 5. The true east extent of either the terrace or the building was not determined. Complete excavation along the south line of the terrace might have provided such information, but the terrace surface was missing where the addition was broken away. The floor of the terrace extended beneath the plinth, with a later floor tying in with the north plinth. After the building had been removed, probably at the time of the low wall

166

remains in this area, a floor had carried over the plinth to the north and south. The fire pit and squared stone flagging found in this area may have belonged to the late structures in this area rather than to the addition.

The West Addition provided only fragmentary remains, and perhaps even these belonged to some later structure rather than to an addition built at the time of the masonry used in the vault construction. The few remaining stones of the north wall and plinth, where they joined the northwest corner of the Southeast Annex, veered considerably to the south in their westerly course. The wall may have served as a late connecting unit from the Southeast Annex to the rear of the East Building of the Southeast Court.

Early East Buildings

The excavated and partially repaired buildings which formed the east and north sides of the East Court (bounded on the south by the Southeast Annex and on the west by the East Wing) were on the approximate level of the surface of the East Wing and La Iglesia basements. An earlier series of structures had occupied this area, and traces of these had been found below the present court level. The earliest building, which rose from, and seemed a part of, the East Court Terrace or Basement, had its west end slightly west of the front line of the present East Building. The wall had broken away at the line of the face of the East Building.

The area west of this early building had later been filled in to the level of its floor line. Traces of buildings remained on the fill west and south of the repaired East Building. Extensive excavation in this area and under the East Building would probably have provided a clarification of the picture at this level.

The Third Addition to the East Wing Basement had apparently been built later than the buildings represented by the wall remains under the East Building level. At a still later time, the area between the basement supporting La Iglesia and the long west face of the sub-East Court buildings had been filled in, possibly in several stages. This work could have either preceded or

East Building and Las Monjas, from northeast, 1934 (Photograph by Raul
Cámara)

East Court, East Building, from Southeast Annex

North Addition to East Building before excavation of East Building, 1934

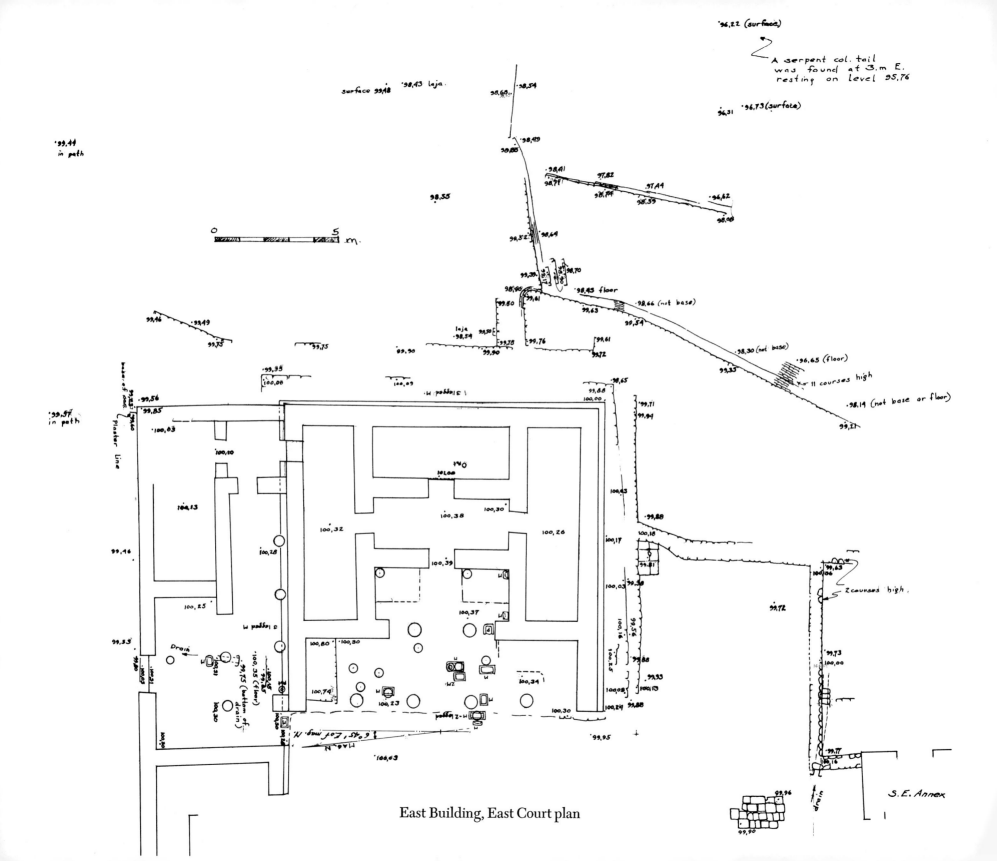

East Building, East Court plan

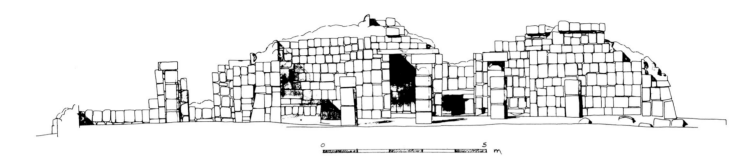

East Building, East Court, west elevation

followed the demolition of the early east buildings. On the axis of the East Wing, a series of square-faced flagstones were found on this fill; to the north of these, in the fill, were found an incensario and two fragments of mask nose motifs, one similar to the tip of the nose of the south mask of La Iglesia flying facade.

EAST BUILDING

The walls of the East Building were found in varying conditions of repair. The vaults had collapsed, and the debris from these protected the inner walls almost in their entirety, with even a few courses of the vaults and vault ends standing. The outer walls had suffered more, and were generally to the height of their talus base when uncovered.

The four columns had been set with the west faces of their capitals in the plane of the west face of the building. None of these columns was standing to full height. The lintel supported by the two columns had undoubtedly been of timber.

The lintel of the opening from the portico into the vestibule was supported by two columns similar to the outer ones. These two columns and the jambs of the opening had been undisturbed by the collapse of the lintel and vaults. Their capitals had not been moved. These capitals were beautifully worked plain stones with sharp arrises and flush surfaces. The timber lintels over the two short spans of this opening had evidently disintegrated after the vaults had collapsed and filled the openings.

A single door penetrated the east wall at its center line. Wooden lintels had doubtlessly been used in spanning the openings.

The hall had a door in the center of each wall. The one from the vestibule was opposite a similar door into the east room.

The north and south rooms extended along the ends of the vestibule, hall, and east room.

A single exterior door opened into the north room through its north wall.

171

East Building, wall sculpture found in debris

East Building, cornice detail found in debris

The only cord holders found were in the north and south rooms.

In addition, in the hall, midway between the north wall and the east and west doors, were two holes that may have held cord holders.

Upper Zone. A few remaining vault-end wall stones were approximately in situ. The only capstone found had traces of plaster.

No remaining section of the exterior facades included the medial cornice. It was possible that the north wall was in places standing to its original full height, and that the cornice rested at this level. This would place the medial cornice at the line of the top of the wood lintels.

The exterior upper zone could be described only by conjecture. The area between the moldings was decorated with low-relief sculpture; one of the moldings had a decorative fascia. The northwest corner of the fascia was found in the debris above the bench in the north end of the portico. It had two fillets on either side of a recess. The bands, or fillets, carried over the end, forming a corner stile. The cones were found in the debris on all sides of the building. Square stones were set with their faces back from the bands, and acted as spacers and background for the round-faced stones. The faces of the conical stones bore traces of green, while the square stones and the setback on the oblong pieces bore traces of red.

Although several low-relief stones were found, their patterns could not be ascertained. They were probably related to the disk and pendant motifs, and may have been festoonlike elements connecting these. The central motifs varied. Some contained crescents; others, star-shaped figures with spiral centers. One had a profile head and shoulders of a human figure wearing a headdress, earplug, and shoulder ornamentss. This figure was encircled by a crescent. The signs were apparently those of the moon and Quetzalcoatl.

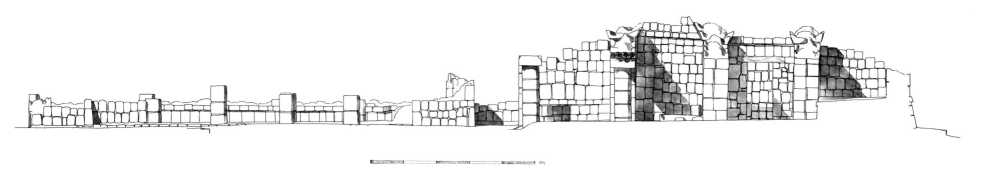

North Building, East Court, south elevation and section through East Building

Other low-relief sculpture included an eagle clutching a heart in its claw and a grotesque skull.

A fragment of what had probably been a roof overflow spout was found at the north in the debris above the drain.

A small animal carved in the full round with a tenon projecting to the rear was found in the debris west of the entrance.

Color was in evidence on the disks and pendants as well as on the built-up decorative fascia. The colors varied, with one combination having a blue-green circle about a red field and with blue-green streamers terminating in red tassels; another had a red outer circle and yellow inner circle with traces of red on the streamers. There were also traces of color on the incised reliefs.

Color was also used on the interior. Traces of a red-buff were found on the jambs of the entrance to the vestibule. The west face of the doorway leading into the hall had traces of a blue band on either side of the opening; the walls on the north and south had traces of a deep red. The same banding in blue was traceable on the hall side of each door opening into it. Near the south door, the

174

areas on the east and west were of yellow-buff with traces of designs in red and blue. The jambs of this door were painted on both under and finish coats with a deep red. The bands ranged in tones from a deep blue to a light green-blue. The south ends of both the east and west walls of the hall had vestiges of a red-buff dado, above which was a light yellow-buff. The north room had traces of light green-blue to a certain level defined by black lines. Above these black lines were remains of designs in color. The east room had traces of red on the west wall and traces of blue on the east wall. The cornice of the bench in the entrance to the east room was blue.

One capstone had traces of paint on the plaster, which had been applied before placing in the wall. No design could be deciphered from the fragments of light blue, ochre, and red.

North Addition to the East Building. The first addition to the East Building was a room built against the north side. In order to support the south half of the east-west vault in this addition, three columns had been set up against the wall of the East Building. The northwest corner was also unusual in being supported on a column rather than on a wall section. The east and west walls abutting the East Building had been erected without disturbing the masonry of the earlier structure.

The columns and capitals had not been cleanly cut, and so spalls had been employed in setting them.

Several rings with tenons were found in the room debris. These were similar to some cord holders, and may have served in that capacity in this addition or as part of the exterior treatment of the north facade of the East Building.

Three floors had been laid in the room, all having a red-buff color. The lower floor rested on a concrete of gravel, small stone, and mortar covering the large, loose rubble fill.

Northeast Annex. The building forming the north end of the East Court had been built as the second addition to the East Building. There was no break in the masonry to indicate that the rear, or north, wall of the single-room building had not been built simultaneously with its extension to the east. This north wall, which was also the north terrace line for the additions north of the East Building, extended east to the line of the east facade of the East Building and then carried south to connect with that face of the earlier building. This construction completely encircled the first addition.

The Northeast Annex was built on the same level as La Iglesia, but principally on later lateral extensions to the basement supporting the latter.

The opening in the south facade had four columns, and on the room's east-west center line were four more columns placed behind those of the entrance.

The west part of the entrance had been blocked in with a wall built of roughly dressed stone. Across the entrance was a high step or plinth in line with the base of the talus. The base of the talus was on the level of the top of this plinth, but rested on small-stone concrete rather than on a plinth. A bench ran along the rear and east walls of the room.

The only color found was a light blue on one of the circular stones, which was probably a fragment of a column, and on the face of the cornice to the bench.

The columns probably supported timber lintels with two east-west vaults. Many specialized boot-shaped vault stones were found in the debris. Some of the conical-shaped stones used in the decorative fascia attributed to the East Building were found south of this addition, and it is possible that the motif may have been used. However, the debris of the two buildings was mixed in places, and since none of the cones was found on other sides of the Northeast Annex, their use on the south face alone was a matter of doubt.

The east portion of the second addition to the East Building appeared definitely to be a part of the Northeast Annex. It was divided into two sections, with a north-south wall tying into the north wall of the first addition. This left an L-shaped room to the east, which had been divided into two rooms by the building of a wall, with a door, in line with the north wall of the earlier addition to the East Building. No special vault stones for turning a corner were found in the debris, and yet the wall subdividing the room had every appearance of having been a later construction.

A single door remained in the north wall a little east of the center line of the interval between the two columns in the north wall of the first addition to the East Building.

At some time, the north door of the East Building had been blocked in.

Several wall fragments were discovered about the East Court, but their use could not be determined.

SOUTHEAST COURT BUILDINGS

The Southeast Court was bounded on the south and east by two buildings with columned entrances. In this respect, they differed fundamentally in plan from the East Wing and its South Addition, which formed the other two sides of the court. All the buildings

Southeast Court during excavation, 1932

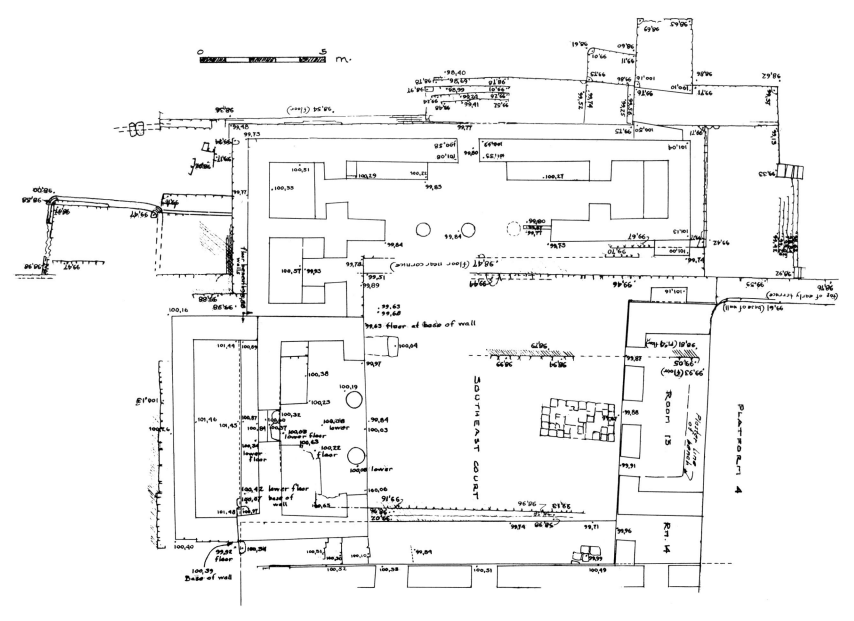

Southeast Court plan, South Addition to East Wing, South Building, and East Building

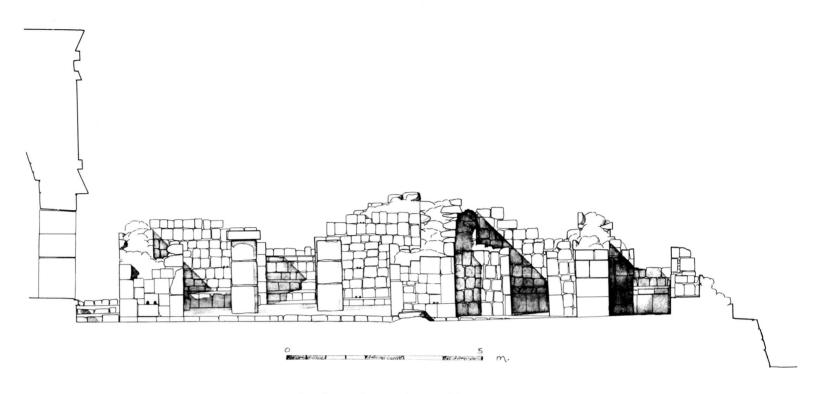

Southeast Court, East Building

were built on or above the level extending out from the top of the East Wing Basement. The north end of the plinth of the South Addition rested directly on the East Wing Basement, and from there it sloped down to the south. The plinth for the west elevation of the East Building of the Southeast Court likewise rested on the East Wing Basement at the north and sloped down to the south. Both these buildings were built within the confines of the primary basal terraces, resting on what was probably the Basal Terrace 4 vertical addition to Basal Terraces 1 and 2.

The South Building of the Southeast Court was built on a basal terrace extension to the south of the primary basal terraces,

with the exception of its northeast room, which overlapped the earlier terraces where it abutted the East Building of the Southeast Court.

There was no evidence other than the building itself to date the South Addition to the East Wing as being earlier than the East Building of the Southeast Court. The buildings could well have been contemporaneous if it was assumed that in the South Addition the builders were guided not only by the offset of Platform 4 for their vault but also by a desire to make the building seem a part of, and not separate from, the East Wing. Both were single-room buildings in their basic form, with room widths the

East Wing and Southeast Court, 1933

same as in the East Wing and having approximately equal lengths. The South Building appeared to have been later than the East Building, and probably later than the South Addition, although again there were no floor or wall proofs of this relationship.

East Building of the Southeast Court

The building on the east side of the Southeast Court was built in two major phases, with several minor changes. The west room of the building was the earlier section. Both the door and entrance must have had timber lintels. The north wall extended east of the face of the east wall of the first unit of the building. This strange protrusion was never satisfactorily explained.

The building stood on a plinth course that formed the step of the west entrance. The west walls were flush with this well-trimmed course of masonry. At the northwest, the corners of the plinth and the building coincided; at the southwest corner of the building, the plinth continued to the south. Perhaps there had been an earlier corner to the plinth within this area, but at some distance from the wall, for the stone of the plinth passing beneath the corner of the building extended south of the building. Then too, there remained no evidence, where investigated, that a plinth course had extended east within such distance from the wall that its removal would have affected the base of the wall. There was some probability that the plinth south of the south wall extension to the east was on the line of the original plinth, and that this section was the remains either of the original or of its extension. The east line of the plinth and the original character of the east facade remained problems. Several stones that resembled a plinth course formed a line south from the east end projection of the north wall. These were on the approximate level of the west plinth. Further excavation might have revealed their full extent and function. The east door had a step-up to the east, with the riser being in the west plane of the wall. This step had indications of having belonged to the original construction, the earliest floor tying in with its base. The walls, however, remained

180

at the lower level, indicating that a floor may have been missing to the east. The floor level of the top of the step was approximately the same as that of the base of the outer face of the walls to the east addition. At the northeast corner of the projecting north wall, remains of a floor were found that corresponded to the level of the base of the plinth. Although no definite floor was found at this same level east of the first unit of the East Building, the possible plinth course extending south from the protruding wall rested on this same level, and indicated that a floor and plinth here were at one time a phase of the building.

Walls. Only a portion of the central and south walls remained to their full heights. On the south wall, where protected by the adjoining building, parts of the lower apron and of the fascia of the medial cornice remained; on the central wall, two stones of the first course of the vault were in situ.

The masonry of the building was of better quality than that found in most of the small structures in the complex.

A portion of the plaster cap of the wall was found on the south half of the center wall on a level with the bottom of the remaining section of the medial cornice and one course below the vault spring, with the top of the wall having been kept in a nearly level plane as compared to the southward declining slope of the plinth.

Vaults. Two stones of the first course of the vault remained in situ on the east face of the south end of the central wall.

Had the building been completed as a single-room structure, the medial cornice would have rested on the plaster cap of the wall. On the south, the tenon of the lower apron extended less than halfway through the wall, making it possible for the east cornice to have been removed without disturbing the west room vault.

The vault stones found in the debris were of the specialized boot-shaped type. No plaster marks were found on the capstones to indicate their span, or whether the vault had a flat cap; and since the stones were roughly dressed, it was possible that these rooms might have had peaked caps, like the East Wing, the South Addition to East Wing, La Iglesia, Southeast Annex, and nearby El Caracol.

The only possible trace of a vault beam was a hole in the course below the two remaining vault stones.

Cord Holders. Cord holders of the U type were found in the north and west facades as well as within the rooms. The west facade had one cord holder on each side of the entrance.

No cord holders were found on the end walls of either room. On the west wall of the west room, a small cord holder was found. No counterpart to this could be found south of the entrance. The east wall of the west room had a row of cord holders.

The east wall of the west room had two more cord holders at the level of the bench south of the door. These were beneath the upper holes. Similar holes may have been in the north half of this wall beneath the level of the bench.

In the east room, the only cord holders found were in the west wall.

Floors and Benches. The floor from the top of the plinth in the west entrance sloped up to the base of the step in the doorway at the east of the west room. This firm, red plaster floor, still in good preservation, passed beneath the two columns of the entrance. The later floor tied in with the column drums above the earlier floor. Near the south jamb of the entrance, this top floor was of a red-buff color. The two benches in the west room belonged to the period of this upper floor. The floor sloped up to the east to the top of the early step.

One bench was found in the southeast corner of the west room. The floor of the room tied in with this bench, and carried up and over to form its surface. Two sculptured meanders carried the west face of the bench to the south. The meander patterns, with their floral spacers, were highly decorative. This type was not seen elsewhere in the complex. The background for the blue

relief was of a deep red. The first stage of this bench had a bright blue band around the top of the faces.

The fragmentary remains of a north bench indicated at least two periods of construction.

NORTH PASSAGEWAY

The passage left between the East Wing and the East Building of the Southeast Court had been filled in to the level of the East Wing floor. Three risers, with the first in the line of the west wall of the East Building, had been used in ascending to this level from the Southeast Court. The apparent east line of this fill was the line of the east facade of the East Wing and the northeast protrusion to the East Building. Only one stone remained of this edge.

South Building of the Southeast Court. The South Building was built upon a terrace that seemed to have been specifically erected for it. On the south and east, the top of the terrace served as the plinth course; on the west and north, the plinth was a separate element, but had been built with the terrace.

A later north plinth, at the same levels as the first, was apparently built after the erection of the gateway between the South Addition to the East Wing and this South Building of the Southeast Court.

The northeast room of this South Building acted as the L of the structure, and formed the connecting unit with the East Building.

The main entrance to the building had three sculptured columns to support what had probably been a wood lintel. The columns were of three drums each. The columns, their capitals, and the jambs were all decorated with low-relief sculpture. None of the columns was standing to full height, but the missing elements were found.

Several fragments of low-relief sculpture were found in the area near this building, but nothing that could be definitely ascribed to this structure's upper-zone treatment. At pavement

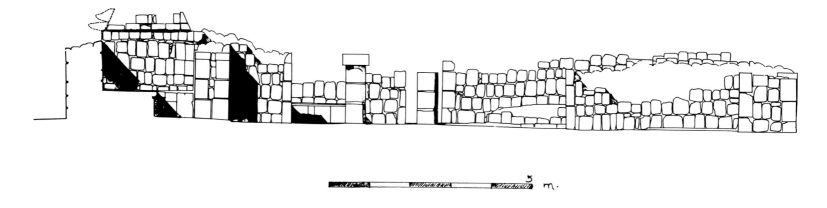

Southeast Court, South Building

level and near the door to the northeast room, the feet and base of what had probably been a full-round figure were found. Nothing that could be associated with this fragment was found elsewhere in the excavation.

The northeast room offered the only possible opportunity for beam holes in the course below the vault spring, but none was found.

No cord holders were found in the walls of the building. One U-type stone was found in front of the northeast room, but this may have fallen from the East Building.

Benches. Benches were found in all the rooms of this South Building. In the central room with the columned entrance, there were two benches against the south wall, one on either side of the center door. The east bench was beautifully carved on face and end in low relief with five pairs of figures on the north and one pair on the west. On this bench, against the east wall, was a talus. The plaster top of the bench carried up onto this sloping construction.

The west bench in this room was of approximately the same dimensions as those of the east bench, but had neither the sculpture nor the talus. Two courses of small, rough facing stones had been used. The reused low-relief sculpture from the south addition to the bench in the northeast room of this building was of the correct height for this bench. Not only did it face in the opposite direction from the figures in the east bench but it was strikingly similar in the character of the carving and detail. Another companion piece was found in the west coping to the stairway south of the east addition to the Southeast Annex. These two pieces appeared as strong evidence that the west bench in the vestibule to the South Building of the Southeast Court had originally been sculptured, as had the east bench, and that these two stones had come from there. Perhaps, on the other hand, the sculpture had been precarved or borrowed for these benches, and that only the east bench had been installed.

The northeast room originally had had a bench similar to those in the other two small rooms. Later, the area in front of the bench and on either side of the door had been filled to the level of the bench. These secondary additions to the original bench had no cornices, and had been built up of one and two courses. The south one of the two contained the sculptured stone assumed to have belonged to the west bench in the vestibule. This bit of sculpture had apparently been given a wash of red.

The meticulous drawing, by Fred P. Parris, of the sculptured bench gave a far more accurate description than words can convey. Several points should, however, be emphasized. The failure of the sculpture to carry over from stone to stone smoothly, and in some cases not at all, made it apparent that the sculpture had not been executed in position. The two west stones of the north elevation were obviously a pair, with all the details carrying across the joint. These two must have been carved side by side. The next pair of stones had obviously not been carved together. The only line that appeared to have carried through was that of the cord from the forward to the rear figure. The height of the panels were not the same; nor did the scrolls from in front of the rear figure carry over onto the west stone. The panel height of the west end of this pair did not match with that of the west pair of figures.

The absence of a left-hand borderline suggested that this might not have been the complete panel, and that the whole bench had perhaps been borrowed from another structure. Failure in design, execution, or determination of the proper scene length might also explain the indefinite end.

The low-relief sculptures on the two jambs to the entrance were strikingly different, even at first glance. The jambs were similar in that each bore a single figure with appurtenances, and each of these figures faced the north or outer edge of the jamb.

The west jamb had been excavated some years before the systematic study of the complex. The top of the jamb was missing, and was not recovered in the debris.

Some trace of color remained on the jambs. On the west jamb, the border band had been painted a light blue, while the background about the figure was a deep red. Yellow was noted on the feathers of the headdress, with occasional spots of red.

The figure on the east jamb had the attributes of the Mexican god of obsidian called Tezcátlipoca. The figure was in full front view, except for the head, which was in profile and faced north. The right foot of the figure had been replaced by a rosette, from the center of which projected the body of a serpent. The serpent carried down, then forward, and finally up to where the head was close to the border of the jamb. The mouth of the serpent was open, displaying the upper and lower fangs; a bifurcated tongue projected and touched the panel border. A groove along the lower side of the body of the serpent probably represented the ventral scales.

The figure had traces of two buttonlike nose plugs. The headdress seemed to have been a bird, from the top of which projected an elaborate system of finely executed feathers, which extended upward and then down toward the rear of the panel to the level of the knees.

A large, bifurcated scroll began near the forehead of the figure and eventually filled the upper north corner of the panel. Another scroll embellished the south upper corner.

The border of the jamb was a light blue. The background of the panel had traces of a deep red. The feathers ranged from light to dark green; the scrolls retained traces of blues and yellows. The body of the figure had apparently been of yellow with traces of red, and on the waistband were traces of blue. The bird or animal head forming the crown for the headdress was a light blue, while the round earplug or cover was green. On neither jamb did any large color areas remain intact. The color schemes given here were taken from small remaining sections, which in many cases were so faint that only a vague idea of the original color could be ascertained.

Each of the three columns had two figures with elaborate meander designs to fill the spaces between them. Fortunately, the lower drums of the east and central columns remained in situ, giving the positions of the figures on each of these as being on the east and west sides of the columns and facing north. The west column had been previously moved to the museum in Mérida,

South Building, Southeast Court, entry column and capital (Photograph by Raul Cámara)

without the capital, but it was assumed that the two figures on it were similarly oriented. Each column was made up of three drums, and was banded at top and bottom by a fillet. The joint between the center and top drums, unfortunately, occurred at face level on all the columns. Considerable chinking was also used, the wide joints accounting for the loss of considerable sculptured detail.

The two figures on the east column were somewhat similar. Each of these figures carried a small rectangular shield with a field of geometric designs. The east figure on the west column carried a somewhat similar shield. Both east-column figures wore simple hats from which projected feathers.

The center column had suffered more than had the east one.

The figures were smaller, but the scrolls and meanders were larger, than those on the east columns.

The figure on the west side of the central column wore a bird headdress, probably representing a hawk.

The east figure on the central column seemed to have had large ornamental disks on the front and back of the chest. A series of semidisks hung from a waist band, with a maxtli hanging in front to below the knees. The two figures faced one another, and it was assumed they had been facing north when in place in the building.

The headdress on the east figure appeared to be a death mask, with a bladelike nose plug and circular ear motif.

The column capitals had been sculptured on all four edges,

each panel containing a figure of a warrior designed to fit the horizontal area.

SOUTHWEST GATEWAY TO SOUTHEAST COURT

A construction which postdated both the South Addition to the East Wing and the South Building of the Southeast Court had been erected between the two, forming a passage or entrance to the court. This gateway had been built over the first plinth to the South Building before the erection of the second plinth and the subsequent filling of the court. The west face of the construction was a continuation of the west face of the South Building.

The masonry closely resembled that of the South Building.

When the court had been filled to the level of the top of the South Building plinths, the west plinth of the South Building was extended north with a single course of vertical stones to form a west line for this fill west of this southwest entrance to the court. Later the terrace west of this was filled to this one course. Only two stones marked the south line of this increase in height. The filling in of the passage to a higher level preserved a portion of the firm, light-red plaster floor at the lower level.

North Building. This adjunct to the complex underwent exploratory excavations in the process of evolving the sequences and limits of the basal and stairs terraces. As a result, information was only fragmentary, and it remained as a portion of the problem to be undertaken when the area about Las Monjas, El Caracol, and Akabdzib would eventually be excavated in order to provide the definite relationship of these and the smaller structures in this area.

The south wall was found to be later than the eastern lateral addition to the Main Stairs Terrace.

The floor level of the building extended to the north, forming a plaza level which passed beneath the Temple of the Wall Panels.

The only remains of a north wall and room construction were encountered at the east. The east jamb of the north entrance was near the east end of the room. A single drum was found, which was probably part of one or two columns that may have supported the beams over the portal. A sculptured stone with cylindrical base was found next to this drum, and was at first thought to have been a Hathor-type column capital. It may, however, have been a large incensario.

The absence of vault material and the wide span of the room, with relatively thin walls, led to the assumption that the roof may have been of timber and mortar construction.

STRUCTURES WEST OF MAIN STAIRS

There were several phases in the remains found in the angle between the west end of the Main Stairs and the north faces of the main platforms. Before any of these constructions had been built, the area west of the stairs had been filled to the approximate level of the terrace north of the stairs.

The first of the later constructions was a wall built against the stairs and the platforms, and so had only a single face.

No other walls were found related to this L-shaped construction at its early level, thereby making any conjectures as to the original plan rather futile.

West of the stairs, walls had been built extending north from the above-described construction. Between the ends of these two walls was a row of stones with a south face that appeared to be the remains of a north wall of a room. These few stones had probably been preserved by the bench that filled the east end of this hypothetical "room." The column drum found north of the east room was in line with this north wall fragment. There were no plaster floor marks to assist in determining whether this drum was in situ.

West of the northwest corner of Platform 4 was a course of five stones, all that remained of a north-south wall facing the platform.

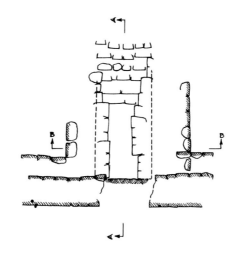

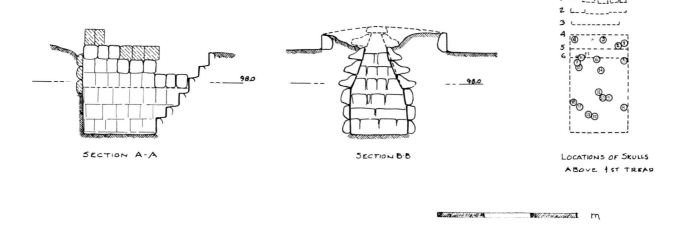

SECTION A-A   SECTION B-B   LOCATIONS OF SKULLS   SKULLS & POTTERY
                                          ABOVE 1ST TREAD   BELOW 1ST TREAD

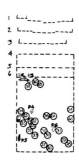

m

Burial vault, Northeast Terrace

7. BURIAL VAULTS

BALL COURT

The small chamber south of the northeast corner of the Ball Court east stairs may have been for burial purposes. The chamber was apparently erected at the time of the filling in of the area east of the Ball Court stairs. The walls had been built in three courses. Three specialized vault stones were found in their original positions. Two flat stones were found that had probably been capstones for the vault. No plaster was found on the walls; nor was the means of opening the vault determined.

The lower riser to this Ball Court east stairs was missing at a similar distance from the south end, and the finding of a face and capstone there gave rise to the belief that a similar burial chamber may have occupied a balancing position here, but no other evidence of this was found.

NORTH BUILDING

The burial chamber built in the approximate center line of the North Building was in fairly good repair, and contained forty distinguishable human skulls as well as many other disintegrated human bones. In addition, seven ceramic objects were found, several of which were almost complete. One broken plate appeared to contain a child's skull associated with it. Of unusual interest was the remains of a layer of plaster covering the bones found on the second tread from the bottom, the plaster rounding over from the riser below that tread. This was the only definite plaster level or surface found within the chamber.

The burial chamber had most likely been built after the single course of stones was laid in front of the upper remaining level of the North Building south wall, for this course of stones appeared to have been modified to carry around the top of the vault.

8. FIREPITS AND FLAGGINGS

Within the area formerly occupied by an east addition to the Southeast Annex was the better preserved of the two firepits found in the complex. Traces of a plaster lining were found, and on the west these were at the approximate level of the floor of the former room. No definite relationship between this plaster and the room floor could be found, the floor being absent at this location. Each of the north and south sides of the pit was faced with a pair of stones. The proximity of this firepit to the surface of the debris in this area resulted in a paucity of charred refuse. Fire discoloration was, however, evident within the pit. The disintegrated condition of the floors in this area made association of this pit with the room or later levels impossible.

The only other definite firepit was found east of the southeast corner of the South Building to the Southeast Court. The hard, charred plaster floor of this pit was on the level of the top of the second or top riser just south of it. On the south and west, several face stones remained of what had probably been a course about the pit. The only refuse found was several small pieces of burned wood and one burned shard. A mano (corn-grinding stone) was found nearby.

Three uncovered flagstone areas had evidence of having been used as fire hearths. The largest of these flagstone areas was in front of the center door to the South Addition to the East Wing. The central stones in this group were badly disintegrated, as though they had been calcinated by intense heat.

An area west of the north column to the East Building entrance was laid in the last floor level. Twenty face stones were used in this regularly laid paving. No evidence other than a burned-over appearance could be found of fire in this section.

Fragments of a flagstone paving were found in the northwest corner of the Southeast Court. The few stones found were on the level of the floor in the north room of the South Addition to the East Wing, and so were above the last definite pavement level found in the court.

North of the Main Stairs were a series of face stones set face up in a single row forming a hollow square.

9. BUILDING DETAILS

DRAINS AND WEEPS

Many of the drainage canals and weep holes have been described, but a general summary of these important features seems justified at this point.

The longest drain found was the one between the Southeast Annex and the Southeast Mound. This was traced from its outlet, through the east face of the Southeast Terrace, west to where it carried beneath the two steps just east of the southeast corner of the Southeast Court Terrace. No definite plaster side lining to this drain was found, but its bottom was the second surface level of the Southeast Terrace. The inlet was not found, but the level and location where last uncovered gave the impression that the drain had been designed to serve the Southeast Court.

The west drain serving the north playing area of the Ball Court has already been described. The masonry used was better cut than that of the above-described drain. As in the latter, no definite plaster lining was found other than the floor which belonged to the earlier pavement upon which the drain was built. In each, the floor already had the slope required for drainage, a factor which the builders always provided for in their roofs and pavements.

East of the Ball Court drain were the remains of what had apparently been an earlier drainage canal serving this area. Only traces of the side walls remained.

Two drains had been provided for the East Court when that area was brought to its last level. These drains are well formed, and had four plastered sides. The drain which had its inlet north of the northeast corner of the Southeast Annex had side walls of face stones and bottom and top courses of well-trimmed flat slabs. Its outlet was probably the similar drain uncovered east of this corner of the Southeast Annex. The wall over the inlet made this drain imperative in order to take the runoff from this area before it accumulated and entered the Southeast Annex.

The area in front of the East Building of the East Court was served by a plaster-lined drain which came from a sump west of the center of the building's entrance. This drain was on the level of the earlier floor level below the final surface. The outlet was not found, but the direction of the inlet would lead it toward the outlet to the drain from in front of the Southeast Annex. These drains had apparently been provided for at the same time, and so a common outlet would not have been improbable.

A section of a drain was found beneath the North Addition to the East Building. This had apparently been provided when the terracing for this addition was built, for it did not extend south within the terrace supporting the East Building. No definite opening was found in the floors above the present south end of this drain, although earth and some shards were found at this point; on the north, the drain was clean, as though it had never been used. The roof overflow spout found in the debris above the floor may have come from the East Building.

RUBBLEWORK IN THE PLATFORMS

A comparative study of the rubblework of Las Monjas complex

Drain east of La Iglesia

must not lose sight of the function which the masonry under consideration played in the structure. The three main groupings were: the low terraces, of one to three meters in height, supporting Las Monjas and the adjacent buildings; the platforms; and the buildings supported by the terraces and the platforms.

The low terraces usually had a fill of uncut and unweathered stone confined by walls of ashlar or rubble masonry. The last depended upon and varied with the wall and vault construction, and was a rubblework confined by ashlar.

Three of the platforms were of a shell-type construction—that is, they were built as masonry walls filled with rough stone laid without mortar. Obviously the masonry of the shell structures was likely to have been laid in courses, since the sections were built as walls and required more care than in a solid structure, in which the stone could be easily thrown into place. In the latter case, there would have been no necessity to select and lay large, regularly shaped flat stones, since the mortar and small stones would have filled the interstices.

The earliest known Las Monjas platform offered the best example of rubble in the complex. Only flat stones had been used, and the interstices were filled with the hardest mortar and the least amount of chinking found anywhere in the complex.

The Second Story Basement was of masonry throughout, but was less than two meters in height. No coursing was employed, and the stones were smaller and the mortar inferior to those in any other rubble in Las Monjas. This basement, beneath the Second Story, was faced with the finest coursed ashlar in Chichén Itzá.

A circular ring of stone formed the inlet to a drain between the Northeast Annex and La Iglesia. This stone was set flat in the surface halfway between the southwest corner of the former building and the rear center line of the latter. The drain leading north from this point passed beyond the north line of the East Wing Basement Addition supporting La Iglesia. Here the cornice of the basement had been removed, the bottom of the drain being at the level of the top of the medial wall band. The top of the cap-stones for the drain was in line with the surface of the basement. The drain continued north of this line, dropping down to the level of the floor supporting the basement. The full northern extent of this drain could not be determined.

Near the north center line of the Northeast Terrace was a heptagonal cist or sump. The north side of this construction was in the plane of the south wall of the North Building. This may have served as a drainage sump for this area. No evidence of a cover or remains of artifacts was found within it.

Weep holes encountered in the course of the excavations probably represented only a small percentage of those actually installed by the builders.

CORD HOLDERS

Cord holders found in the complex are of four types: U-groove, spool, ring, and tongue.

The U-groove type cord holder was the most common in the complex as well as the simplest in construction. Grooves 0.02 m. deep were cut into the side of a wall stone, with the open end of the U at the face of the stone, and the spread between the two grooves generally about 0.08 m. Sometimes two stones were similarly grooved and placed together, each stone therefore containing half of the circular groove.

The spool-type cord holders were generally square holes in the wall with spool-shaped stones at the face of the hole. The type of spool varied, some being of the U shape and some of the L shape, found in situ in the Southeast Annex.

The ring-type cord holder was much like a ballcourt ring, with the tail of the ring inserted into an opening in the wall. The sizes of rings varied.

The tongue-type cord holder was an elaborate U-groove type. These were generally cut on smaller wall stones, about 0.20 m. by 0.25 m. From one of the smaller ends projected a tongue 0.10 m. square and 0.5 m. deep, with the surface of the tongue flush with the wall.

Cord holders were most commonly found near doors. Us-

191

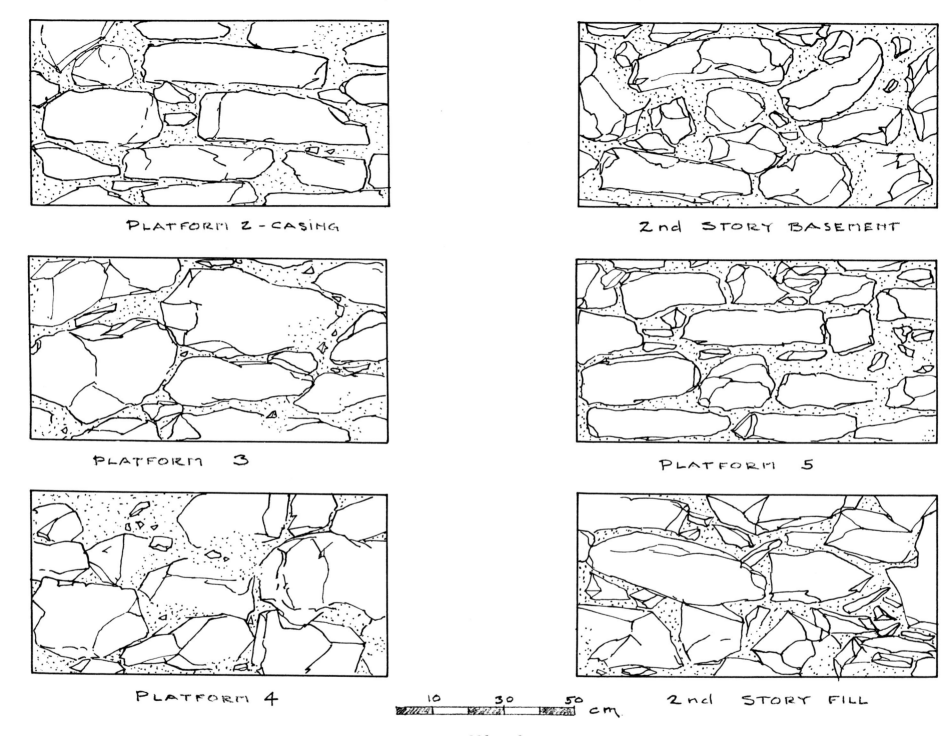

PLATFORM 2-CASING

2nd STORY BASEMENT

PLATFORM 3

PLATFORM 5

PLATFORM 4

2nd STORY FILL

10   30   50 cm.

Rubblework

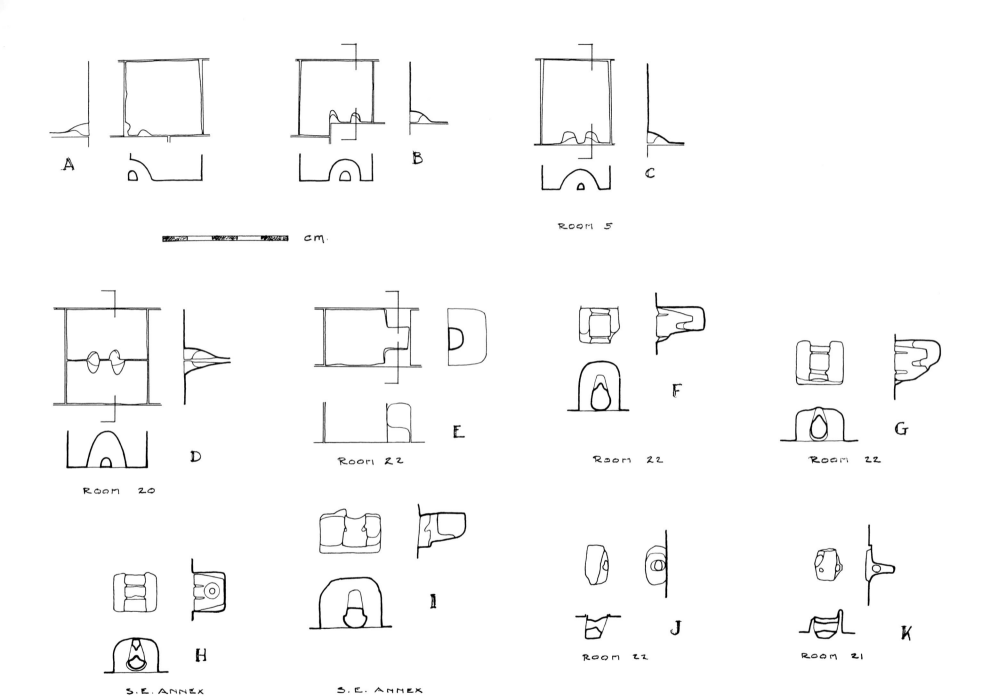

A

cm.

B

ROOM 5

C

ROOM 20

D

ROOM 22

E

ROOM 22

F

ROOM 22

G

S.E. ANNEX

H

S.E. ANNEX

I

ROOM 22

J

ROOM 21

K

Cord holders

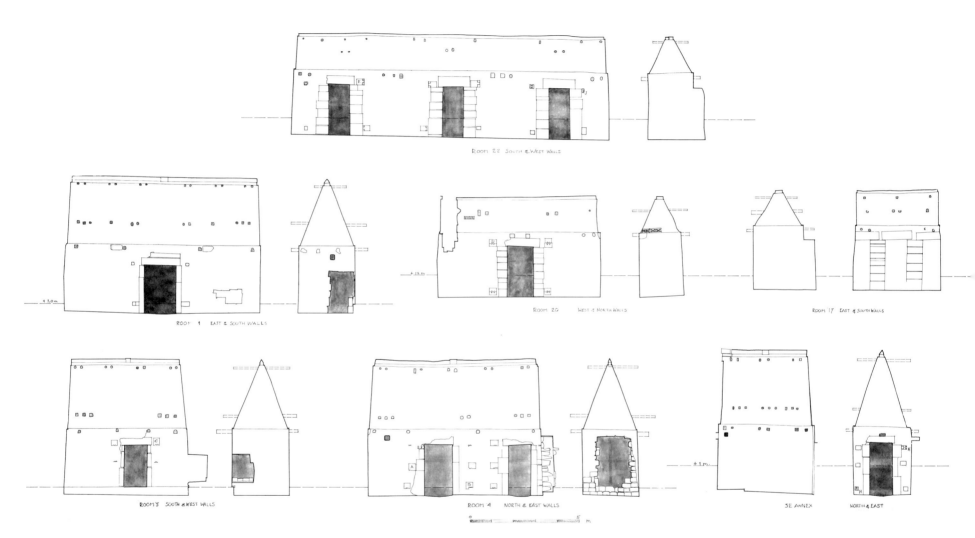

Room elevations and sections, with beam holes and cord holders

ually there were three, from 0.40 m. to 0.75 m. inside the doorways to the buildings. Interior doorways had only the upper two cord holders, on both wall surfaces. The top pair was on a level with the soffit of the lintel; another pair was at mid-height; for the outer doors, the lower pairs were within half a meter from the floor. Although cord holders were in pairs and usually near doors, some had their mates directly across the room, but in no definite relation to the room that could be determined.

BEAM HOLES

Beam holes were the result of the disintegration of timbers in the vaults. Only in a few places in the complex, mainly in La Iglesia, was there any evidence of the beams themselves. These were set in the vaults during construction, but their use could not be ascertained.

Beam holes were generally found to occur in three rows: the lower row near the vault spring, either above or below it; the second row, somewhere from one-quarter to one-half the way up the vault; the third row, somewhere near the capstone. The beams were most often regularly spaced, the measurement between beams varying, depending upon the size of the room. However, irregular patterns often appeared, and sometimes the central portion were lacking in the lower row of beams. The lower and middle beams were usually of the same length, the upper beams being somewhat shorter.

In 1962, permission was obtained from the Mexican Government for removal of beam samples from La Iglesia and La Casa Colorada. E. Wyllys Andrews of the Middle American Research Institute, David Bolles, and Señor Galvéz of the Instituto Nacional de Antropología e Historia removed sections of two beams from La Iglesia and one from La Casa Colorada. In April 1963, John B. Chandler, Research Scientist for the Texas Bio-Nuclear division of Kaman Aircraft Corp. of Austin, Texas, reported the radiocarbon age determinations to be A.D. 600 plus or minus seventy years for the upper beam sample from La Iglesia. The beam from La Casa Colorada was dated as A.D. 610 plus or minus sixty years.

Had carbon-14 dating been available in the 1930s perhaps dates could have been obtained on other charred remains, such as in firepits.

10. MURAL PAINTINGS

SECOND STORY PAINTINGS

Color was used in many places throughout the complex: on the floors and pavements, on exterior and interior wall surfaces, in combination with the sculpture, and for small capstones. Pictorial representations in paint were, however, limited to the paired capstones in the ground-level standing rooms, the fragments on the walls and doorways of the East Wing and South Addition to the East Wing facades of the Southeast Court, and two of the Second Story rooms. Other areas may have been treated as beautifully as the walls and vaults of the two Second Story rooms, but it is doubtful that little of such material can ever be recovered.

All the mural and capstone decorations were painted on the dry plaster wall, and so are not true frescoes. The work was outlined before the areas were filled in with flat colors. Details and corrections were often made with over lines. In most of the designs, only the sienna or so-called reddish copper-tan outlining remained; in others, only a black outline could be seen. In the larger fragment in Room 22, the long central chamber of the south range of the Second Story, both sienna and black occurred separately on the same motif. The impression here was that the artist was either not particular about his choice of outlining color or had forgotten to complete the drawing the first time and, when adding latter details, had carried out other parts of the design. Some details, such as the lines of the roof thatch, were painted in black lines after the red-outlined area had been filled in.

The line work was generally narrower on the figures than on

the architecture and the backgrounds. The flat background colors, where distinguishable, were painted with extremely narrow strokes. Rooms 17 and 22 of the Second Story contained remains of mural paintings. In both of these, the fragments were sufficiently large to give some conception of the effect of the completed room. No traces of paintings were found in the other rooms of this building, other than the red hand prints found on the face of the pier between the two southern niches of Room 16. The paintings in Room 17 were applied to the hard and smooth but irregular first finish coat of plaster of the room. In Room 22, faint traces of paint were found, in the east end of the vault and in the east niche, which had been made on the first overall hard plaster coat of the room. The large painting fragments in this room were on the second finish coat, which, like the first coats on both Rooms 17 and 22, was hard and smooth but irregular.

The infiltration of moisture from behind the plaster surfaces had weakened their bond with the walls and vaults, with the result that the few fragments remaining were in perilous condition and might at any time be lost. Repairs were made to the building roofs to prevent the seepage of moisture, but only careful removal and restoration could prevent the irreparable loss of these magnificent examples of pre-Hispanic American art.

The west wall of Room 17 was painted, as shown by the fragments, from floor to ceiling, with the painted surface unbroken by the vault and end-wall offset and the room corners. A large fragment on this west wall extended from below the spring over onto the side wall. Some of the designs carried over the corners. Below the spring line of the vault, there were two rows of figures and the head of a figure which apparently belonged to a third row. There were four figures in the upper row, and two in the lower. Traces of other figures could be seen in each row. The background for this scene was green and deep blue, and the red-yellow figures were outlined in black. A narrow black line was used to define the background areas of green and blue. These areas may have been used for representation of specific conditions, or the designers were probably conscious of the effects to be achieved in color as well as in object composition. The figures were all facing north; the two lower row and northern upper-row figures held dull-red trumpetlike objects to their mouths. These objects may have represented blowguns. They tapered from the mouth out, and had a flare at the outer end. Two hands were needed to hold them to the mouth—the left hand next to the mouth, and the right along the instrument. One figure in the upper row held a stick in his right hand as though beating a drum. Each figure wore a white headdress with two or three forward-projecting white feathers. Each wore white, round earplugs; their black hair seemed to hang down forward and back of the earplugs in long braids. Each figure wore only a breechcloth, was bare-footed, and stood with his left foot forward. The eye of the head of the lower figure had been gouged out, a condition that was especially common in Room 22 paintings. Perhaps these missing eyes might have been inlays, but no binder material was found; nor were such insets in place.

Beneath each row of figures was a roughly horizontal line. A number of red, yellow, and green scrolls, and several pufflike red splotches occupied a considerable section of the background.

On the east wall of Room 17, little remained other than some distinguishable red lines on a blue field. At the east end of the south wall, near the base, was a tree. Below the spring of the vault in the southeast corner was another tree. These trees had red trunks and branches; green balls or puffs represented the foliage.

The field of the south wall and vault painting was also of blues and greens. Over the center line niche were a number of flowing meanders in yellow and a group of feathers that might have been the remains of a headdress. A few traces of paintings remained in each niche, near its top, but only sufficient to show that the sides bore designs on blue and green backgrounds. A narrow red line ran around the top of each side, leaving the soffit of the niche lintel for the bordered panel which might have contained painted glyphs. These were especially clearly defined in Room 22.

The paintings in Room 22 had evidently extended over all the walls, vaults, capstones, and niches. The wall and vault paintings were separated by a cobalt-blue band outlined with a dull-red line above and a black line below. This band extended from below the spring of the vault to above the spring line. The vault soffit scene was bordered at the top by a wide, black-outlined blue band. This upper border remained only above the large scene on the north vault soffit. At this point, there was no definite capstone offset; the remaining blue border or design-separation lines were at the tops of the niches and in the center of the east vault end wall. In all cases, these were narrow, dull-red lines.

Although not containing the largest scene in the room, the east end wall offered a good opportunity for a description, since it was the only place where a vertical scene-separation line remained. This line was in the center of the vault end. Above the vault spring line, the painting remained legible for only a short distance; to the north of the division line, the fragments were too meager for description. In this end of the room, no design could be seen in the blue border. The lower portion of a figure walking toward the north stood upon the dull-red border line of the blue band. His right foot was forward. Nothing of the figure remained above the waistline. He wore a short skirt, which left the well-drawn legs exposed below mid-thigh level. A sash was tied about his waist, with an end hanging down to the calf of his leg. The line drawing was in dull red. No flat body colors remained. Above the border was a smaller figure, with head missing, facing to the south, and with the left foot forward. This figure was one of the

Mural in Room 22, 1934

Part of the Painting in Vault of large Chamber. Casa de las Monjas. Chichen Itza. Yucatán.

Scale ¼.   A. Br

Mural in
Room 22
(painting by
A. Breton)

199

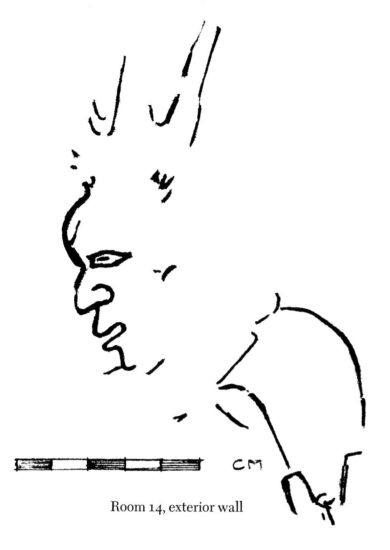

Room 14, exterior wall

forearm extended at an angle of around forty-five degrees. The inside of the forearm and hand was shown, exposing the inner face of a shield the figure carried. Two straps were used to hold the shield—one over the upper forearm, just below the elbow, and the other across the palm of the hand. The thumb and the small finger—though possibly by error—did not pass under the strap. In addition to grasping the strap of the shield, the figure was holding spears in the left hand, these projecting forward and back of the body at an angle of less than twenty degrees from the horizontal. Their tapering points were forward and down. The spears in shape resembled modern billiard cues, with no pointing apparent other than at the tapered end of the shaft. South of this figure were traces of others. At the rear could be seen similarly held shield and spears of a fourth figure in this row. Traces of the sandal on the right foot of the second figure from the south could be seen. A flowing, furcated meander tied the design together behind the figures. Only the red outlines remained in these paintings.

Below the spring end and on the south half of this east wall of Room 22 was another fragment. The blue border carried around under the spring line offset of the wall and down onto this lower wall. Below this was evidently a decorative band. Two apparently reclining figures, similar to those carved on the column capitals of the South Building of the Southeast Court, faced one another. Only the profile of the south face remained. The headgear had a trailer at the rear. Around the ear was the trace of an earplug or part of the headdress. What appeared to be an upturned foot could be seen south of the face. The headdress of the north figure was larger, painted a deep blue, but its outline was difficult to discern. The right elbow of the north figure appeared to be resting on the border of the motif, while the forearm extended forward and up, placing the hand close to the chin. This hand held what appeared to be a long fiber brush between the thumb and index finger. On the wrist was a large, semicircular, sectioned bracelet. The figures were outlined in red; the background was painted a light blue; and the flesh color of the figures

best-drawn in the room. The lines of the right leg and the handling of the arms—particularly the left hand holding the shield—were those of a master delineator. The figure wore a short-sleeved slip-over shirt that fell to just below the buttocks. Two thin lines formed a band hanging from the rear of the shirt and appearing to be a tail to the costume. The fragment of a figure in front of this one had the same tail motif. In his right hand, this latter figure held a throwing stick, with the back showing, the long end forward, and with the back of the hand with three fingers forward, leaving the thumb and small finger to close around the handle. The left shoulder was forward, the right pulled back. The left

200

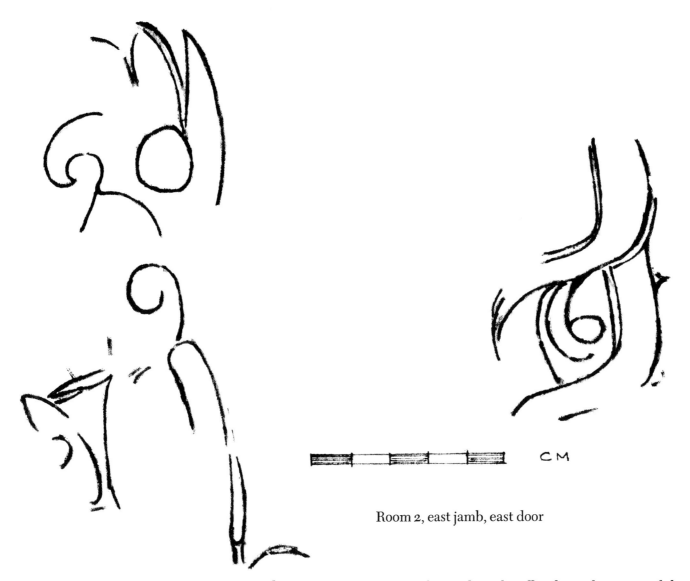

Room 2, east jamb, east door

was a reddish yellow. Between the faces was an indeterminate pattern in deep green, deep blue, light blue, deep yellow, and light red. In a rectangle within this area were three small buttons from which hung two and three streamers. The upper half of this tiny rosette and feather panel was in yellow, while the lower half was red. The lines were all red.

On the south vault soffit, above the spring of the vault, were the fragmentary representations of two buildings and two figures. These were on two levels. The lower level was the same scene as that on the east wall. The figure was facing east, or in the same direction as was the lower figure on the east-vault end wall. Both figures were apparently of about the same size. The figure in the

201

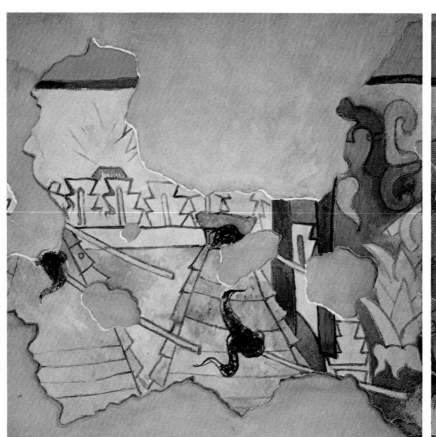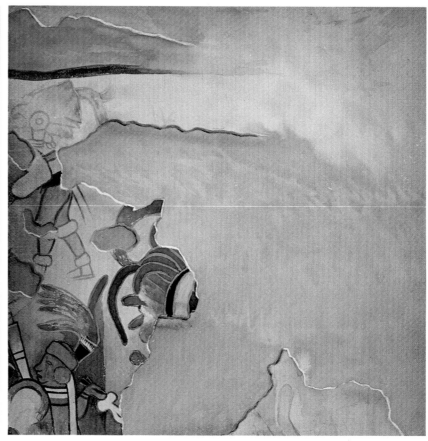

Watercolor in Room 22, Las Monjas, by Jean Charlot.
Courtesy of Jean Charlot and Peabody Museum, Harvard University.

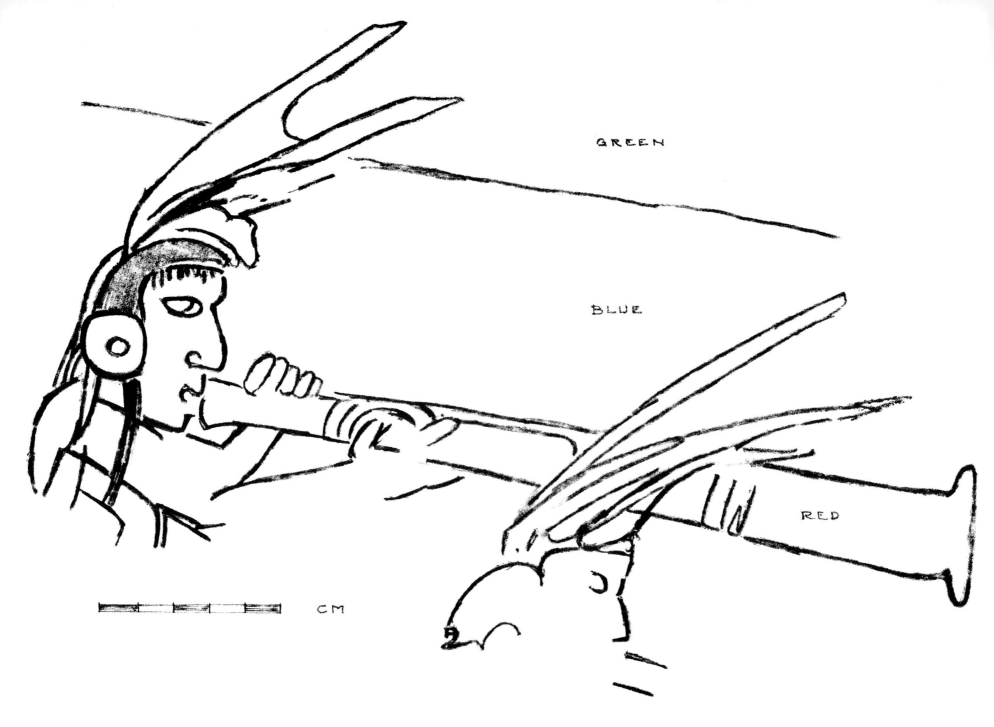

GREEN

BLUE

RED

CM

Room 17, west end below vault

204

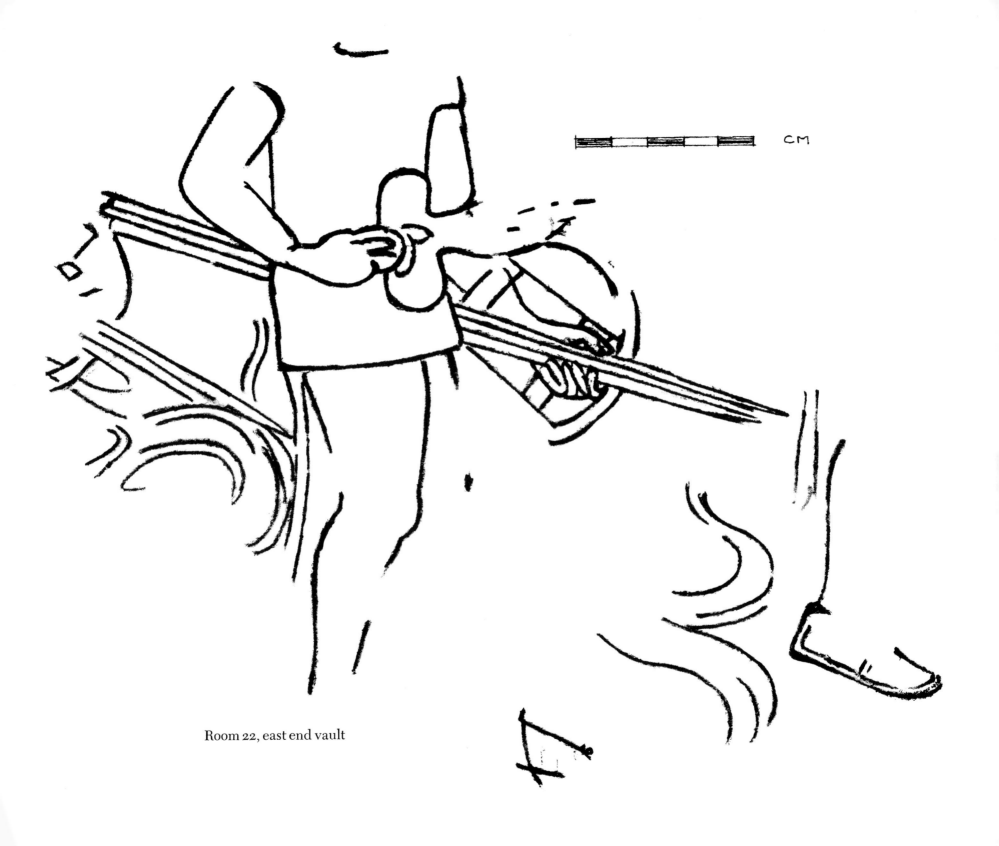

Room 22, east end vault

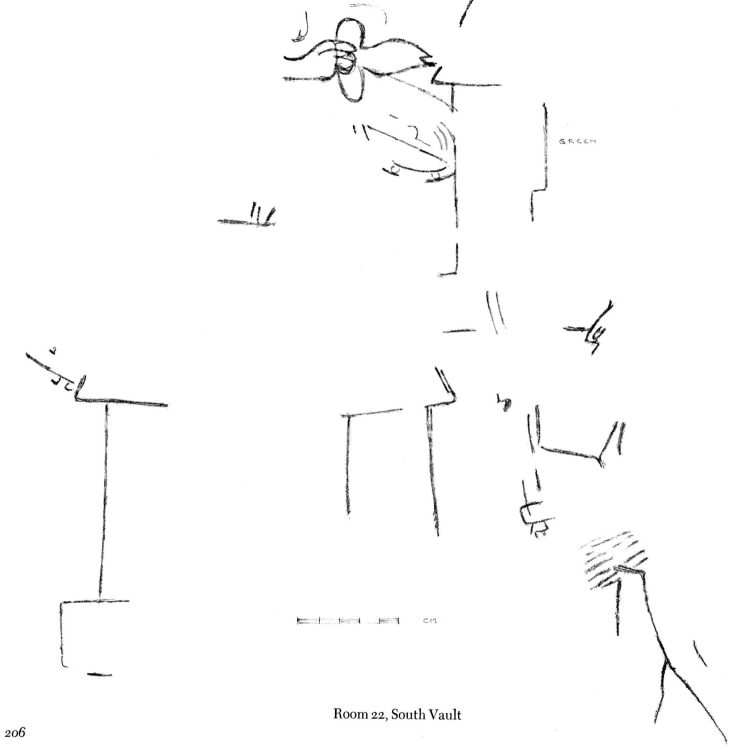

GREEN

Room 22, South Vault

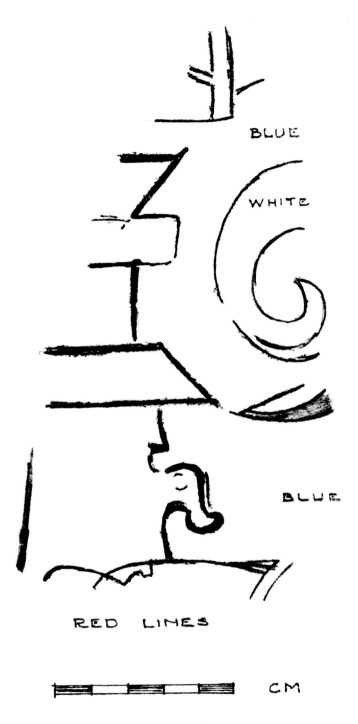

BLUE

WHITE

BLUE

RED LINES

CM

Room, second story

upper row could be ascertained only by means of his throwing stick, shield, and spears. These were all in the same relative positions as were those held by the figure in the upper row on the east vault-end wall. Both figures faced to the west. In front of each figure were the remains of houses. One house in the lower row, on a high stereobate, had one edge of an opening in the wall remaining. The sloping roof and eaves line were clearly seen. The upper house was in front, or west, of the figure in the upper row, who was apparently passing behind it. Except for a small section of green on what was probably the doorway of the upper building, no color remained except the red outlining of the design. The scent was certainly a continuation of that on the east end of the room.

Over the interval between the east and center doors of the room were a number of fragments of richly colored paintings on the vault soffit. Unfortunately, all these were of such small areas that they disclosed nothing more than that figures and buildings did occupy the scene that had been portrayed here.

On the south-vault soffit between the center and west doors was a section containing fragments of what was doubtlessly a sacrificial scene. The sections remaining carried down over the spring of the vault onto the wall below. The blue border remained here, and carried down onto the wall. Above this blue band was a field in dull yellow-green on which were some ten or eleven figures. These were rather poorly drawn in a reddish yellow. The two figures at the right appeared to have their hands bound in front of their bodies, and were nude. They were possibly being led to the sacrifice. The other figures, lying in various positions, were all nude. Blood was spurting from a wounded left breast. The blood was painted in a deep red. The eyes were not drawn on any of these figures. The hair had the forelock brushed forward with the remainder brushed back and hanging shoulder length behind. The background and bodies, though not well drawn, presented as pallid a scene as could be imagined.

The sacrificial field was bordered above by a deep-red band. In the Jean Charlot tracing of this scene, this was shown as a pos-

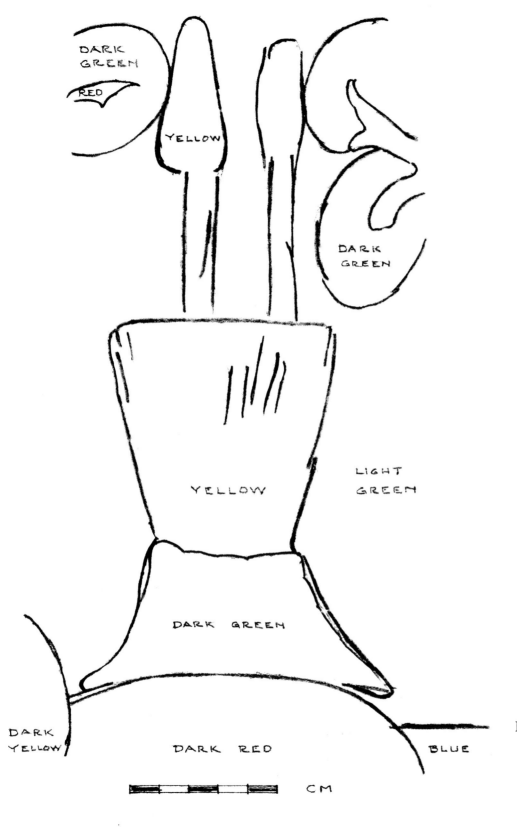

DARK GREEN

RED

YELLOW

DARK GREEN

YELLOW

LIGHT GREEN

DARK GREEN

DARK YELLOW

DARK RED

BLUE

CM

sible platform. Above this line was a figure, apparently squatting, without headdress. The hair treatment was similar to those in the field below. The eye had been gouged out of the plaster. This figure was painted in dull reds and yellows. In front of this west-facing figure were what appeared to be bushes and the trunk of a tree. Behind was another figure wearing a blue slip-over shirt of mid-thigh length having no sleeves and with a high collar and painted an indigo blue. This figure was seated, had the left arm upraised with a band on the forearm, and wore a turbanlike headdress and circular earplug. The legs and arms were a light yellow outlined in dull red.

East of this last-mentioned figure was the edge of a building with only parts of the west line and of the high apron of the cornice remaining. Charlot showed a red-painted opening just below the cornice that occupied the position taken by windows in such structures as the East Wing. The remaining section of the building was white with a red outline.

No other fragments of painted plaster remained on this south vault soffit. On the wall below was one small, indeterminate design fragment in vivid colors. It was above and east of the upper east cord holder for the west door, and its presence was sufficient to show that this wall had also been painted with an overall design.

Nothing remained on the west end of the room or on the west section of the north vault soffit. Opposite the sacrificial scene was a section of painting from the spring of the vault up a short distance. Only the red outlining remained, showing two figures running east. The rear, or west, of the two figures was the more complete. The feet, face, and right arm were missing. The figure was springing forward on his left foot, with the right knee raised and forward, the thigh being roughly parallel with the ground. The torso was twisted by the action of the runner in looking to the

Room 17

rear. The left shoulder was high; the elbow, forward; and the left hand, just above his right knee. There were traces of a headdress and possibly a bar earplug. He wore a breechcloth, which had a maxtli trailing to the rear. Traces of a corded shirt or neckpiece could be seen. All that remained of the forward of the two figures was the right foot and a small portion of the leg. The leg was horizontal, and the bottom of the foot was up at the rear. No sandal could be seen. This figure was probably the same as the more complete companion. To the rear of the figures were traces of indeterminate designs having a yellow wash between the red outlines. Above was a small bit which seemed to represent timber construction using vertical, a top horizontal, and two diagonal bracing members. The timbers were painted a pale yellow between the red outlines. The design was broken away below, and so was incomplete. East of this timber design were fragments with horizontal lines and two horizontal red bands. These seemed to have been traces of buildings. Other scant fragments remained in this area.

On the vault soffit over the west of the two center line niches and above the vault spring was a figure standing on the left foot with the right leg relaxed and heel raised. Though the feet were partly missing, the wide top to the sandals remained. The figure wore knee pads; there were traces of a breechcloth, and the feather headdress fell to below the calf of the leg. There were some vertical lines at the rear of the figure. The outlining was in red, with a tinge of yellow remaining on the body of the figure. Below and to the east of this fragment, many small fragments remained with lines which seemed to represent parts of buildings, shields, spears, and figures. Between this central area and the large attack scene on the east end of this north-vault soffit, there were only a few small fragments.

Room 22, north wall

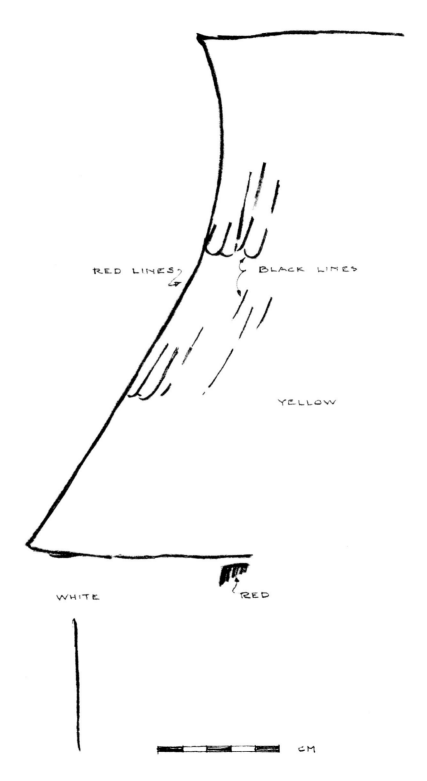

The so-called attack scene had plaster remaining from slightly below the vault spring to the capstones. Large sections were missing in this area, but the continuous areas were sufficiently large to make it one of the outstanding fragments of paintings found in this area.

Many types of costumes, several buildings, and inner and outer city walls were shown.

The scene was bordered above and below by the continuous blue band noted at other places in this room. The lower band began below the spring of the vault and carried up over the offset onto the vault soffit, where it was outlined with a red trim line. The upper band was bordered with a black line.

The first thing to catch the eye was the long sweep of the deep-red band that formed part of the city wall. This continued beyond the fragment to the west. Where it first entered the remaining scene, it was slightly above the vault spring. From here, it carried eastward and then turned upward in a broad sweep near the east end of the fragment. A row of figures partially covered the band. This red band was lined off to represent stone jointing. These were five courses high, with the vertical joints broken. Although the vertical joints were all broken in this painted representation of masonry, in actual construction no great pains were taken to carry out such sound building practice. At the east, the jointing was painted black; at the west, only the red of the stones and open joints showed. This west variation was probably the result of some form of disintegration of the painted joint line which also removed the red background. The figures behind this wall were hidden to hip height by the wall. Five courses of stone wall would have been about that height. Yet the general design usually showed figures much larger in scale than the buildings, so that this particular wall was probably not in scale.

Above the west end of the red wall was a second wall in neutral color. This wall had six horizontal courses of stone. Crowning the wall was a fascia, with a series of roof adornos similar in design to those on the Temple of the Wall Panels, having three "teeth" on each side and a center-line vertical groove. Several of the grooves had been omitted. Near the west end of this inner wall was what may have been an entrance or gateway. The painting was vague at this point, and was also partially covered by a warrior. East of this point, the wall and cornice band were missing, while the adornos and their single base line continued east and then turned upward forming a band. The area between the red band representing the outer wall and the row of adornos was filled by a series of west-facing warriors on a dull-green background. Before reaching the top of the vault soffit, the row of adornos again turned west, forming a band with a top line slightly below the blue border of the wall. Two broad, red vertical bands crossed the line of adornos, where they turned west at the top; between the two bands and west of them were several which had been drawn in a modified perspective. This may have been unconsciously achieved in the difficulty of turning the corner. In the upper row and in the east half of the lower row, the adornos were outlined in black; elsewhere they were defined in a copper-red. In the upper row, the fascia cornice, but not the supporting wall, was repeated.

In the field between the two horizontal lines of the adornos, two buildings could be seen occupying the full height of this area. The buildings and their supporting pyramids were in white outlined in black and copper-red. Their roofs were yellow outlined in black, to represent thatch. The east building had a pyramid platform divided into four horizontal bands. On the west edge could be seen traces of what may have been the stairs. Near the east edge was a second, slightly inward-sloping line. This inner line was in black, as were the horizontal lines west of it. The east edge and the short horizontal lines connecting it with the inner east line were copper-red. All the red lines were at an angle to their black counterparts, giving the effect of being a perspective or isometric representation of the east face of the platform.

The mid-portion between the top of the platform and the roof ridge had broken away. The building, as shown by the steps and the apparent location of the door, faced west. A section of the deep-red door or entrance and jamb remained. A small graffito found on the first finish coat of plaster near the base of the north jamb of the south interior door of La Casa Colorada showed a building on a pyramid with stairs and entrance on the left. The entrance was supported by a serpent column, and the stairs representation was strikingly similar to the angular stairs to this painted pyramid. The building shown in the graffito had a three-member upper cornice and Castillo- and Mercado-type adornos. The thatched roof of the building shown in this painting would not justify the support of serpent columns, and yet such a possibility remained.

The building was outlined in copper-red. Below this pitched ridge line, there remained eight bands defined by black lines and probably representing courses of thatch. The edges were treated in a shingled effect with approximately the same width per course.

Only one section of the roof and a trace of what had probably been the lower east corner of the doorway remained of the west one of the two buildings. The roof was similar to, but possibly slightly larger than, that of the east building. The horizontal thatch markings were closer together, and existed only in the lower part of the roof. The plaster had unfortunately broken away at the place where the two roofs came together, making it impossible to determine relative planes of the structures. The small section of painting assumed to represent the stairs of the east building was beneath the roof center line of the west building, leading to the belief that the east building was in the foreground. The top of the west platform was slightly higher than that of the east platform, and so appeared to verify these relative positions.

On each roof were the flaming points of a pair of spears, which had evidently been thrown from the lower right. The spears were formed by two black lines defining the white shafts. The forked flames were a deep red outlined in black.

The area between the upper row of adornos and the blue border was a dull white of the same value as the adornos and the buildings. The only drawing remaining in this field appeared to be a spiny-leafed object similar to the native henequen plant.

There were more than thirty figures in the area of this scene of the besieged or attacked city. Some figures were nearly complete, while only faint traces or small fragments of others remained. Many of the figures had had their eyes gouged out from the plaster. Nowhere were inlaid eyes found, and so it was impossible to determine if the eyes had had insets or were simply mutilated for some other reason.

Below the existing west end of the red wall band was a figure apparently seated on the ground with a foot pulled up under him. He was on a level only slightly below the red city wall. On the east, a very rigid figure faced east with only the head and torso remaining. The face was stiffly drawn, with tight lips and a projecting square jaw. A large headdress curved down in front of the face and carried down the back of the figure for the full remaining height. This was apparently of red feathers on a yellow and white band. In front of this figure were the remains of what seemed to have been a similar headdress. In each, there was a spot of blue in front of the headdress.

East of these first three figures were traces of four more, the first two being identifiable only by traces of headdress and body lines. The forwardmost of the four—all facing east—was the best preserved. The left foot was forward and bare. Elbows were at the sides, and hands were in front of the chest as though bound. He wore a shirt skirt which hung low over the buttocks and was pulled up in front and tied in a bow. A small turbanlike headdress was on the head. There was a rectangular earplug or flap with a vertical bar through it. The rear figure had feet and hands in somewhat the same position as those of the forwardmost figure. A breechcloth and a light blue sleeveless shirt could be seen.

Between this group of figures and the three vertical bands crossing the red wall were only faint traces of one head. Three slightly curving vertical bands were identical in design except for the notch in the lower right-hand edge of the easternmost of the three. They were pale green in color, each banded with white marks.

Remains of the west end of a multiple-membered cornice of a white building outlined in copper-red were on this same level east of the vertical bands. The cornice was probably of five bands, a lower apron with an upper inverted apron, and a vertical central band bordered by two narrow fillets or fascias. The Breton drawing of this scene recorded the now missing plinth. Below and to

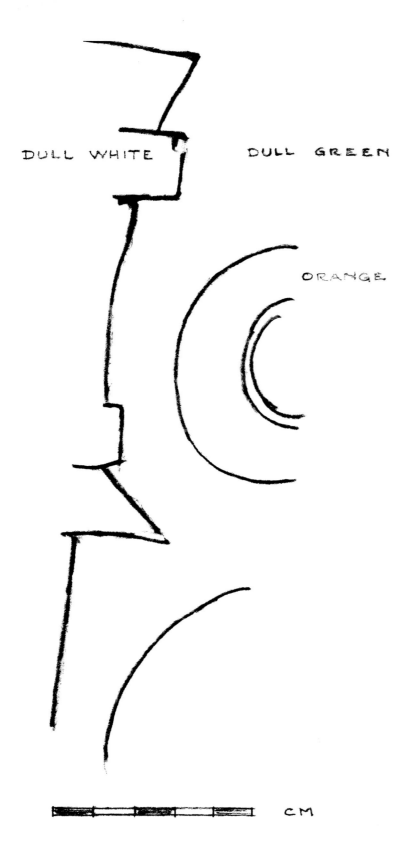

DULL WHITE   DULL GREEN

ORANGE

CM

the left of the plinth could be seen two figures, one with only a hand, spear points, and top of headdress, while the head and torso of the other were clearly shown. This drawing also recorded a now missing section showing a corner of the entrance with a dark lintel which might be meant to represent one of wood. Traces of a figure were also discernible east of this entrance.

Between this building and the vertical bands were three figures seated on a level slightly below the red wall. These three were all facing west. The westernmost figure had the right hand raised forward of the head, and seemed to be holding some object. The left arm was drawn by the side, with the hand holding what appeared to be an obsidian-like blade with handle. There was a small scroll in front of the head, possibly a speech scroll. On the head was a white skull cap with two forward-projecting feathers. Hanging around the neck and down onto the chest was a corded white neckpiece. Around the left bicep was a broad red band. The figure had a double chin and a potbelly. They may have been the result of stylization employed by the artist of this section, for the figure of a warrior directly above and behind the red wall was similar in these two respects. In front of this was a dark form that appeared to be a bound figure. The middle of the three seated figures had the left knee on the ground and the left foot drawn up under the flexed right leg with foot flat on the ground. A red sash about the waist with a white band or tail could be seen. Several white feathers projecting to the rear were all that remained above waist level. The body color was then a dull white outlined in a dull copper-red. The easternmost figure was similar in color. The forwardmost of the three had an orange body tone outlined in black, and appeared to have both knees pulled up with the arms clasped about them. Three vertical feathers could be seen above the head position. Between this figure and the small

Room 22, in wall niche

multiple-corniced building was a bifurcated scroll beginning near the back of the figure and turning up and down close to the building. The lower curl was a dull, deep red, while the upper was half muddy deep blue and half yellow. The dull-green background of the figures ended in a vertical line west of the building. East of this line, the field was a bright green. This field-color change line carried up; but in the upper half of the painting, the east field was a light blue, while the dull green acquired a browner tone.

Beneath the three figures described above and in line with the figure shown on the Breton recording of the scene were some five figures, only traces of which could be seen. Two were seated on an orange-colored bench.

Above the red wall band and west of the three vertical bars were remains of a figure carrying a shield, on the field of which was a design. This warrior faced west, had a feather headdress, and, in addition to the shield, carried three spears.

West of the vertical bars was another shield having a narrow red border and a dull, plain white field. The Charlot drawing showed a second shield west of this plain one. The shield shown in his drawing was similar, except that the field was light blue and had an indistinguishable pattern.

East of the three vertical bars were the three warriors who were concealed to hip level by the red wall band. All three figures faced west, had feathered headdresses, and carried circular shields on their left forearms. The full headdress was missing on the easternmost figure. The other two warriors had spears which were apparently carried by the left hand, as shown on the east wall painting. The spears were shown as three pieces below the shield, but above, these appeared sheathed or as blades. These two figures also carried throwing sticks in their right hands. The middle figure held his stick up and to the rear, as though in the act of impelling a spear, and yet no spear was shown in use. The easternmost figure held the stick up in front of the face. The westernmost shield had a red border and yellow field. The middle shield had a red border and yellow field, but also showed traces of an overall black line design. The easternmost shield had a deep-red border and a blue-black field.

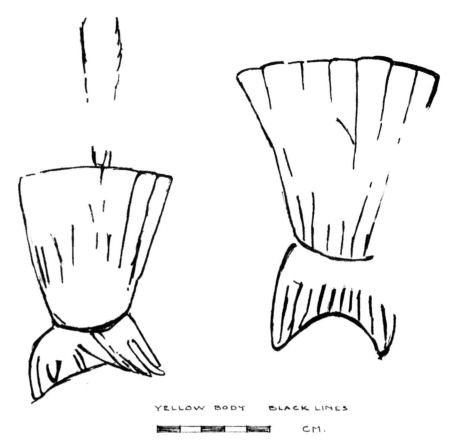

YELLOW BODY   BLACK LINES

CM.

Room 17, west wall vault

The white-tipped black feather headdress of the western-most figure was held in place by a broad white band which covered the ears and carried under the chin. There was a broad blue band about the neck. Following the under line of the left arm was a red band. A white breechcloth with a double band about the waist and tied behind appeared just above the red wall top. The body and face were a brown-black. The headdress of the middle figure was not so complete as that of the westernmost one. The copper-red outline and white field were all shown, except for a twisted, blue, heavy cord just above the forehead, which projected forward. Charlot showed this figure with blue-black body and face. There was a broad white band about the waist which probably supported a breechcloth. The easternmost figure wore a short-sleeved blue shirt with white collar. The face and arms were a pale red.

A row of five similar figures in close order and facing east were on a level just above the roof of the building with the five-member cornice building. The westernmost of these figures formed the termination of the red wall band. Each figure wore an animal headdress that might have been either that of a jaguar or of a wild boar. This headdress was tilted back from the long, receding forehead, and was held in place by a broad tie from the rear which passed beneath the chin, where it was tied in a small bow. Over the ears were green plates, which were repeated, but in larger size, over the breasts. Each figure has the right arm slightly flexed, with the hands in line as though holding a pole that was being carried by all five. On the wrist of each was a broad blue band. None of the figures showed below hip level. The drawing was outlined in copper-red; the arms and faces were pale red; the headdress and what appeared to be shoulder pads were light yellow-red; the ties holding the headdresses were white.

The field near these five figures was a bright green. In this field and above the group was a bifurcated scroll which began east of the headdress of the central figure and extended vertically to where it spread to the east and west, and then each division curved down and back toward the initial vertical member. From each curl was an additional fork, while below the right-hand member was a small circular design that may have been a glyph. The outline of this scroll was copper-red. The vertical section was red on the left and yellow on the right. The yellow was carried around for the right curl or spiral; the red stopped shortly after the left spiral began, and was then continued in deep blue. The projection from this left spiral was red.

Two horizontal, wavy red lines with a deep-green field between formed a band above the scroll and five figures. At the east termination of the red wall band was a figure of a warrior facing downward and probably representing a wounded or dead combatant. He was holding two long spears with obsidian-like blades. His legs were an orange-red. Little else could be definitely de-

214

termined regarding this figure. In the Charlot drawing, traces of a light-green field color could be seen about the body.

Above the deep-green band was a light-blue band containing several eel-like objects. This might be interpreted as a body of water. The outlining here was all done in a pale copper-red. The upper line was one of a pair, forming a straight, wide band upon which stood a series of figures.

Of the figures in this upper scene, the three easternmost were standing facing east with each left foot slightly forward. The westernmost of these three was the most complete. Only the lower legs of the easternmost figure remained. The other two had their right arms slightly flexed, with the fingers forward and palms down. Each wore a mid-thigh-length white, sleeveless shirt brought up in front with a white belt about the waist. The bodies were orange-red. Sandals with ankle and arch ties could be seen. What appeared to be two other figures back to back with a small space between them were slightly west of the other three. The shirts, or skirts—they seemed to serve a double function—were shorter than those on the other figures and had wide green bands about the knees. The toes of what may have been a sixth figure touched those of the west-facing of the probable pair. The Breton drawing showed what were probably the head and shoulder of this figure. Above this head was an elaborate bit of plumage done in blues and greens projecting from a deep-red and yellow body. The outlining was in light sienna.

Just west of this last-mentioned figure and the plumage, the light-blue background ended in a vertical line against the deep-green background which prevailed about the city scene. This break was directly over the end of the red wall band and the muddy-green to light-green field change in the lower part of the wall. It was possible that these had been two distinct scenes with the background colors, rather than definite borders, used to differentiate the panels.

On the level with, and west of, the last row of figures was a fully garbed warrior standing on the roof of a building. The building upon which the figure stood had a three-member cornice. The warrior wore a small blue hat with round blue earplugs or pads. From the top rear of the hat projected a deep-red-and-white-trimmed tuft from which half a dozen long, blue-green feathers extended up and forward. Around the neck were three narrow bands—the top two in white, and the lower in blue. The brown, straight, wide, long coatlike object hanging from the neck to below the knee might have been a protective padding. A white band hung straight down from the headdress. A shield was held up near the chin. From this shield hung a streamer with short red and white tassels. This shield and streamer were similar to the carved decorations belonging to the East Building facing the East Court of Las Monjas complex. Projecting above and from behind the shield was a bladelike object with a square end similar to those carried by the warriors below and within the red city wall. The right hand was back of the head, holding a trifoliate throwing stick. The figure wore sandals, and had a pad on the left knee. The body color was orange-red, while all the outlining was in light red.

Between this warrior and the inner city wall was a tree the base of which was just above the building cornice. The tree had a deep burnt-sienna trunk with a spread base, and at the top expanded into five branches. The bulbous foliage was a deep blue-green outlined in copper-red. This foliage partly overlapped the outlined band of the adornos.

Above the tree and the shield of the warrior was a henequen-like plant, with only the outlines in light red remaining.

Occupying the area above the warrior and the trees and beneath the upper blue border of the vault soffit was another almost complete warrior facing west. This warrior stood with left foot and left arm forward and with torso bent slightly forward. The object in the left hand had one short section projecting forward and the other curving downward. The body position would indicate that the other hand held the end of a long handle to this instrument. The headdress was large, and appeared to have been of feathers projecting to the rear; from the rear center, two longer feathers carried out and down. A blue color was used on this

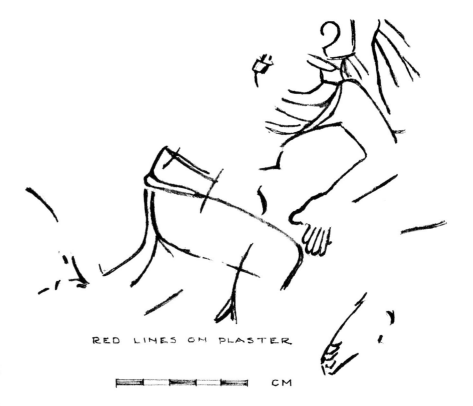

RED LINES ON PLASTER

CM

Room 22, north vault

headdress. A round earplug or pad had a central hole, from which hung two short objects. The figure wore a short shirt with a deep-red, narrow band for the bottom hem, from which a taillike object hung. The left arm was padded to the wrist, and both knees and ankles had thick paddings. On the feet were sandals. In front of the head was a double scroll, commencing near the head, extending west, and then bifurcating. The upper section was yellow, and the lower red. Attached to the west face of the upper-swinging yellow scroll was a forward-projecting red scroll, which also appeared to split toward the west.

The only other figure in this large area of painting was identified by a small blue skullcap type headdress and blue circular ear pad. This fragment was just below the door of the building on the west pyramid within the city. Three short reddish bars

215

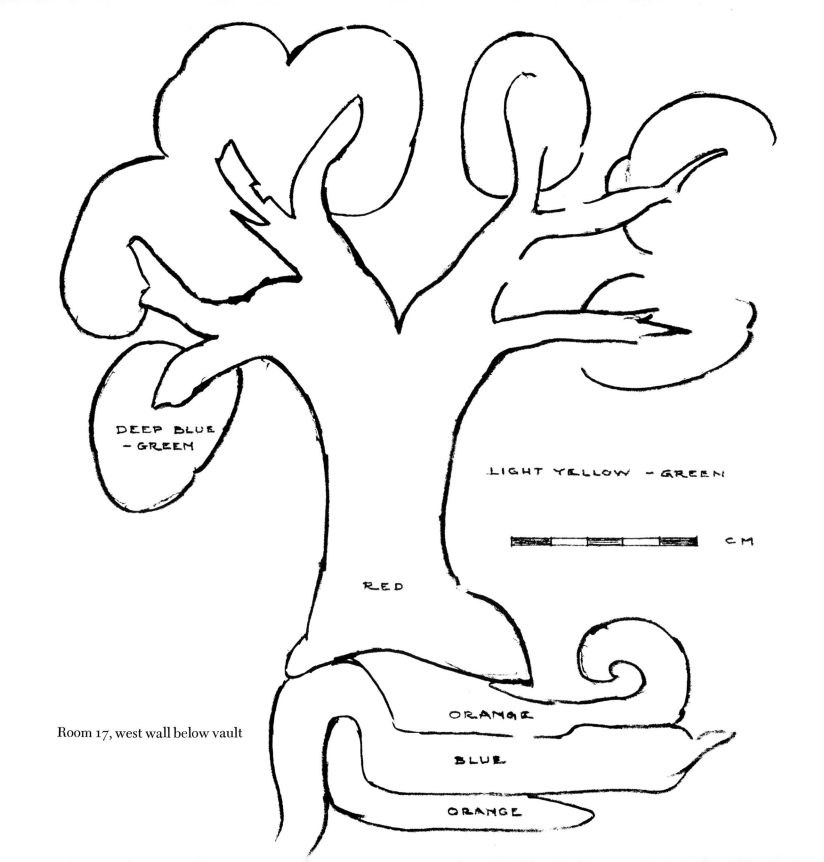

DEEP BLUE
- GREEN

LIGHT YELLOW - GREEN

CM

RED

ORANGE

BLUE

ORANGE

Room 17, west wall below vault

projected from the rear half of the hat, and two reddish featherlike objects hung from the ear pad.

On the lower zone of the east pyramid was a snake or eel-like object similar to those in the scene east of the wall.

Between the large attack scene and the east end of the room were several small fragments of plaster bearing paintings. One fragment showed the upper cornice and a corner mask of a building. The cornice was similar to those crowning the East Wing and La Iglesia, but no design was seen on the short, vertical, recessed plane of this cornice. The mask was identified by the projecting nose.

Near the east end of the room were several fragments containing a number of figures. In the corner, a narrow strip of plaster remained for the full height of the vault soffit, but the only legible painting was at the base, where there was a blue border with a black outline on which was a figure. This figure had relaxed knees, was apparently nude, was painted yellow with red outlines, and faced west.

Above the spring line of the vault and an equal distance from the east wall were the legs of a barefoot figure walking east. This figure was shown in a tracing by Charlot, in which the body was depicted as crouching. Above this were the legs and feet of a number of figures. These appeared to have been five or more figures, who faced in both directions, and who were all barefooted. Just below and near the east wall were the legs of another figure, with the legs up as though falling or lying on the ground. Next to this figure was a spot of vivid pink. The field color was a blue-green. Above the row of legs was the leg of another figure, having a sandal and padded knee band.

A few of the capstones for the vault retained traces of color, and from these the evidence pointed toward there having been a bold, plumed-serpent meander pattern running the full length of the room. The colors were alternate red and green bands of plumage with a dark, almost black, field color.

On the north wall and in the niches were a number of small areas containing remains of paintings. The wall plaster to which the paint had been applied was somewhat rougher than that in the vaults, while in other places it was so thin that the painting was practically on the stone.

In places, the blue spring line band carried down onto the wall, where it was bordered by a narrow black line.

Between the lintels of the first two niches from the east, some traces of paintings remained but were too vague for study. Over the second niche was what was undoubtedly one of the finest examples of profile head representation to be found in Maya art. The flowing line was so positive and so smooth that it was difficult to do it justice in tracing. In this one head, the artist had summed up all the characteristics of Maya art and had, in a few deft strokes of his brush, portrayed a masterpiece. In front of the head, which faced west, were scrolls in red, yellow, and blue on a green background.

Above the third niche from the east and around the west end of the lintel to the fifth niche were traces of painting. In the first of the two locations were red-outlined patterns in all the primary colors.

Near the upper-right corner of the third niche from the west was the painted remains of a thatch roof. The roof was outlined in red, while the yellow thatch was overpainted with black lines with their scalloped ends in horizontal rows. Toward the ends of the roof, the thatch lines took on the angle of the roof. East of this niche and below the level of this roof was the west end of another yellow thatch roof. Beneath the eaves was the west end of the white building supporting the roof. The upper-left corner of a door or window was shown east of the wall end. The opening was painted red. The roof was marked similarly to the one described above. The end curved out at the ridge.

Over the second niche from the west was an area of light blue on which appeared traces of a meander in dull red. The plaster was at its thinnest at this point.

Traces of paintings remained in four of the niches—the first two niches from each end of the room. In the easternmost niche, traces of an earlier painted plaster coat were found, over which the final painted plaster contained designs similar to those in the other niches. This earlier layer had been broken away, either accidentally or intentionally, before the last coat was applied, and so the only remains were in a very fragmentary condition. On all the niche walls, the field, or background color, was a dull green.

Other than traces of scrolls and feathers, the only legible design on the under layer of the easternmost niche was on the north wall. With its top slightly below the lintel was the east end of the upper zone of a building. This upper facade area was banded by an apron and fascia below and a fascia and inverted apron above. On the outer plaster level, traces of a dark figure remained on the east wall. The head faced south. The eye had been gouged out after painting. There were traces of a blue feather headdress, ear-plug or pad, and a waist sash and maxtli. Behind this figure was a two-branched tree.

On the walls of the second niche from the east were traces of the field colors in blue and green.

The westernmost niche of this room had painted plaster remains on its north and west walls. The background was blue-green outlined in both red and black, the black lines outlining the drawing, which appeared to have been originally laid out in the red. A large yellow scroll and a three-branched tree remained on the west wall. On the north wall were two west-facing figures and the headdresses for two others. The east figure had a black face, an ear ornament, and a headdress composed of five erect to retreating white feathers. In front of his face was a group of three featherlike objects. The lower sections were a deep blue, above which a narrow white band separated this color from the yellow-divided tips. The figure in front of this was yellow, and appeared to have had no headdress. The section about the ear was missing. The arm was raised to the rear, holding a spear which was in line with the head and declining to the west. The two headdresses in front of this face had four feathers each. Upright weapons or standards were associated with each of these two missing figures. In the northwest corner was a henequen-like plant, with vertical, spiny leaves, painted a dull green rising from a red base.

In the second niche from the west, only traces of the top red border to the blue field remained on the walls.

The lintels of all but the westernmost of these four niches bore traces of what appeared to have been hieroglyphs painted on their soffits. The soffit of the second niche from the west had an unpainted band at the north and a similar band on the west. Inside this plain border was a red band about a dark brown-black field. On this background, a series of lines formed three rows of square patterns that may have been hieroglyphs.

On the soffit of the lintel to the second niche from the east was a similar treatment. Only a trace of the dark field remained. The lintel soffit of the easternmost niche bore definite traces of hieroglyphs similar in size and execution to those in the second niche from the west. In this niche, the hieroglyphs appeared to have been painted after some of the plaster had broken away. The plaster was very thin, but even where broken away, the painting carried over the rough edge and onto the stone. The overpainting, after the apparent intentional removal of earlier paintings in this niche, was reminiscent of the Hatsheput-Thutmose affair in the XVIII Egyptian dynasty, when one effaced the name of the other and replaced the destroyed cartouche with his or her own.

EAST WING PAINTINGS

Traces of line paintings were found on the finish coat of plaster given to the exterior of the East Wing and its South Addition. The paintings were on the plaster which carried onto the addition, and so were later than that structure. These were under at least three later colored wash coatings, and remained principally where protected under the overhanging medial cornice. Above and north of the entrance to Room 14 was the profile of one face with traces of the headdress and shoulder. The line work was in black, with no body colors remaining.

On the east jamb of the east door through the south wall of Room 2 were traces of line drawings on the finish plaster coat, which was here likewise covered with later wash coats. Traces of a guilloche pattern and a possible headdress and shoulder of a figure could be distinguished. The existence of these fragments of design on the exterior and a doorway of this ground-level series of rooms indicated the possibility that such drawings had been used extensively on the exterior surfaces of buildings. The areas noted were in faint condition even though protected by later washes and where the wall surface did not receive direct weather or manhandling. The striking feature of these exterior fragments was their small scale, approximately the same as that used on the walls and vaults of the two decorated Second Story rooms. This led to the belief that the designers relied more on their color masses and groupings than on the portent of the scene or the details. Such was true of the architecture and sculpture where bold areas of design and a play of light and shadow, plus the use of large areas where the whole was either sculptured or plain, showed the effects of a vigorous handling. There was every reason to believe that the painters would all be classified in the same "school." The influence of the skill of line work learned in manuscripts was brought out in the painting.

On the exterior faces of the lintels to the west door of Room 2 and the door to Room 14 were traces of areas of deep-red paint with touches of light blue. That on the Room 14 lintel was on the rough coat of plaster—the only remaining plaster—while the paint on the Room 2 west-doorway lintel was on one of the later wash coats.

The rear wall of Room 15 had had paintings in red and green areas with black outlining on the finish plaster coat. Over this, at least one coat of thin plaster had been applied, and this too bore faint traces of paintings.

The artists assigned to the painting of the capstones were probably not those employed for the large mural scenes. The murals could have been from almost any period during the occupancy of the structures, while the dedicatory capstones were painted prior to their installation during the erection of the building.

Only two of the painted capstones were removed for study—the pair in the center of the Room 2 vault. The scenes were bordered by a band containing hieroglyphs. These borders were outlined by two narrow lines, while the hieroglyphs and the

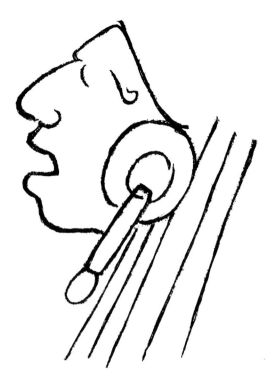

Room 22

scenes within the panels were painted with brush lines generally less than a millimeter in width—in some places, the line was as narrow as that drawn by a fine pen. The right leg and arm of a seated figure could be seen on the north capstone, with traces above of what was probably a headdress. Behind the arm could be seen a part of the costume that looked like a bird's wing. On the arm and leg were painted embellishments of several concentric circles having a solid center. On the south capstone were traces of a left leg of a similar figure that, like the one on the north capstone, appeared to be seated on a bench. This figure had the left leg drawn up under, and upon the calf could be seen a concentric circle pattern. The only colors remaining were faint reds and yellows.

None of the other dedicatory capstones were removed, but those on which some trace of painting remained were similar in design to the pair in Room 2.

219

11. SCULPTURE

Most Maya sculpture can be classed as bas-relief work, with an occasional admixture or separate piece in the full round. Some of the bas-reliefs used the full and three-quarter round in many of their elements, such as the projecting nose and the ornamental head between the eyes of the mask panels. All of the mask panels and remnants of masks belonging to Las Monjas complex were drawn in detail by Russell T. Smith.

The Ball Court playing benches and the benches, columns, and jambs of the South Building of the Southeast Court offered fine examples of low-relief carving. The face of the lintel over the west entrance to the East Wing was an unusual example of low and bold relief on the same stone. The line work on the low-relief hieroglyphs was better preserved here than in most other places about the complex, and displayed a remarkable sureness of line. The hieroglyphic lintels of the Second Story had generally suffered more than had this East Wing lintel, and did not appear to have been so well executed. The quality of stone used in all cases had a great deal of effect on the final object. Yet there were definite artistic craftsmanlike qualities to some works regardless of materials.

The East Building had been adorned with disks and pendants on its upper zone. These, it appeared, had been tied together with grooved lines cut in the face of the building. The disks or shields and the feathered pendants were on raised surfaces

East Wing, east door lintel

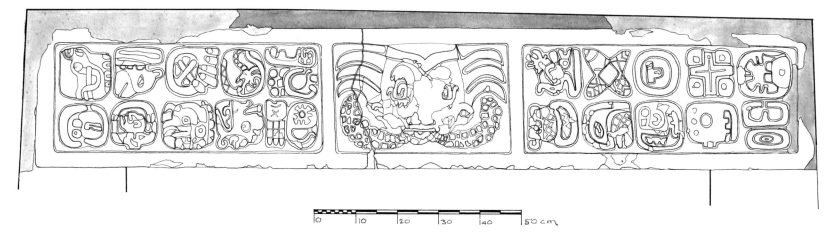

0   10   20   30   40   50 cm

Ball Court, West Bench north cornerstone

with the backgrounds at the face of the building. In most of the other bas-reliefs, the face of the bench, lintel, or column was the face of the carving, with the background cut into the stone.

The small truncated pyramidal block found in front of the Third Story entrance was carved in low relief on all four sides and the top. This stone had been badly weathered, but two figures could still be seen on each of its longer faces—a single figure on the small faces, with a possible figure on the top.

Several unrelated fragments of low relief were found in the south and east areas. Some of these were in raised relief similar to the upper-zone shields of the East Building; others were in incised bas-relief.

Considerable color remained on the Ball Court sculpture. This, coupled with that found on some of the masks, bore out the belief that most of the sculpture had been enlivened by the use of color. In the Temple of the Warriors, where more complete and earlier demolition had preserved the sculpture, this was found to be the rule.

The sculpture of Las Monjas complex had evidently been carved in much the manner described by Jean Charlot in *The Temple of the Warriors*, by Earl H. Morris, as being the probable method of carving the bas-reliefs for that structure. The suggestion is offered that some of the carving tools may have had hardwood points, the relatively soft material to be worked not necessitating stone tools for use in abrasive carving. The backgrounds in the low-relief sculpture appeared to have been cut out with a hammer tool, having the same pockmarked appearance common to the finer finished masonry work. The outlines were probably cut in first with a V-shaped line, and the background was then removed. In some of the carving, the tool marks remained. On curves, the line was formed by a series of straight sections with traces of these tangential lines carrying out and onto the recessed background. The detail on the surface of the figures was both scratched and grooved.

Sculpture in the full round was represented by only a few pieces. The semiattached figures on La Iglesia facade may be included in this classification. The Chac Mool, or jaguar altar, found

South Building, Southeast Court, west entry jamb

at the foot of the Main Stairs was the largest piece of free sculpture discovered in the complex. The small monkeylike figure from the refuse pit in the northeast corner of the Ball Court was one of the smallest. A standard holder had been carved in the form of a seated jaguar holding a ring in his front paws. A nearly identical figure in the Mérida Museum probably served as the companion piece to the one which was found in front of the East Wing facade. In the Southeast Court, the legs and feet of what appeared to have been so-called Atlantean columns were found. In the debris south and west of the East Building, a disintegrated lower section of an almost life-size kneeling figure was uncovered.

Of all the full-round sculpture, only the seated jaguar standard holder is nearly complete. The head and shoulders of this figure had been broken off, but were recovered and replaced. As in the jaguar altar, the spots on the animal were represented by circular grooves. The altar had spots on the left side only. Each had the tail carved against the stone, but, except in the Mérida Museum specimen, the tails were badly disintegrated. Both heads had lips drawn back, baring the teeth. The whiskers were represented by lines receding from the lips. The altar was found lying on its right side in the debris in front of the Main Stairs. The breaking of the tail and the loss of the head may have occurred in a fall from the main platform. Neither the head nor the tail fragments were found.

The torso of a figure was found in front of La Iglesia doorway, and had no definite relation to any particular phase of the complex. The right arm was brought up across the chest, and the right hand grasped what appeared to have been a scepter held at an angle of forty-five degrees across the body. An ornamental disk was carved on the back between the shoulders, with somewhat similar but smaller disks on each upper arm. The figure appeared to have been bare to the waist with a belt, which was looped front and back, serving to support whatever garment was worn below this line.

The small figure found in the debris in the northeast corner of the Ball Court north playing area was kneeling on the left knee, with the right foot resting in line with the left knee, and the right hand appearing to rest on the right knee. The left arm was broken away near the shoulder. The figure appeared to have worn some sort of headdress. The large, deep eye sockets and the long groove representing the mouth gave the figure a monkeylike facial expression. It was found on the floor level at the base of Basal Terrace 1 beneath the great quantity of debris, mostly shards and black earth, which had been dumped in this northeast corner of the Ball Court.

Several incensarios were found about the complex. One had a simple geometric rosette about the semispherical depression in its top, while the others bore facial designs. One incensario was found in front of the last eastern addition to the East Wing Basement. It had been buried here, along with a fragment of a mask nose, when the East Building constructions had brought about the leveling of the East Court and the covering of the basements to the East Wing. Two incense burners were found as unrelated surface debris. A fourth object, which may have been either an incensario or a column capital, was found in the entrance to the demolished North Building.

A serpent-column tail piece lay on the surface east and south of the southeast corner of the East Building. The supporting pier had apparently been square. The vertical section of the tail must have been a separate piece, and was not found. The sides of the tail were carved with low-relief panels over the pier section. Out from those extended feathered treatments, while the rattles commenced near the end and carried up onto the missing vertical element. This piece was similar in design to those of the Temple of the Warriors, but was wider, thinner, and shorter. The vertical and horizontal sections of the tails on the Temple of the Warriors had been carved from one piece; this one seemed to have been a two-piece assemblage. This serpent-column tail belonged to no known phase of Las Monjas complex, but may have come from the associated mound east of the East Building and south of the Akabdzib.

Southeast Court, South Building, bench sculpture

223

South Building, Southeast Court, East Bench

Ball Court, bench detail

Ball Court, bench details

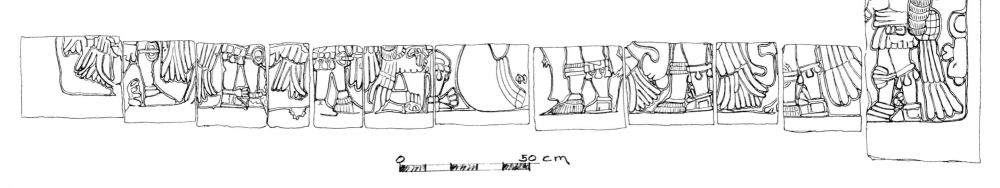

Ball Court, north panel (above), and south panel (below) of west playing bench

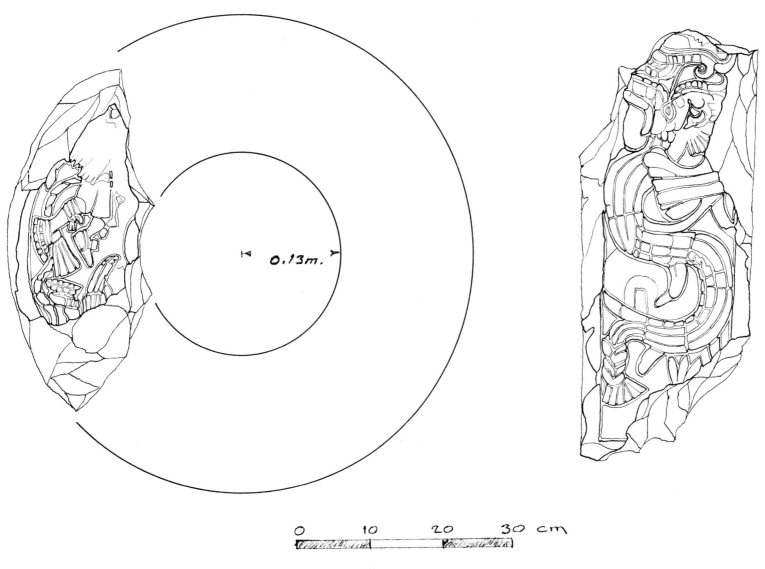

0.13m.

0   10   20   30 cm

Ball Court, ring

Chac Mool found at base of Main Stairs in debris

East Wing, east elevation, sculpture over door

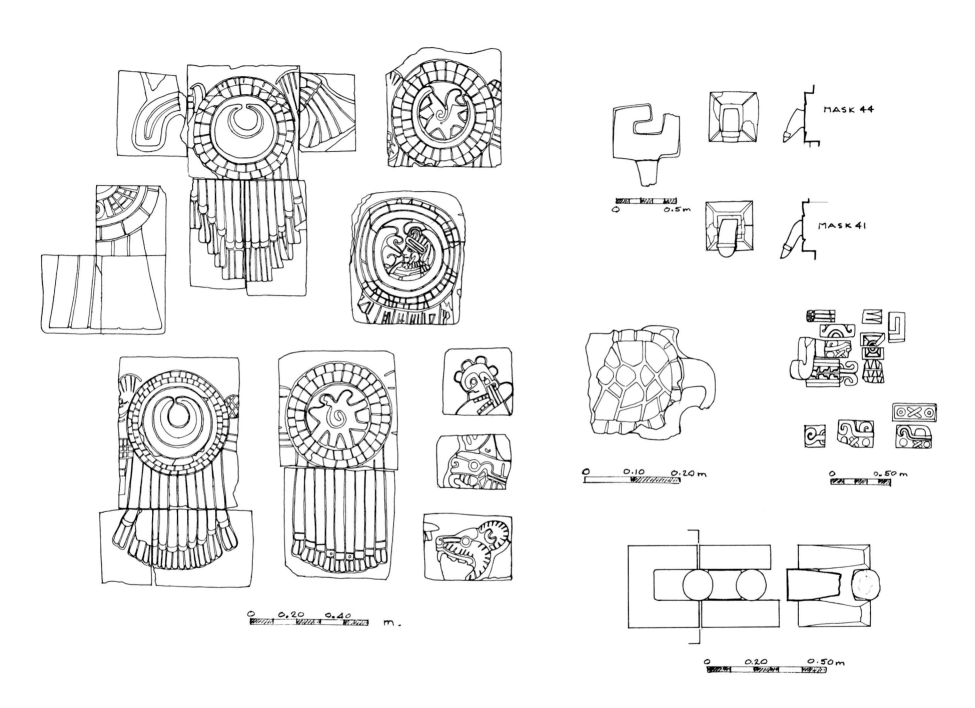

MASK 44

MASK 41

0   0.5 m

0   0.10   0.20 m

0   0.50 m

0   0.20   0.40   m.

0   0.20   0.50 m

East Court, East Building, sculpture

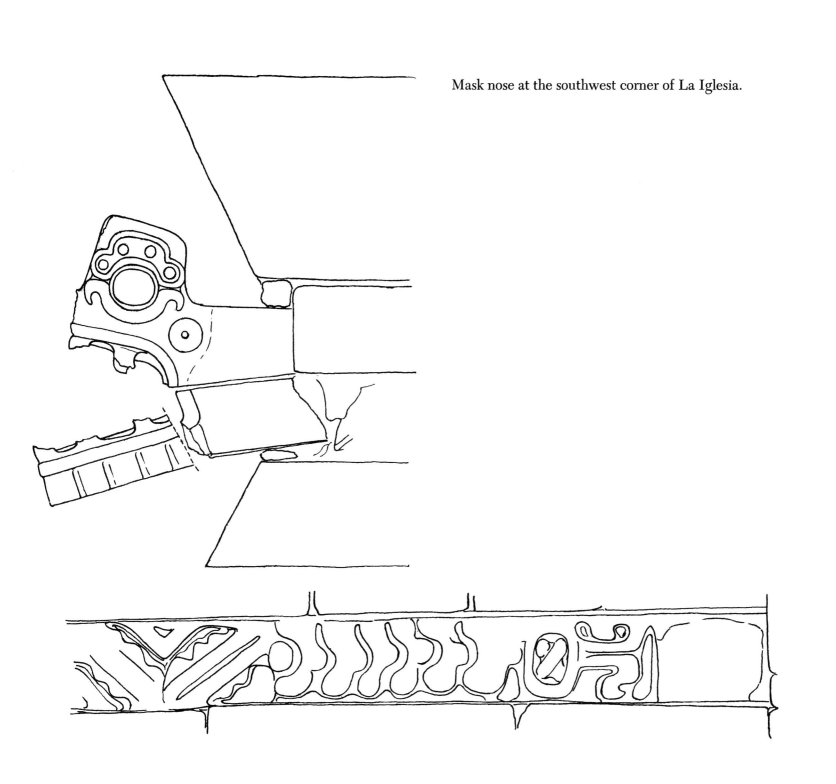

Mask nose at the southwest corner of La Iglesia.

12. ARTIFACTS

GRINDING STONES

One hundred and eighty-six grinding stones were cataloged during the course of the excavations. One long mano was found with a three-legged metate on the east mound. In cross section, most of the stones were roughly elliptical, though some were circular and others nearly rectangular. Many stones could be identified as having a definite number of grinding surfaces, the greater number of these had single and double surfaces, while a few had three and four working faces.

More than one-third of the stones were found in and about the Southeast Court buildings, principally in the debris in the court and about the rear of the two buildings flanking the south and east sides of the court. The East Building excavation accounted for about half as many as the Southeast Court.

No differences could be determined in the general characteristics of the definitely related and surface debris grinding stones.

The stone found in La Iglesia fret gave rise to the possibility that these stones had been used for smoothing and rubbing down the plaster as well as for corn grinding. In rebuilding a new roof to the hacienda, the workmen used similar stones for the laborious process of wetting and rubbing down the plaster surface.

METATES

Fifty metates or fragments of metates were cataloged, including two pelas and two fragments that appeared to be from pelas rather than from metates. Like the grinding stones, the locations

and sizes varied widely, and yet no apparent development could be noted between those found within the heart of Basal Terrace 1 and those encountered on the surface of the East Building debris. In general, use seemed to have been made of rectangular blocks, in many cases obviously old building stones, and the grinding grooves were worn into the planed surfaces. The more specialized three-legged metates were found in and near the East Building and the Northwest Addition to it. A miniature three-legged metate was found in the entrance collonnade to the South Building of the Southeast Court. The East Building and additions offered a group of metates which appeared to have been placed there as ceremonial offerings.

The finest metate and mano found in the complex came from the talus debris just east of the east wall on the center line of the East Building. This three-legged metate and long grinding stone had been cut from black stone, and were the only ones of this material found. Both retained their high polish.

HAND TOOLS

Five nearly complete celts, as well as two objects that were possibly fragments of celts, were found in the course of the excavations. They were all highly polished and had sharp cutting edges. The smallest of the tools was of jadeite, while the others were of a dense black stone.

Two stone axes came from the fill for the later terraces southeast of the East Building. Both had grooves about their midpoints, and were roughly cut.

Manos from excavations

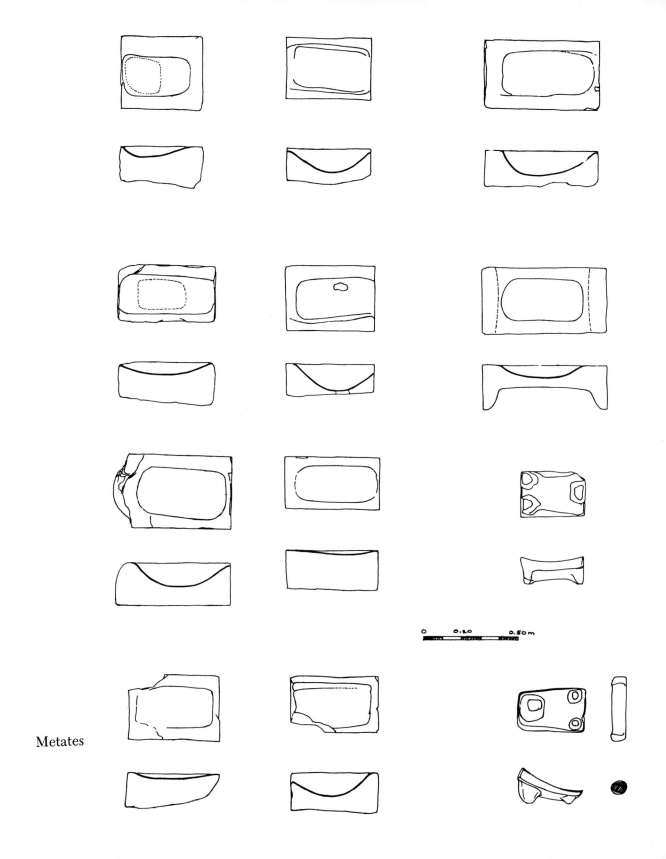

Metates

Several stone balls were unearthed. They appeared to have been used for grinding purposes.

ARROW AND SPEAR POINTS

The points found in the course of the excavations were divided into two groups—arrow and spear. The first group were so classified because of their generally smaller size, and possessed shoulders. Only four so-called spear points were found, and these may well have served as knives or as points for the multibladed battle axes shown in paintings. Several materials were used, flint being the most common. The largest spear blade was of chert; the longest arrow point was a beautifully worked piece of clear black obsidian.

OBSIDIAN BLADES AND FLAKES

The refuse pit in the northeast corner of the north playing area of the Ball Court produced thirty-three obsidian fragments. In the Third Addition to the East Wing Basement, three similar obsidian-flake fragments were found along the east face. The obsidian varied from a nearly clear gray to a dark bottle-green and black. Others were found about the complex in surface debris, but in no such concentration as in the refuse pit. One fragment was found on a skull in the tomb north of the Northeast Terrace.

WHORLS

All the whorls found were made of pottery; only one of the thirty-one had a glazed surface. They all bore designs on at least one face and often on the edge. Some were discus-shaped, while others were similar to a bowl in cross section. Geometric, floral, and animal designs were used as decoration on the whorls.

ORNAMENTS

Most of the costume ornaments found were of either jadeite or shell. Two jadeite beads were found, as well as a jadeite part of an earplug or nose plug.

A number of shell ornaments and fragments of ornaments were found.

A group of blue paste beads were found near the metate in the southeast corner of the vestibule of the East Building. These were soft, and could be crumbled by finger pressure.

A conch shell was found just outside the entrance to the northeast room of the South Building to the Southeast Court.

A fragment of a sculptured bone came from in front of the east face of the Third Addition to the East Wing Basement.

A large bead made from the core of a conch or other shell was made to represent a face by drilling holes for the eyes and mouth and by carving between.

CERAMIC OBJECTS

Great quantities of shards were found in the excavations, and all were recorded in relation to the area and section of the complex in which they were found. Complete utensils were, on the other hand, limited to two urns, two vases, and five shallow bowls. Of this group, the two vases and two of the flat bowls or plates were found in the tomb north of the Northeast Terrace center line. These, along with a shallow bowl found above the floor in the east room of the East Building, had three hollow or cascabel-type legs. One urn with two horizontal loop handles was found mouth down in the debris against the north wall exterior of the East Building.

The two vases were of redware. One was decorated with incised rectangular panels containing incised designs. These panels were of a darker tone than the body color of the vase. Horizontal painted lines of this same tone carried around the base at the top and bottom levels of the incised panels.

An urn found in Platform 5 was of a striated porous ware. It was nearly spherical in shape. A section of the outward flaring rim remained.

The shards found ran the full range of wares common to the city. Considerable slate ware was found beneath the surface of the passage between the Second Story and the upper stairs, as well as elsewhere about the complex. The collapsed section of Platform 3 produced quantities of the so-called and supposedly

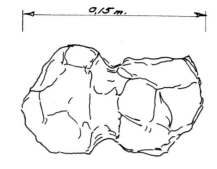

0.15 m.

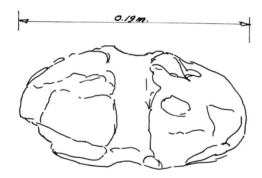

0.19 m.

Stone tools

late incensario ware, with many fragments of pottery faces, torsos, arms, and legs. Two fragments of human skulls and a few body bones were found with the shards from this area. Below the incensario ware, the loose masonry contained considerable slate ware shards. The refuse pit in the northeast corner of the north end zone of the Ball Court was, along with the Platform 3 cave, one of the more prolific producers of shards. Red and buff ware were common to this dump, with some shards of other types occurring.

Whorls from
excavations

Hand tools from excavations

Arrow and spear points from excavations

Ornaments and artifacts from excavations

Pottery from excavations. Striated pot from below surface in front of Room 17, painted pot from debris above floor in North Room of East Building

Pottery from northeast burial vault

Pottery from northeast burial vault

13. MASKS

Russell Smith, in his studies and detailed drawings, has a count of sixty masks, which includes missing ones at the west end of Platform 5, and the remains of corner ones found in the debris of the North Ball Court Temple.

Smith has five main classifications, although he does break the largest group, Type 1, into three parts. Type 1 include: the six upper-frieze masks of the east end of the East Wing, carrying around onto the north and south elevations for one panel; the four central masks of the East Wing lower wall; and the two masks on the Southeast Annex.

Type 1A are the four corner masks of Platform 5, all the north masks of that platform, and all but two of the east masks, which belong to Type 3 along with all of the south masks.

The masks on the main frieze about La Iglesia constitute all the Type 1B group.

The lower corner masks of the East Wing are assigned to Type 2.

The three west masks of the north face of the East Wing constitute Type 4.

Type 5 are the two remains of masks found in the debris of the North Ball Court Temple.

A study of the Smith's drawings and the photographs should be more helpful to the general reader than his thorough stone-by-stone analysis which is available.

Much of the confusion attendant upon the excavation and study was the result of the lack of knowledge of the years covering the many phases of occupancy of, and architectural changes

in Las Monjas, as well as the sequences in the design and building processes.

It should be borne in mind that the Maya appeared to have carved their mosaic pieces of sculpture away from the project; they were often incorrectly set by the masons, and then all was covered with plaster; borrowing and reusing of sculpture were prevalent during most periods of the development and occupancy of the site.

The remaining portions of this discussion of the masks have been excerpted from Smith's study, which covered two years of work. Copies of Smith's complete reports are available from the Peabody Museum at Harvard University.

The major part of the decoration of the buildings of the Monjas complex consists of the so-called mask faces; for example, as a single band encircling the upper part of the main structure, and as a complete facade at the east end of the East Wing. In order to identify readily the different masks, distinguishing one from another, it was necessary to number them in some consistent manner. And although the whole or the larger parts of ten masks are missing, these missing masks are included in the numbering to give a complete picture of the decoration of the complex. There were in all probability sixty masks divided up among the present excavated buildings. No elements were found to suggest more than two masks on the north wall of the Southeast Annex. The remains of two corner masks were found in the debris of the north temple of the Ball Court. No elements were found in the debris on the southwest and west sides of the main platform. Almost all of the elements of the incomplete masks of the north facade of the main platform, as well as of the incomplete mask of the flying facade of La

Iglesia (which remains on record for us in the photographs of Charnay), were found.

The masks of the complex may be divided comparatively easily into their separate elements. The lateral ear motive is divided into either two or three parts, the upper and lower, with or without a central dart. The inferior ear element and the lateral mouth elements sometimes overlap each other in actual placing, but never fail to carry their significance in the design. The eye motive varies among the different types and inside each type, perhaps more than any other single unit of the mask. Never made up of a single stone, it may be of two to five stones set carefully to suggest a single point of interest. The forehead band comes in three parts, the central band, and the right and left parts which end the motive, resembling the "clasps" that may have held the band in place if the band was taken from the adornment of a human. The superior nose ornament may be of three or four general forms, namely: a human face, masked or natural; a human seated figure; a dome-shaped convex stone; or a stone resembling a bundle of sticks of equal length tied tightly together in the center by a wide band so that they splay out at the sides. Bolles often expressed his belief that these were portrait heads, similar to those carved by the artisans of the Romanesque and Gothic periods of Europe.

The nose plugs generally appear at the upper sides of the nose ornament, but in some cases they project from some part of the nose itself. The jaws of the mouth are divided into the upper and lower lips with teeth. The lateral mouth elements are of two kinds, those representing, as Dr. Spinden says, the "curled fang at the back of the mouth on more realistic representations," or the tongue of the serpent rolling out of the mouth to the sides. In certain types of masks, both of these elements may be used.

As a general rule the indications are that the stones were grooved out by the continual rubbing of some other material, whether stone or hard wood. Such a process would give the rounded bottoms to the grooves and the rounded sides to the relief work, which can be seen in almost any part of the mask decoration. The exterior sides of the stones often were carved with a lip at the position where they were to join the general line of the wall of the facade.

Over a single stone, the surface is generally level, but over a number of stones or the length of a facade, the cornices and mouldings were not kept level. This may have some bearing upon the fact that the work of carving in the quarries was done by a sculptor while the work in assembling was done by masons. The assembler apparently had the use of a plumb but not of a level.

There is a little question that the design, once set, was followed for some time without change. Apparently after the size had been determined, and the general design had been set, all the masks were carved at the quarries, brought to the building, and erected by a mason who was adept at spacing the elements in good proportion. Thus it would be possible to have the difference in the spacing of the elements, the difference in the length of the masks, without changing the design.

The facing generally carried only its own weight. None of the heavy building loads were imposed upon it, even though it was comparatively thick. The areas of facing were divided into smaller sections by the use of continuous mouldings and stiles, which were used as bond for the whole facade. These bonding courses often, as for example the Medial Band of the building, ran completely through the wall, and would thus transmit the whole load above to the core.

In the mask section of the building, the bond courses did not run further than to the rough core, but this distance, of course, varied according to the position above the Medial Band.

The system of tenoning in the stones changed considerably through the period of the life of Las Monjas complex. The stones on Las Monjas proper and La Iglesia were much heavier and more deeply tenoned than the stones on the Southeast Annex.

The lower walls of the buildings did not have bonding courses.

In all probability some of the noses were similar in design to the remaining complete nose of Mask 48, where the curve turns up and out at the top. Masks 1, 3, 5, 15, 48, and 58 could be put in this class. All the butts are extremely heavy and wide, yet they broke in their wide parts. This would indicate the possibility of a large mass of stone extending beyond shear capacity.

Of the type of Mask 51 there were undoubtedly many. These, when analyzed, could well have been broken off more in the form of Mask 25. Masks 9, 10, 12, 16, 25, 34, 35, 36, 37, 51, 52, 53, 54, 55, 56, 57, 59, and 60 could be put in this class. The slant of the break and the size of the stone at that point seem to indicate a different curve and load.

Then in a third class, which might be well represented by the crudely formed reused stone of Mask 50 [of La Iglesia] may be placed all those noses which did not extend very far, and which may have had only the end broken away. Masks 11, 13, 14, 17, 18, and 33 could be put in this group. The breaks are more horizontal than in the former types, and the stone is not very thick at that point. According to Schellas, this type is represented in the codices by the nose of God B.

Little can be said about the next class of break, the nose broken

247

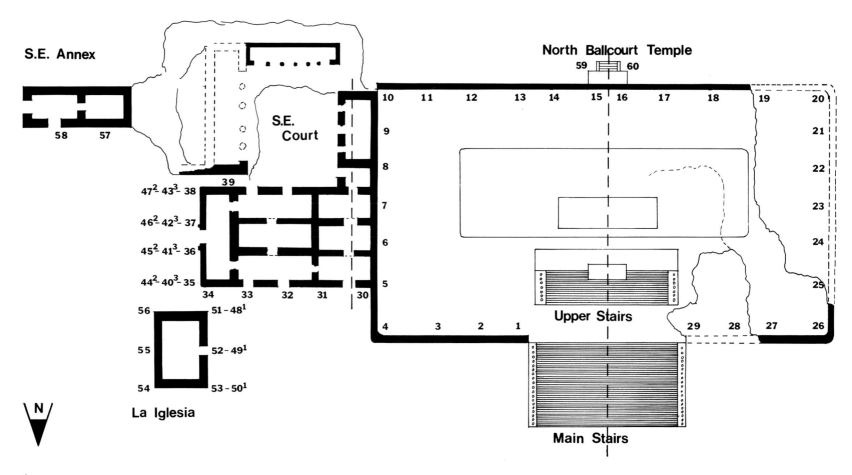

S.E. Annex

North Ballcourt Temple

59 60

S.E. Court

10 11 12 13 14 15 16 17 18 19 20

9

21

8

22

7

23

6

24

5

25

58 57

39

47² 43³ 38

46² 42³ 37

45² 41³ 36

44² 40³ 35

34 33 32 31 30

Upper Stairs

4 3 2 1

29 28 27 26

56 51 – 48¹

55 52 – 49¹

54 53 – 50¹

La Iglesia

Main Stairs

N

¹ UPPER FACADE

² LOWER BAND

³ MIDDLE BAND

ALL OTHERS IN MAIN FRIEZE

Mask numbering system

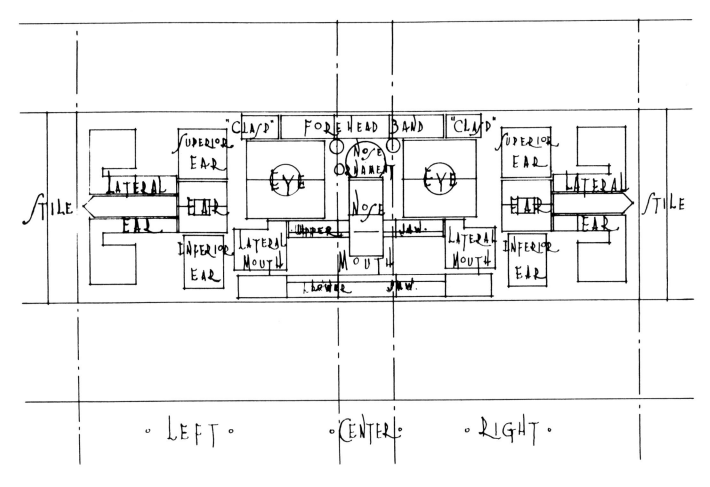

Mask element diagram

at the wall line. It may have been either one of the first two types, probably not the third. Masks 4, 6, 7, 8, 39, 41, 42, 45, and 46 could be placed in this class of unknown type.

The fourth class of break is represented by four excellent examples comprising two types of noses, both of which have one feature in common, that the nose plug holes were drilled and plugs inserted into the curve of the noses. In every case the nose broke through this weakened point. Masks 30, 31, 32, and 40 could be placed in this class. The noses of the first three masks mentioned above were probably similar in design and shape to that of the Caracol masks, except that the plugs were inserted rather than cut from the same stone.

Mask 40, it is natural to suppose, is the exact type of all four of the corner masks of the east facade of the East Wing. It is obvious that the weight of the nose would cause the break of the noses of Masks 43 and 44, at the wall line. Mask 47 is missing completely, but was unquestionably similar to the other three masks. The nose of Mask 40 was broken in such a way that the design of the nose can be indicated. The holes drilled for the nose plugs are clearly visible, and also a small section of the finished surface on the top of the nose is left. Thus, it is quite clear that the nose did not go on indefinitely in this case but turned into a short end, close to the broken surface that remains. . . .

As a general rule the color remains on the Monjas masks where the plaster has not fallen. It is found on the north faces of the building more than on any other side.

The other places where color remains are the protected spots, hollow carvings, such as mouths, eyes, ear plug holes, and in the niche of the East Wing, and along the grooves of the carving, not only on the mask elements but also on the mouldings. This color in the grooves of the elements and on the mouldings shows very clearly that they were "striped." The grooves were made to stand out by the use of color. The designer did not depend entirely upon the shadow or change in plane to give the effect of the design. This can be clearly seen on the snake band on the upper cornice, north elevation, of La Iglesia. The red color was carried along in the central groove of the zigzag stones and then continued on the sides of the zigzags so that the design became one of a striped snake rather than a saw-tooth snake, as one might suppose at first glance. The clean-cut edge of the red paint can be seen to stop at the surface, coming up from the bottom of the grooves of the ear and eye elements of Masks 54 and 55. But on the lid of the eye of Mask 55, the color seems to have covered the whole area.

The backgrounds were, generally speaking, a warm yellow chrome which may or may not have been a painted color. It is very possible that the yellow chrome tone was produced by the ageing of the plaster. However, it covers much of the plaster that still remains, and it does not sink deeply into it. When the plaster is broken, the color is seen in section to be on the surface. On the east side of the building, especially in Mask 35, this theory of plaster ageing is shown,

for where the sun has continually worked on it the color is a cool steel blue rather than the yellow chrome. This steel blue was also noted as the color of the stone on the masks of the south side of Las Monjas proper. Where the plaster remains in almost perfect condition, however, on the lower masks of the east elevation, East Wing, there is a slight feeling that the color was blended out from the center. That is, that the niche over the doorway, and the doorway mouth were brilliantly colored, that the masks to the sides of the doorway were also colored, and that the corner masks and the side masks of the niche carried away the color into a yellow chrome and even a pale yellow at the edges. This is, however, very uncertain because no definite color line or tone remains besides the brilliant colors of the niche and of Masks 41, 42, 45, and 46. If this coloring were present, the design of the east elevation of the East Wing would be greatly changed, and would be nearer the idea of Bolles that the elevation represents the open mouth of the serpent.

There appears to be no consistent coloring for single masks or elements of masks, nor a definite uniform color used for snakes or frets. Red was the most used color on Las Monjas masks.

The color was applied directly to the first coat of plaster, showing that the mask was colored from the first, as on Mask 41. In the case of Mask 45, the hard yellow chrome plaster covers a plaster which was painted. The yellow chrome plaster may have been painted at one time, and the plaster worn off by the elements. On Mask 54 the color on the eye and in the pupil is covered with two unpainted coats. The color coat of plaster is paper thin, probably just a wash coat.

Above Mask 56 there is a considerable amount of black-on-white drawing. It may be that many of the blank areas above the masks of La Iglesia were painted with small figures. Of course, this small area may have been painted at some later time.

The use of different colors seems to be limited to the central motives of the facades. There are four sections in which polychrome coloring was found: (1) the masks of the Southeast Annex; (2) the central figure of Mask 52 on the west elevation of La Iglesia; (3) the central figure and niche of the east facade of the East Wing; (4) the small elements of Las Monjas Ball Court masks.

On the Southeast Annex, the color remains to such an extent that a color drawing could be made. The background of the mask was a deep red-purple. This tone is left mainly around the outside lateral ear frets. The insides of the frets were covered with the same deep red-purple. This red-purple was used inside the ear peg hole, under the mortar that later held the ear plug peg. This would at least show that

Mask 4, Type 1A, northeast corner of Platform 5

Mask 9, Type 3, east elevation, Platform 5

Mask 10, Type 1A, southeast corner of Platform 5

Mask 1, Type 1A

SECTION A-A

Mask 33, Type 3

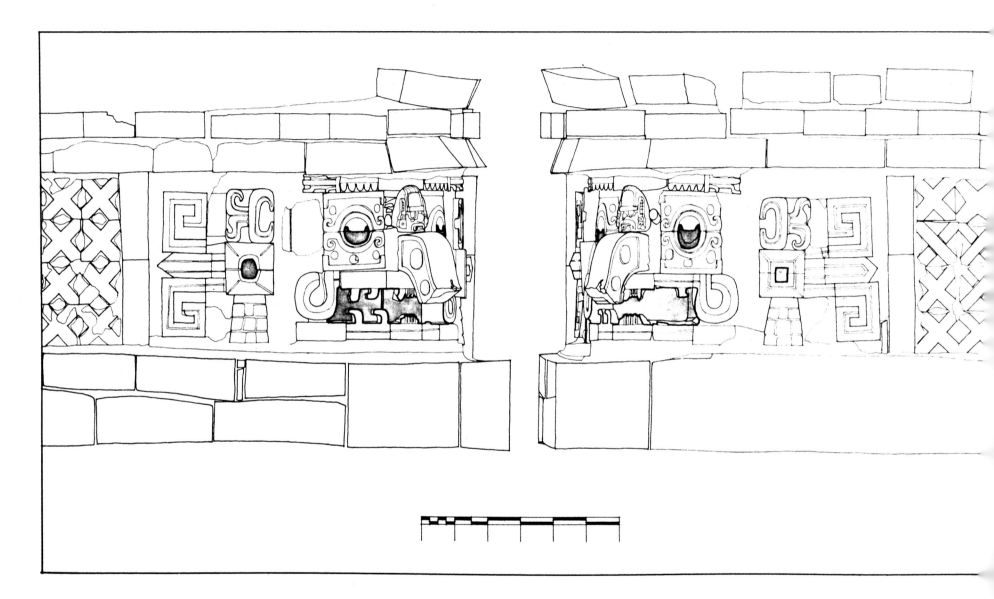

Mask 10, Type 3

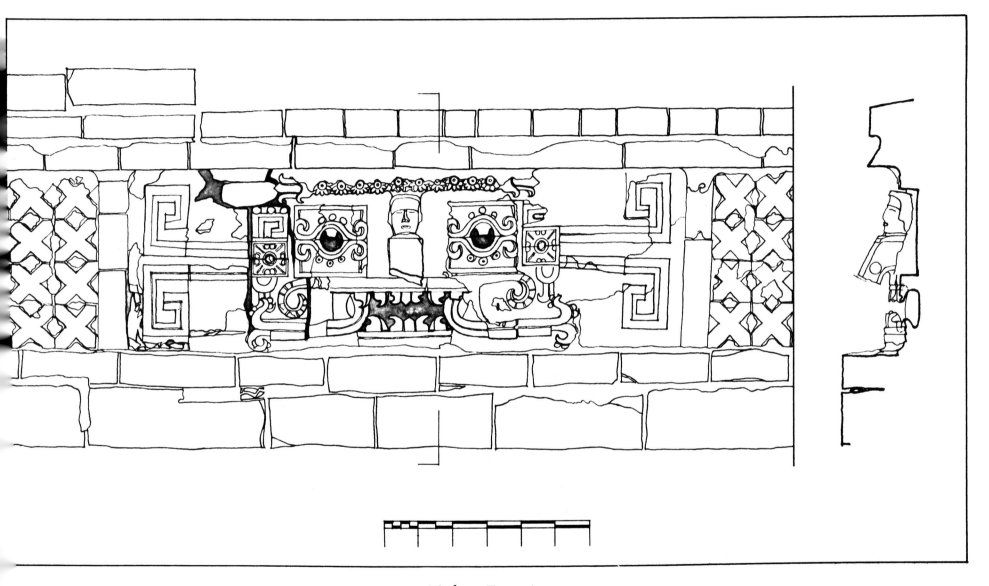

Mask 11, Type 1A

257

some time elapsed, for the purple paint is under the peg, which has always been considered a Maya design. Certainly the pegs were put in after the color. The red-purple tone came out almost to the edge of the hole, where it joined a bright blue-green color. The blue-green continued out on all sides from the hole for a short distance. It was then picked up in the groove around the hole, but not on the diagonal grooves. Blue-green appears again at the top of the inferior ear, continuing for the width of the upper quarter of the element. Yellow appears on the next quarter down, beginning on the groove below the blue-green. Purple shows again on the third quarter down, and probably covered it. The inside of the mouth is painted a strong red tone. No color remains on or in the eyes. No color remains on the forehead band, the nose, or the nose ornament. The X motive between the masks is deep red-purple.

The sixty masks of Las Monjas complex may be divided into five types or groups, within each of which the masks seem to have a considerable likeness in feeling, size, stone cutting, and element design. In general, the first type includes the east facade of the East Wing except for the more elaborate lower corner masks; the north frieze and the east frieze of Las Monjas proper except for Masks 8 and 9; the Southeast Annex; La Iglesia except for Masks 49 and 50; and the first masks contiguous with the east facade of the East Wing on the north and south. In the second type are only the four elaborate corner masks of the east facade. The third type includes all the remaining masks on Las Monjas proper and Mask 33 of the north facade, East Wing. The fourth type comprises the three remaining masks of the north facade, East Wing, being the three farthest west on that wing. In the fifth type are the two masks, made up of smaller elements, of the north temple of the Ball Court. The last group, which can hardly be called a type, is that of masks built up of re-used stones which obviously were not cut for their present positions and which seem to have been set in the masks simply because the size of the stone was correct.

Type 1B masks vary considerably from Type 1 and Type 1A. In fact, except for the resemblance in the design, it would be wiser to segregate them to another type number, such as Type 2, for the sizes of the elements change, the cutting changes, some of the elements change, and some elements are omitted entirely in the mask motive. Nevertheless, the feeling of the mask, the squareness of the ear plugs, the stone jointing, and perhaps more especially than any other, the sizes of the elements are nearer this Type 1 than any other on the Monjas complex because they are larger, and all the other types are smaller than Type 1. However, it should be realized that Type 1B is

258

Masks 59 and 60, Type 5

not as close an analogy to Type 1 as Type 1A, and that in many respects it closely resembles Type 3.

There are three masks in Type 4. All are located on the East Wing, being the three masks nearest the main platform. They have very little relation to the three types described. Many features have a distant relationship to those of other masks, such as the general idea of the pendant shape for the inferior ear element, or the realistic face of the superior nose ornament, but even in these, changes must be noted. These are the "portrait heads" upon which Bolles based his concepts.

It is more likely that these masks, which seem to resemble the Caracol masks more closely than they do Las Monjas, follow the masks in this type order. The lower eye carries the design of the La Iglesia Type 1B masks, the teeth seem still to be the Type 1 teeth, yet the tongue is found in the masks of Type 3. It might be possible to see a connection between Mask 25 and this type where 25 omits the outer teeth of the lower jaw to make a place for the flat tongue, yet is still of the hooked tooth type. The ear plugs are a short step away from some of the variants of Type 3.

Masks 49 and 50 can hardly be placed in a type class, unless one might call a miscellaneous group of elements, definitely thrown together simply to fill up space and in some way approximating a mask, to be worthy of a type basis. Where the elements came from, why they resemble some of the masks of the types previously described, is uncertain, but the fact that some of the elements are not found elsewhere in the complex, or elsewhere in Chichén Itzá, makes them considerably more important.

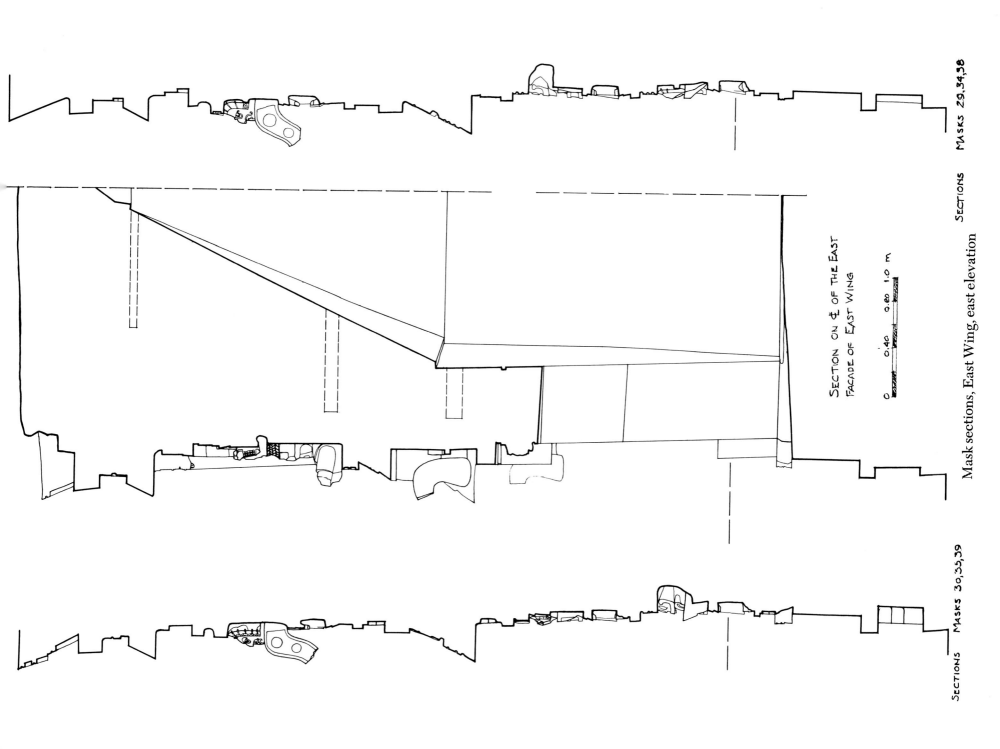

Section on ℄ of the East
Facade of East Wing

0   0.40   0.80   1.0 m

Mask sections, East Wing, east elevation

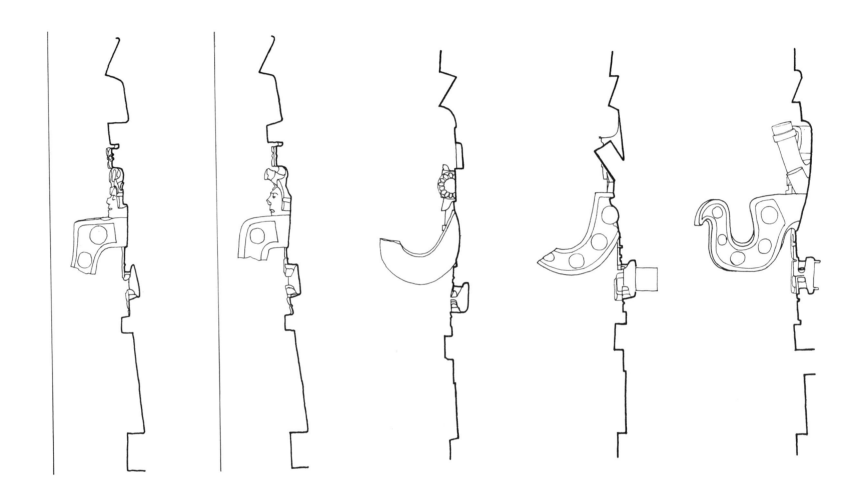

Mask sections, Southeast Annex and La Iglesia

14. HIEROGLYPHIC LINTELS

A study of the hieroglyphic lintels and the painted capstones would require a research program of its own. The lintels have been reproduced in many documents since the earliest visitors to the site. Of particular importance were: the work of Hermann Beyer for Tulane University from 1928 to 1932; the rubbings by Jack Denison for Carnegie Institution at the time of the excavations; and the studies by E. Wyllys Andrews III, who did his first work with Jack Denison and went on to become head of the Tulane projects in Central America.

The most recent analysis by J. Eric S. Thompson is included herein. His dating of A.D. 889 for the dedication of the Second Story and for the East Addition capstone fits well with the apparent architectural developments. New beam tests with the latest techniques might well show that La Iglesia and La Casa Colorada were of this same date, not a hundred or so years earlier.

All the Second Story doorway lintels, with the exception of those over the south facade entrances, were inscribed with hieroglyphic panels on both their soffits and exterior faces. The face of the lintel over the east doorway to the East Wing was the only other discovered example of this type of work. Some of the lintels over the niches in the Second Story rooms were painted with what appeared to have been hieroglyphic panels, and a frieze of hieroglyphs modeled in plaster extended around the single room of La Iglesia just below the vault spring. Four of the face panels of the Second Story lintels were divided into four blocks containing groups of hieroglyphs. On the faces of the lintels to Room 20 and the center line and east doors of Room 18, the hieroglyphs were separated into five groups.

The soffits of the north facade doorways to the Second Story were all carved with a border of sixteen glyphs blocks. The panels contained additional hieroglyphic carvings, some with only three blocks, others, such as the center and east doors to Room 18, had two rows of four blocks each. The soffit of the Room 16 doorway lintel had four east-west panels of four glyph blocks each. The narrow bands between panels were roughly the same width as the border bands of the soffit, which was rather badly disintegrated. As with several of the other lintels, the failure of the panel lines to parallel the plane of the door jambs bore out the belief that the carving must have been done before installation in the building. The execution would have been extremely difficult on the soffit, owing to the overhead position and the interference by the jambs. The Room 20 lintel soffit was divided into three east-west panels, each containing two rows of four hieroglyphic blocks, for a total of twenty-four.

All the lintel soffits were intended to be read with the bottom of the panel at the room edge of the lintel. The background was cut out around the individual hieroglyphic blocks. The details of the hieroglyphs were both scratched and cut into the surface.

The lintel to the East Wing east entrance, as described above, had a projecting head as the central motif; the two lateral panels each contained two rows of hieroglyphs, with five hieroglyphs to the row. Each of these two panels was intended to be read with the base of each inscription as the outer ends of the lintel. These hieroglyphs were beautifully executed, each having completely carved or worked, rather than scratched-on, details. It required a true sculptor to execute this splendid lintel. Not only were there definite space requirements to fulfill but had in addition the projecting head and the two lateral panels—all of which was executed with admirable craftsmanship and design.

THE HIEROGLYPHIC TEXTS OF LAS MONJAS AND THEIR BEARING ON BUILDING ACTIVITIES
By J. Eric S. Thompson

Hieroglyphic texts of Yucatán differ in several important respects from those of the Central area (southern lowlands).

Initial Series are very rare and, of those reported, only one records a date later than 9.16.0.0.0 (A.D. 751). The exception is the Initial Series lintel at Chichén Itzá, dedicated at 10.3.0.0.0 (A.D. 889). All Christian-era dates in this section are according to the Goodman-Martínez-Thompson correlation.

Dates linked by distance numbers, such a feature of texts of the Central area, are unknown in Yucatán, where not a single example has been reported.

The custom, so prevalent in the Central area, of recording the end of a katun by giving it number, the day Ahau on which it ends, and the corresponding month position, is replaced in Yucatán by a mere record of the day Ahau on which the katun ends together with certain affixes almost certainly with the meaning "Lord" or "Lord Owner." For example, 19 katuns, 9 Ahau 18 Mol" of the Central area would have been written "Lord Owner 9 Ahau" in Yucatán.

The emblem glyph, apparently giving the name of an individual ceremonial center, with affixes probably indicating "Lord ruler of," has not as yet been identified in Yucatán inscriptions.

Glyphs of the Central area are almost invariably carved with great care. They are symmetrical with gently rounded corners and affixes carefully fitted into spaces adjusted to avoid distortion and retain the standard mold. Glyphs in Yucatán, with few exceptions, are assymmetrical, slovenly laid-out and poorly carved, so that they leave the impression that little care was taken in seeking a pleasant appearance. Treatment of the former reminds one of that of the sleek cattle in a Cuyp landscape; that of the

262

latter, of charging bulls in a comic strip. Other diversities confirm that we are faced with two different traditions.

Chichén Itzá did not follow the Puuc custom of recording coefficients of month signs one day less than in the Central area (e.g., recording 1 Kan 1 Pop in place of 1 Kan 2 Pop of the Central area (See Proskouriakoff and Thompson, 1947).

Of the seven hieroglyphic lintels of the Second Story of Las Monjas, five (2–6) span doorways on the front (north) of the structure; 1 and 7 are over doorways on the east and west sides, respectively. All have texts on the front and underside. Texts on the front lintels are arranged in a fashion peculiar to Chichén Itzá. On the underside of each lintel, the first part of the text occupies an outer rectangular frame. The inscription opens at the top left corner of the frame and proceeds counterclockwise to terminate with the glyph block immediately to the right of the starting point. The text then continues in one or two horizontal columns, each of three or four glyph blocks, in the rectangle thus framed. An almost similar layout characterizes the water-trough lintel of Chichén Itzá.

In contrast, Lintels 1 and 7, over side doorways, carry no such frame and rectangle arrangement, but have the glyphs on their undersides arranged in four and three double columns of glyph blocks. Furthermore, whereas Lintels 2–6 commence with the same Calendar Round date, Lintels 1 and 7 open with a non-calendric Kan sign. Those differences raise the possibility that Lintels 1 and 7 are reused, having come from some demolished building. However, style and content rather argue against that possibility.

Maudslay (1889–1902, p. 4, Plates 12 and 13) reproduces drawings from casts by Miss Annie Hunter of Lintels 2, 3, and 4 and parts of Lintels 5 and 7.

Beyer (1937, p. 34) draws the complete texts, depending on his own studies of them in situ in 1928 and 1932, Miss Hunter's drawings, and ink rubbings made in 1933 by J. H. Denison.

An amusing but disturbing story concerns those rubbings. They were lent by Carnegie Institution of Washington to Beyer

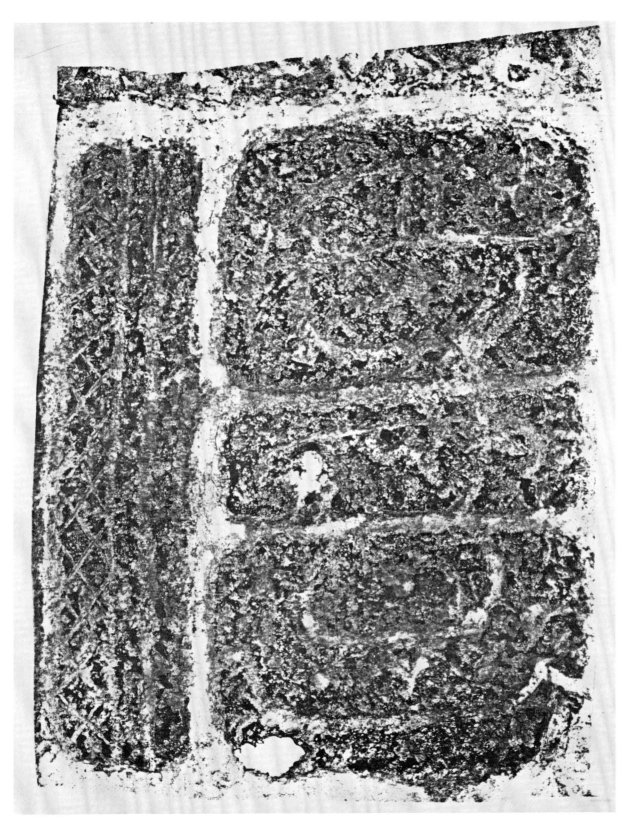

Rubbing of hieroglyphic
block on face of Lintel 7

at his request to aid him in his great study of the inscriptions of Chichén Itzá, an outstanding pioneer exercise in methodology (Beyer, 1937). After publication of that work, Morley asked Beyer to return the rubbings. On opening the package, Morley found not large rubbings covering the best part of a whole inscription but bundles of hundreds of small squares and rectangles of paper each with a single glyph. (In 1936 Bolles received an envelope from Tulane containing the cut-up rubbings, Lintel 7.) Beyer had cut up the texts for his glyph-by-glyph study. The splendid collection of rubbings had been ruined beyond redemption. They had cost Denison much time and effort, and he was not available to make a fresh set.

The next time Morley was in New Orleans, spluttering imprecations against Beyer, he asked Beyer why he had cut up the rubbings without even asking permission to do so.

"Vell," replied Beyer, "I didn't ask your permission because I knew you would refuse it. I did it for the advancement of science."

That answer left Morley, surely for the first time in his life, speechlesss. It seems never to have occurred to Beyer that he could have had photographs made of the texts and cut these up, instead of the originals, thereby both advancing science and keeping Morley's blood pressure short of the explosion point. It was long before Morley could tell the story calmly.

Drawings of the texts of all seven lintels were recently made in situ by Ian Graham, who most kindly has placed copies of these at the writer's disposal.

All lintels have weathered to a greater or lesser extent, as Maudslay noted on his visit to Chichén Itzá in 1889. Accordingly, it is very fortunate that we have the three sets of drawings, each backed by some advantage: less weathering and light casts, which could be moved to get any cross light for Miss Hunter; comparative studies of all Chichén Itzá texts for Beyer; artificial light for Graham.

Beyer's studies of the Monjas lintels, in bringing out for the first time duplicated or parallel phrases in the total glyphic litera-

ture of Chichén Itzá, was a highly important contribution to hieroglyphic investigation.

Thompson (1937), in setting forth the method of recording dates in Yucatán, discussed dates on lintels of the Monjas, a matter referred to below.

Barthel (1955), in a review of non-calendrical glyphs at Chichén Itzá covered much material from the Monjas lintels.

The purpose of this short contribution is not to discuss non-calendric texts but to review dates recorded on lintels and capstones which may aid us in deciding when the Second Story of the Monjas was built.

The texts on the undersides of Lintels 2, 3, and 4 open with a clear day 8 Manik (most unusually, the Manik hand of Lintel 4 lacks a cartouche). The first glyph of Lintel 5 is a day Manik with a weathered head numeral replacing the bar and three dots of Lintels 2–4. The maize element on temple and cheek seems to be present. As that is a characteristic of the head of number 8 (the maize god) and in view of other correspondences with the Calendar Round, there is every reason to accept a reading of 8 Manik, as, indeed, did Beyer. On Lintel 6, the first glyph is again Manik, but the numerical head attached to it is almost beyond identification. Comparison of the Calendar Round again makes it nearly certain that this also was a record of 8 Manik.

In all cases, a kin sign (symbolic or personified) follows directly the day sign. In Yucatán texts, this kin "day," glyph almost invariably follows the day sign, a piece of tautology, a vice to which the Maya were incurably addicted, since there could be no doubt that the preceding glyph indicated the day.

Postfixed to this kin sign on all five lintels is Affix 92, which really belongs with the next glyph, a good example of the careless writing which marks texts in Yucatán. It probably has the value *tu*, a contraction of *ti* and *u* (*ti*, "at," *u* converts the following number from cardinal to ordinal (Thompson, 1950, p. 57).

There follows, as one would expect, the month position corresponding to 8 Manik. The number is expressed on Lintels 2–5 by a head number. The head in all cases has the tun headdress,

264

found only with heads for numbers 5 and 15; A bared jawbone is visible on Lintel 2 and almost certainly on Lintel 4, and gumless teeth are recognizable in all four cases. Such symbols of death make it clear that the heads represent 15 (death symbols—a death head is the symbol for 10—convert 4 to 9 to 14 to 19).

In the case of Lintel 6, the number is expressed as a numerical bar for 5 above a weathered head with an unusual kind of fountain of water before it and with Affix 23 below. The combination of numerical bar and dots or numerical head with the head of the number 10 to the right or below it is a known feature of texts of the Central area (Thompson, 1950, fig. 5, no. 53). In fact, the two heads representing two digits are placed side by side instead of having the characteristics of each digit combined in a single head, as on Lintels 2–5. Clearly, then, all five lintels record the month number 15. Also, in all five cases, Affix 23 is postfixed to the number. This is a characteristic of the death head for number 10, and appears only with heads for 10 or teen numbers 14 to 19, further confirmation that in all cases the number is 15.

The month sign to which the number 15 is attached is rather worn in all five cases, but in all examples the main element comprising the crossed bar sign (*kat*) is readily recognizable, evidence that the month sign must be Uo or Zip. The superfix of the month sign on Lintel 6 is without serious doubt, the black element (G1. 95), which characterizes Uo, and that of Lintel 3 are probably the same element. The outlines of the remaining three superfixes are too round to be those of Zip (G1. 109), and lack the lateral nicks of that sign.

There can therefore be no reasonable doubt that the Calendar Round date is 8 Manik 15 Uo or, more correctly, 8 Manik on 15th Uo.

As a Calendar Round date recurs every 52 years, it was necessary to place it securely in a longer period when dealing with memorials of state or church. In Yucatán, by adding the number of the 360–day year (*haab* or *tun*) in which it fell and the day Ahau on which the current katun ended, one has a combination which will not repeat for over 7,000 years. This system is fol-

lowed on several of the Monjas lintels (Thompson, 1937, pp. 179–81). The day Ahau marking the day on which the current katun ended was the common method of naming a katun in the Books of Chilam Balam: "4 Ahau was the katun when they sought and discovered Chichén Itzá"; "2 Ahau was when the eruption of pustules occurred"; "Katun 11 Ahau was the beginning of the katun count"; "It was in the first tun of 11 Ahau, that was the katun when. . . ." Scores of such entries can be found in those books (Roys, 1933). The day Ahau and its number which records the katun were differentiated by the addition of prefix 168 and postfix 130, a combination which in all probability signifies *Ah nal*, "owner" (Thompson, 1972, pp. 64, 65).

As in the case of the date 8 Manik 15 Uo, the glyphs giving the current tun and current Ahau katun are weathered, and only by comparing the four passages which record those details can we safely reconstruct the whole passage.

On the front of Lintel 4, well-preserved glyphs read: Forward to completion of 11 haab (360-day year) falling in unnumbered Ahau, Owner [of the katun].

On Lintel 2 (A4–A5), immediately following the 8 Manik 15 Uo clause, occur badly weathered glyphs "within (?) 11 Haab (the tail and infix are recognizable) falling in damaged numerical head Ahau, Owner [of the katun]. Beyer (1937, fig. 683 legend) reads the damaged numerical head as 1.

On Lintel 6, similar information follows immediately the recording of 8 Manik 15 Uo, but again is badly weathered. The block which should record "within 11 haab" is badly weathered. The characteristic tail of haab is clear as is the sign tentatively read as "within." As to the numerical head, Beyer shows a curving incised line descending from about where the eye should be. At the time he made the drawing, the distinctive feature of the head for 11 was unknown; it was only in 1931 that its characteristic, the query mark of the Caban sign, was established. He could therefore not have been seeing what he wanted to see, but his curving line agrees reasonably well with the lower part of the Caban query mark. We can, accordingly, accept this as the head for number 11, in agreement with the haab coefficient of Lintel 4. The outline of Owner Ahau and the falling in affix are clear. Again, the number of the day Ahau is in head form. The protuberance on the forehead, the apparently youthful face, and traces on temple and cheek of the woman's lock of hair make it rather more than probable that this is the head for 1. The whole can accordingly be restored as "within 11 haab, falling in 1 Ahau, Owner [of the katun]."

The corresponding phrase on Lintel 5 is again weathered. It can be restored as "within 11 haab falling numerical head Ahau [Owner of the katun]." The damaged numerical head is again youthful and has a forehead element resembling that of the head for 1, and so, in view of the parallel passages, we are on good grounds in accepting the reading 1 Ahau, Owner.

Lintel 3 has no corresponding phrase.

Drawing the above material together—the following statement was originally carved without much doubt on Lintels 2, 5, and 6: "8 Manik on 15th Uo within Haab 11 falling in 1 Ahau, Owner [of the katun]." Lintel 4 reads: 8 Manik on 15th Uo, forward to completion of Haab 11 falling in Ahau, Owner [of the katun]." Here the Ahau number is omitted. It is to be understood that "falling in" and "within" are tentative readings, but the general sense of the glyphic elements is not in doubt.

The only date which will meet those conditions is 10.2.10.11.7 8 Manik 15 Uo, which duly falls in a haab or tun 11 in a katun 1 Ahau—that is, 10.3.0.0.0, 1 Ahau 3 Yaxkin. Such an arrangement will not repeat for several thousand years. That position of 8 Manik 15 Uo corresponds to February 6, A.D. 880 in the Thompson variant of the Goodman-Martínez-Thompson correlation.

One may suppose that the Second Story of the Monjas was dedicated at the katun ending 10.3.0.0.0, the equivalent of May 2, A.D. 889.

These dates are just over a century later than the Carbon-14 readings of A.D. 780 ± 70 and A.D. 600 ± 70 samples of beams taken for Bolles by his son David and E. Wyllys Andrews in the adjacent La Iglesia (Andrews, 1965, p. 63). At the time those samples were taken, it was not realized that only the outside ring

of a tree trunk gives the date of felling. In the case of zapote beams, for instance, there could well be a century or more between a sample taken from the core and one taken from the outmost rings. That factor together with the 1 sigma range could bridge the gap between Monjas and Iglesia should there be reason to suppose them to be approximately contemporaneous.

Of the crude glyphs on the front of the lintel of the East Room of the East Wing, little can be said. Arranged in two horizontal columns extending outward in both directions from an embossed central mask, these are to be read outward from the mask, and so are awkwardly at right angles to the observer, who must twist his head first in one direction and then in the other to read them.

The line of carved stones between the lintel and the seated figure above form a planetary band, a feature common in the Central area and in the hieroglyphic books, where they decorate the stylized bodies of Itzam monsters. Recognizable are symbols representing stars in general or the planet Venus in particular, a moon sign and celestial (conjunction?) crossbands. In addition, various creatures—a peccary or wild boar, a turtle, two birds, a sort of crocodile-snake, a probable scorpion, a death's head and two weathered beyond identification—are attached to the Venus symbols. As several of these animals are known constellation symbols, it is probable that the whole design represent conjunctions of the planet Venus with various constellations.

Both painted capstones of Room 2 once carried dates of a similar kind to those on the lintels—a Calendar Round date, the haab in which it fell, and the day Ahau Owner of the then-current katun. Unfortunately, both have suffered extensive damage.

The north capstone date reads: ? Imix, the day on 14th Zip, ? haab, 1? Ahau, Owner [of the katun]. The coefficient of the month Zip is formed of a death's head, representing the number 10, surmounted by dots or a bar, which might read, 2, 3, 4, or 5. As the day is Imix, which calls for month positions 4, 9, 14, or 19, the number must be restored as four dots, which, combined with the head for 10, gives the reading 14. Note that we have already encountered this combination of a head for 10 and a numerical bar on Lintel 6. The coefficient of Ahau, Owner, is badly damaged. The circle at bottom on right is like that commonly found at the wrist of a hand used as a glyphic element. Sometimes a finger or thumb stands for the number 1 and, when thus used, invariably has the circle at its base. There is, accordingly, a good chance that this damaged coefficient is 1 expressed as an upright thumb. Moreover, one would expect a capstone date to fall in the same katun (1 Ahau) as that recorded on the lintels of the building.

The south capstone, even more damaged, reads: damaged day sign, day, *tu* destroyed month, 14 haab (4 dots over death head representing 10), falling in ? (the affix here resembles Affix 96, with value *yol*, "in the heart of").

If, as is not unlikely, the same date is recorded on both capstones, thus paralleling the lintel dates, this can be partially restored as: ? Imix 14th Zip within 14 haab falling in ? 1 ? Ahau, Owner [of the katun].

On the assumption that the number attached to Ahau is, indeed, 1, in agreement with the katun of the lintels, the whole text can be restored and given the long count position 10.2.13.13.1 4 Imix 14 Zip, corresponding to February 24, A.D. 883, just over three years later than the lintel date. In support of this reconstruction, one may note that there is only a one-in-four chance that a day Imix will correspond to 14 Zip in a given haab. Nevertheless, the reading cannot be accepted as proved.

According to the writer's reconstruction of Yucatec history (Thompson, 1970, p. 14), the Putun Itzá seized Chichén Itzá on 10.4.9.7.3 2 Akbal 1 Yaxkin, April 26, A.D. 918 in our calendar. It would seem that the old rulers of what may then have been called Uuc Yabnal (Roys, 1933, p. 65), who ordered the building of the Second Story of the Monjas, had little time to enjoy that pleasant structure; within thirty years they had been overthrown. Perhaps no second story was built over the East Wing, because the Itzá arrived before work had advanced beyond filling in the ground-floor rooms to bear the weight of a projected Second Story. Reused stones in the Third Story room indicate that that came later still.

Illustrations of Lintels
By Ian Graham
Explanation

Nomenclature Beyer's numbering of the glyph blocks (Beyer, 1937) has been preserved and also that of the surfaces of the lintels themselves, except that arabic numbers are substituted for his roman numerals; thus the soffit of Lintel 1 is referred to as Lintel 1, and its front surface as Lintel 1a.

Photographs are reproduced at the scale of 1:10. The sources of these are as follows:

1. I. Graham	4a. Maudslay cast, I. Graham
1a. Carnegie Inst. Wash.	5. I. Graham
2. I. Graham	5a. I. Graham
2a. I. Graham	6. I. Graham
3. I. Graham	6a. I. Graham
3a. Carnegie Inst. Wash.	7. Graham cast, I. Graham
4. I. Graham	7a. Graham cast, I. Graham

Drawings are reproduced at a scale of about 1:8. Both surfaces of Lintel 6 were drawn by Wesley Wong, the remainder by Ian Graham. The drawings were based upon the following sources:

Field drawings by Ian Graham of all the lintels, refined under illumination at night.

Photographs of some of the casts made by A. P. Maudslay, preserved in the British Museum.

Casts of both surfaces of Lintels 6 and 7 made from latex moulds taken by Ian Graham.

Rubbings made by Carnegie Institution personnel and now preserved in the Peabody Museum, Harvard University, of the following surfaces: 1a, 2, 2a, 4, 4a, 5, 5a, 6.

Photographs in the Carnegie Institution files (Peabody Museum).

Reference: H. Beyer, "Studies on the Inscriptions of Chichen Itza," *Carnegie Institution of Washington, Pub. 483, Contrib. 21* (Washington, 1937).

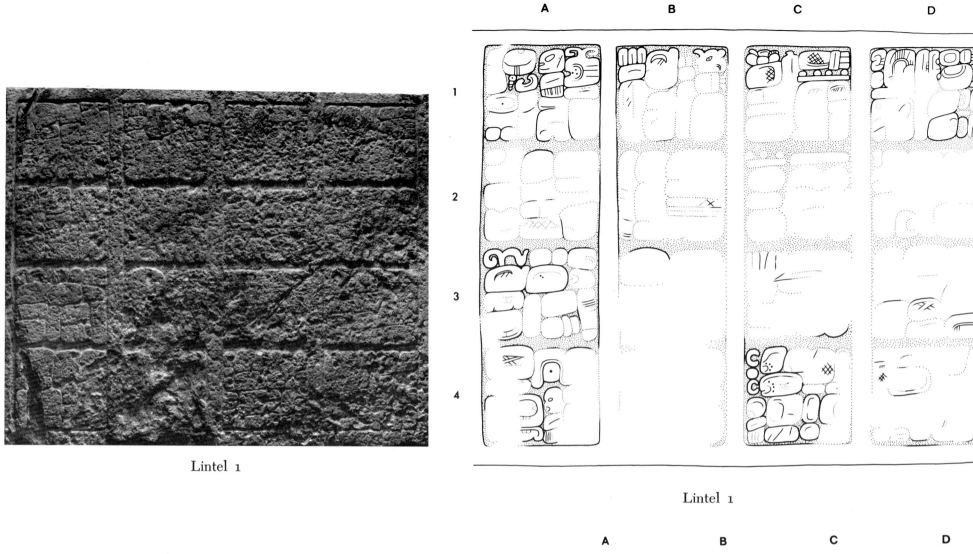

Lintel 1

Lintel 1

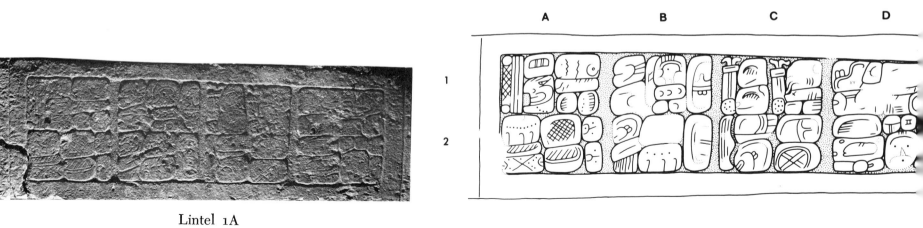

Lintel 1A

Lintel 1A

Lintel 2

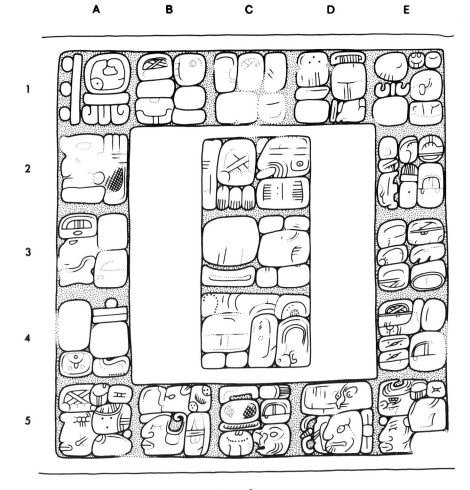

Lintel 2

Lintel 2A

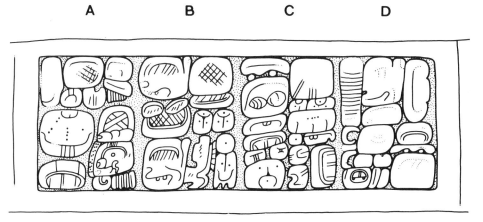

Lintel 2A

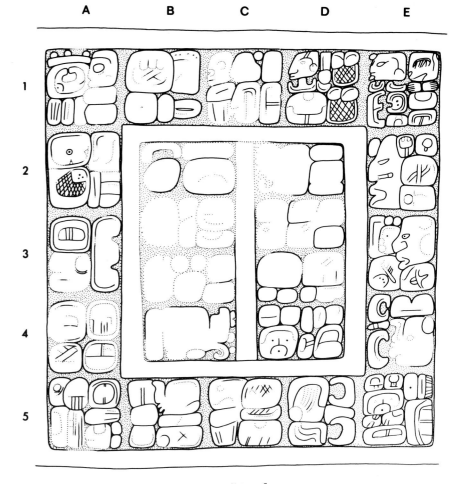

Lintel 3

Lintel 3

Lintel 3A

Lintel 3A

Lintel 4

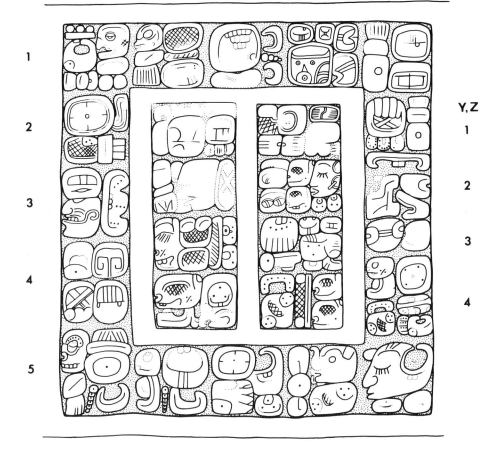

Lintel 4

Lintel 4A

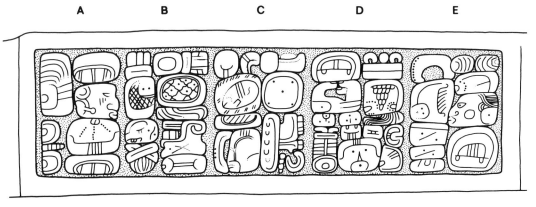

Lintel 4A

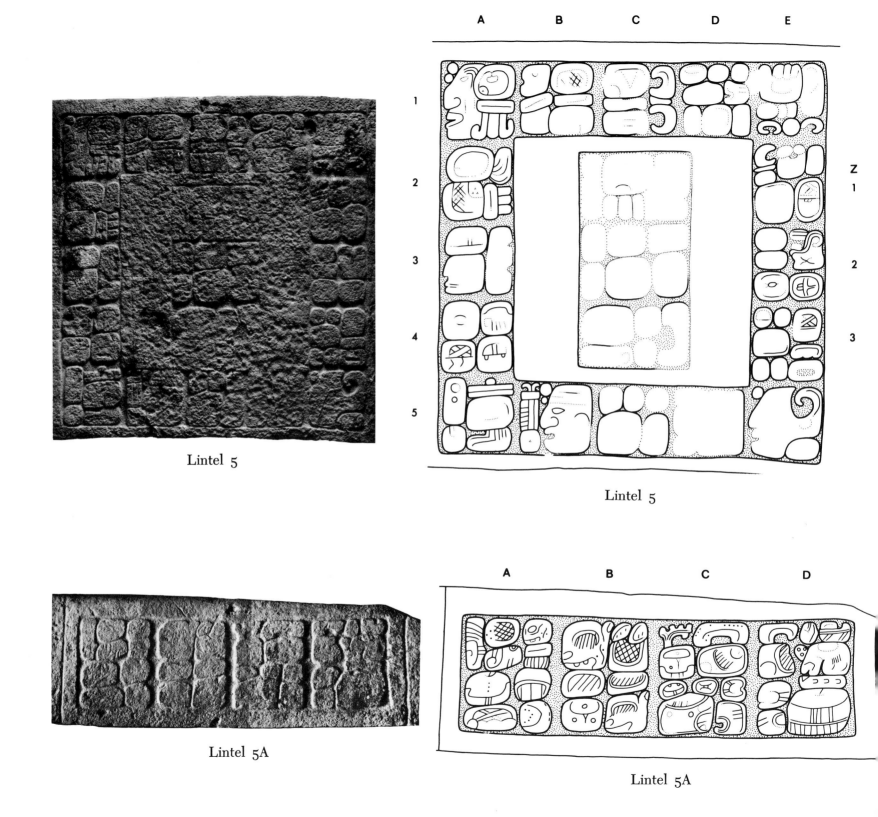

Lintel 5

Lintel 5

Lintel 5A

Lintel 5A

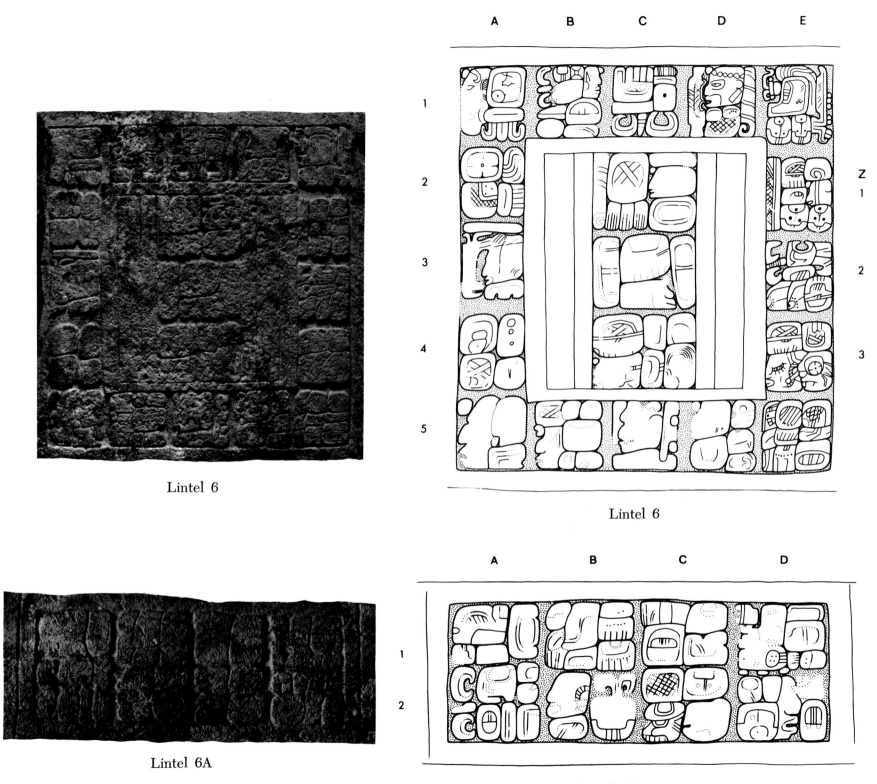

Lintel 6

Lintel 6

Lintel 6A

Lintel 6A

Lintel 7

Lintel 7

Lintel 7A

Lintel 7A

AGE SEQUENCE BASED ON STYLE (*After Hermann Beyer*)

1. Akabtzib ⎡Cauac old, pure Old Empire Style
           ⎣Ahau old.

2. Initial Series ⎡Cauac old. Old Empire Style.
                 ⎣Kin is different from Old Empire Style

First Stage

3. *Jalacal Cauac two dotted symbols.

4. Red House ⎡Sometimes above and sometimes tending to the new form.
            ⎣The Kin is Old Empire.

5. Monjas ⎡Double form of Cauac
         ⎣neither old nor late.

Second Stage

6. **Temple of the Two Lintels ⎡New Cauac
                               ⎣Kin only with one line

7. Caracol
8. Water Trough
9. Yula

Third Stage

10. Four Lintels ⎡Both new Cauac
                ⎣and new kin.

Fourth Stage

* Hieroglyphic Jambs Cauac looks old. Stylistic criteria not safe. Four doubtful cases, unclassified. Hieroglyphic jambs. High Priest's Grave.

** Caracol Circular New Cauac and Old Cauac in Mérida. Circular Stone, Caracol. Temple of the One Lintel.

APPENDIX A : TOPOGRAPHY

Finally, a few words about the geographical site of Las Monjas complex. Las Monjas was built on the south of a flat stretch of terrain, requiring a minimum of fill in order to obtain a level plaza for a group of structures. Aside from Las Monjas, this area included such buildings as La Casa del Venado, La Casa Colorada, El Caracol, and the Akabdzib. East and south of the Akabdzib were deep depressions, from which a series of low sinkholes extended south of Las Monjas, swinging to the northwest toward the deep depression west of the complex. Extensive quarrying operations were obviously carried on in the sinkholes to the south and west; probably most of the stone for the complex came from these.

The highest elevation within the complex was at the northwest corner of the main platform (Platform 4). From the excavations, where they reached to bedrock, it was apparent that the remainder of the complex had been built on a comparatively level site. East of the East Building was a slight elevation sloping off rapidly to the southeast. West of the Ball Court behind Las Monajs was a small knoll of about the same height as that of the northwest corner. Extending west and north from the northwest corner of Platform 4 were low ridges.

The region was of limestone of varying degrees of hardness. In many places there were pockets of soscob (a powdered limestone used as a binder with lime to form the plaster used in construction). The digging of this material had left many caves.

The surface of the limestone was lined with small crevices filled with earth and humus. In most of the low areas, a layer of cancob (a deep red material that appeared to be a mixture of burned earth and humus) was found over the rock. Potsherds were often found mixed with the material in the crevices as well as in the cancob.

APPENDIX B : SUMMARY OF EXCAVATION AND REPAIR BY SEASONS

THE 1932 SEASON

Work on the project began in 1932 with a survey, including plans and sections, of the known structures. With the assistance of these drawings, doubtful areas were pinpointed and minor excavations undertaken in an attempt to find missing corners and levels.

Among the first problems was to determine the corners of the Third Story. In the search for these corners, the upper stairs leading to the roof of the Second Story Building were uncovered. The single step in front of the entrance was found while determining the floor level at the front of the building. The small altar or bench within the building came to light during the clearing of the center line in an attempt to find the rear wall.

The tracing of the level in front of the Third Story helped reveal the structure of the upper stairs. The construction level at the top of the twelfth riser was found, and the interior construction of the upper section of the stairs was revealed. Of the upper section, no trace remained of the stairs parapets. The niche in the center and the low dais formed by the roof were cleared of debris and indicated on the plans. The foundation line of the stairs and its relation to the Second Story Basement were traced.

Work on the Second Story Building began with the boring of a tunnel into the west door of Room 18 in an effort to find the rear wall and to investigate the possibility that a vault had been erected there. The rear wall was found to be similar to that of Room 22, but with only the original construction plaster. No evidence of a vault was found. The floor was in excellent condition except for a crack caused by structural failure of the platforms. The room had been filled to wall height with large stones fairly well embedded in a lean lime mortar. A rough construction level, entirely of large stones with no binder, was at the

top. The faced stones sealing the entrances to the room had been placed from within as the room was filled. From each of the three doors, a few of these faced stones had been removed by others.

In the construction of the tunnel into the west door of Room 18, the use of timber and then masonry shoring was necessary to hold in place the loose rubble at the top. This masonry was left in place, and the single pier and niches of the rear wall were exposed.

The Second Story Basement had been exposed on the west by the collapse of Platform 4. Trenching into the loose stone fill of Platform 5 exposed the two east corners as well as the north and south center lines. Digging the south center line pit exposed the weep holes in both the basement and Platform 5.

To determine the levels of the Main Stairs in relation to Platform 3 as well as the relation of the foundation lines of Platform 3 and Platform 4, pits were dug at the juncture points of these lines east of the stairs. Subsequent tunneling into the stairs structure along the face of Platform 3 showed that the masonry was solid for nearly the entire length of the tunnel. The base of the stairs was above the firm floor upon which Platform 3 rested, on a loose stone fill. A vertical construction line was found in the plaster facing of the platform.

The work in this area included the first tracing of the Northeast Terrace. The west face was partly analyzed, and the corners and the north line were traced.

Investigation of the junctures of the East Wing with Platforms 3 and 4 revealed the necessity for extensive tunneling operations. Consequently, two principal tunnels—the north and the south—with subsidiary lateral branches, were constructed as the operation proceeded.

The north tunnel, the first to be undertaken, extended along the south wall of Room 5 and west to within the shell of Platform 3. Efforts

East Wing, south
tunnel debris in
Southeast Court,
1932

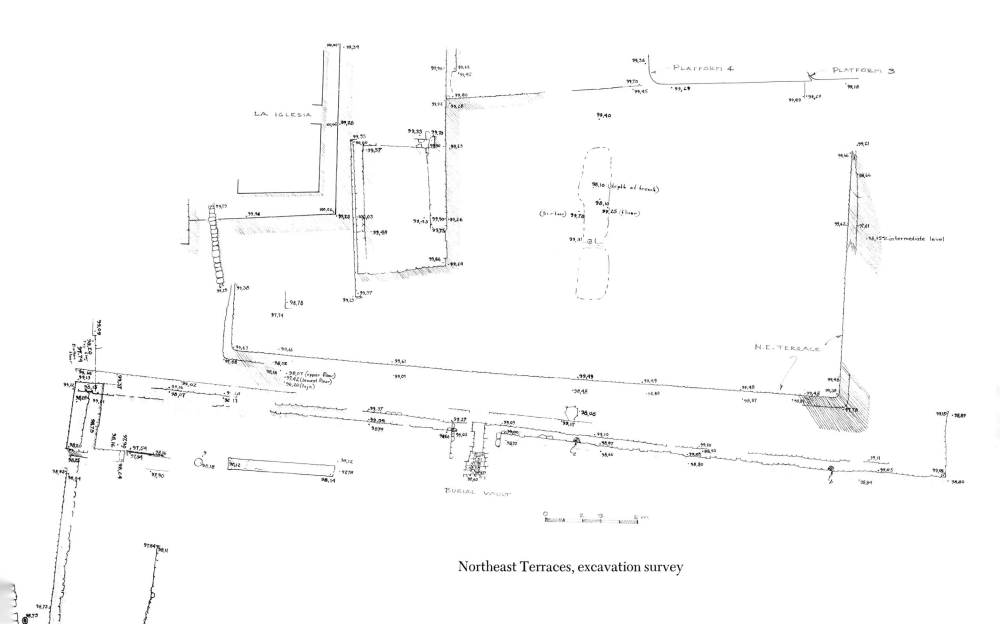

Northeast Terraces, excavation survey

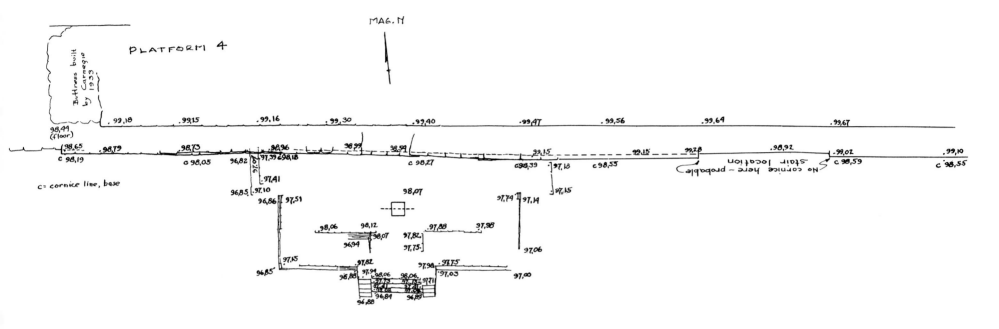

PLATFORM 3

PLATFORM 4

MAG. N

Buttress built by Carnegie 1933

98,44 (floor)

.99,18   .99,15   .99,16   .99,30   .99,40   .99,47   .99,56   .99,64   .99,67

98,65   .98,79   98,73   98,96   98,99   98,59   99,15   99,15   99,28   .98,92   .99,02   .99,10
c 98,19   c 98,05   96,82   97,39 98,18   c 98,27   c 98,39   97,18   c 98,55   No cornice here - probable   c 98,59   c 98,55
Stair location

c= cornice line, base   96,76   97,41   97,15

96,85   97,10   98,07   97,79   97,14
96,86   97,51   97,06

98,06   98,12   97,88   97,98
96,94   98,07   97,82
97,75

97,15   97,82   97,98   98,75
96,85   97,94   98,06   98,06   97,71   97,03   97,00
96,88   97,75   97,15   97,71
96,88   96,84   96,85

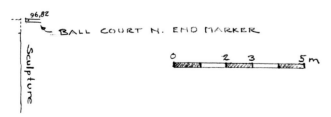

96,82
BALL COURT N. END MARKER

Sculpture

0   2   3   5 m

Ball Court, North Temple platforms, excavation survey

were made to continue further, but the work was abandoned as too dangerous after one section of shoring collapsed. A branch tunnel north through Room 10 exposed the basement relation of the East Wing and Platform 3. The main tunnel could have been continued, but it would have been necessary first to grout the loose stone in this core of Platform 3, where there was no binder. Instead, a wall was built against this fill. Consequently, the question of the connection between Platforms 1 and 2 with the East Wing remained one of the major unsolved problems of the entire complex.

The south tunnel along the south face of the East Wing was carried into the facing of Platform 3, but was abandoned when loose rubble similar to that found in the north tunnel was encountered.

Surface evidence showed remains of a supporting terrace along the south side of the main platforms. The tracing of this terrace, eventually identified as Basal Terrace 1, resulted in the determination of the full extent of Las Monjas complex and became the most intricate undertaking of the project.

Discovery of the Ball Court was one of the first direct results of the tracing of Basal Terrace 1. Most of the remains of the Ball Court were traced in the 1932 season.

The refuse pit in the northeast corner of the north playing area of the Ball Court yielded twelve ten-gallon cases of shards, bones, and a few other objects.

Investigation of the upper courses of the Northeast Terrace led to the discovery of the double row of stones on the north, which were subsequently traced to the Temple of the Wall Panels.

From the East Wing Basement, excavation of trenches to the north revealed the later additions as well as the remains of early buildings west of La Iglesia.

One of the major repair projects was the erection of a support wall in the large cave in the west section of Platform 3. The loose, unstable surface of the bottom of the cave was removed, and a firm foundation was established below the surface of Platform 1. A wall was erected near the west faces of Platforms 1 and 2, and the area west of the wall was filled with loose stones. The wall was built upward to near the top of the cave, and was then flared out so as to form a corbel over the area that was to remain open. The large capstones excavated from El Mercado by Karl Ruppert were used in this corbel construc-

tion, as were the smaller capstones from the vaults of the Southwest Colonnade. The wall prevented further collapse of the roof of the cave, which, in turn, supported the Second Story, and eliminated all hazard to subsequent work in this area.

In the search for the west limit of the complex, the exposed remains west of Platform 4 were excavated and traced, but these were nonproductive.

The floor at the southeast corner of La Iglesia was cleaned to the east. The east cornice line of what was later identified as the Third Addition to the East Wing Basement was encountered east of the East Wing facade. Excavation here led to the partial cleaning of the Northeast Annex and to the first probing of the substructures of the East Building.

Several pits were dug in an effort to determine the possible existence of earlier levels and the depth to bedrock. One of these pits, north of the East Wing and in front of the East Wing Basement addition that extended the north line of Platform 4 to the east, was excavated to a point below the floor level extending from the base of the East Wing Basement. Below this floor, only large, unworked stone rested on a layer of black earth, humus, and gravel above the bedrock. No shards were found in this pit, although some shards—mostly of slateware—were found in another similar pit dug through the floor of the Ball Court in the northeast corner of the north end zone.

A cross section taken through the Southeast Annex led to the digging of a pit south of the building and against the south face of the basal terraces. Several floor levels were encountered in this first exposure of the extensions of basal terraces, and a low wall extending south to a round corner was found related to one of these floor levels. At the time this pit was dug, the relation of the bench to the one south of the building was not anticipated; subsequent new work on the area revealed this possibility. Tracing of the bench was begun in this area.

Permission was received to excavate the Southeast Court, and an area was cleaned in the depression east of the Southeast Annex for excavation debris. Trenches were dug, and the east limits of the East and Southeast Terraces were determined. The debris was carried to a point beyond these terraces. A drain from the southeast corner of the Southeast Court Terrace, which was found to empty through the inner East Terrace, was traced west from the outlet.

The excavations in the Ball Court extended into the west limits of the Southeast Terraces; as was later demonstrated, the Ball Court fill itself was probably another extension of this south terracing.

The south-end sculptured stone from the west bench of the Ball Court was found on the south slope of the so-called Southwest Mound, west of the Ball Court. Except for the rough stone debris, there was no evidence of a building at this mound. Here the bedrock rose rapidly, and may have been a high outcrop combined with the remains of a minor construction. A cave at the foot of the north slope of the Southwest Mound yielded considerable ceramic material and many human bones. Such small caves may originally have been the sources of soscob.

When the south line of the basal terrace was found to pass beneath the mounds bordering the Southeast Court, it was decided to excavate the mounds so that the terrace could be traced. Permission for this excavation was obtained from the Mexican government, and the two buildings forming the south and east sides of the court were cleaned and repaired. When stones were found in position but in danger of collapse, the wall was rebuilt and capped at the height at which it was found when uncovered. Only in the columns were out-of-position stones restored.

Work on the northwest corner of Platforms 1 and 2 was begun after the completion of the support wall in the center of the large cave at the west end of Platform 3. In the early stages of this work, large amounts of incensario ware were found at the approximate surface level of Platform 1. The deposit of shards was most dense west of the corner, and tended to disappear to the south. Black earth was found with the ceramics below the surface level of Platform 1. Below this level, the masonry, which contained some slateware, was apparently undisturbed. Two human skulls were found with the incensario ware. Several other human bones were found with the upper skull.

The excavations around the northwest corner of Platforms 1 and 2 revealed a cavity at the southwest corner of the Main Stairs. This was cleaned and repaired to the depth of the season's excavations.

Repairs of the rest of the west section of Platform 4 were undertaken. The north and west faces were pointed, and some of the lower offset stones were replaced. The foundations were checked, and restored where necessary. The cavity within the section was cleaned and pointed. The tunnel through the north face was lined for support, so

282

that there would be no danger from falling loose stones or pieces of masonry. The condition of the west end of Platform 3, where it appeared within the cavity, seemed to indicate that a breakdown of some kind must have occurred in the foundations. Possibly a hole or weak spot in the bedrock had collapsed and disrupted the foundation course. Within the large part of the cavity, the facing of Platform 3 had been forced out, as though by a combination of pressure from the rear and of loss of bearing below. The pressure was probably exerted by the loose fill behind the masonry shell construction. In the small extension leading north from the cavity, the fill under the west facing of Platform 3 had disappeared. This space was filled with repair masonry to support the facing. The missing part may have been the loose rubble fill of the west extension of the Main Stairs Terrace, which seems to have supported this section of Platform 3.

At the end of the 1932 season, the exploration of the entire Las Monjas complex was well under way but far from complete.

Detailed drawings had not yet been made. Because making these drawings would obviously be a full-time job, it was agreed that the project staff should be augmented for this purpose in the ensuing season.

The 1932 season had been successful in that the probable extent of the complex had been revealed and the obviously dangerous areas had been repaired. Among the major accomplishments were the determination of the extent of the East Wing, the study of the basal terraces, and the discovery of the Ball Court. The excavation and repair of the two Southeast Court buildings would enable a more thorough study of the underlying terraces. The low-relief sculptures found in the Ball Court and Southeast Court were valuable contributions to Middle American art.

THE 1933 SEASON

The second season at Las Monjas began with a continuation of the work begun in 1932. At this time, Russell T. Smith joined the group. Although he spent most of his time in studying and drawing such architectural details as the masks on the buildings, he also assisted in supervising the excavations.

Among the repair works continued were those around the west end of the platforms. The cave in Platform 4 was lined, and the broken

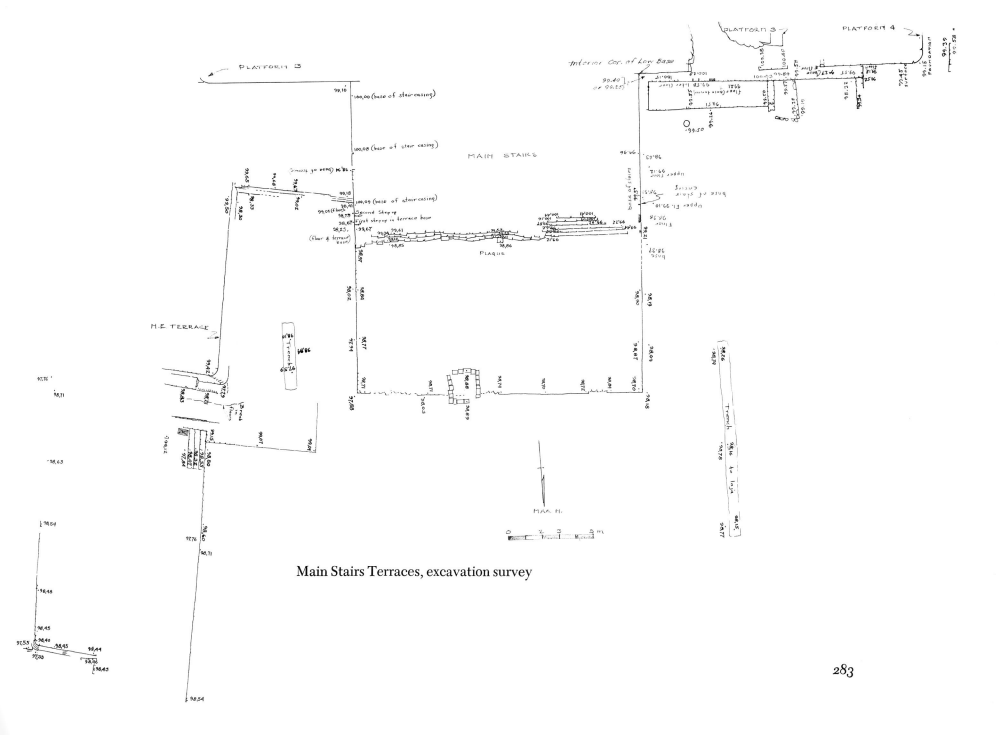

Main Stairs Terraces, excavation survey

283

south face of that section of the platform was given a facing of riprap to prevent further damage by roots and animals and to consolidate loose sections. The broken west face of the south section was similarly repaired. The southwest corner of Platform 3 was cleaned and pointed. New foundations were placed under the footing step-ups, which were investigated for possible evidence of a West Wing comparable to the East Wing. The situations and heights of the breaks coincided with those over the East Wing Basement and plinth. Although excavations were continued here, no wall or foundations of a West Wing were ever found.

Work was continued at the southeast exterior corner of the Southeast Court, where steps, a fire pit, and several small terraces were found. Later, after the east line of Basal Terrace 1 was found, this area was again opened, at which time the rough southeast corner of Basal Terrace 1 was found.

A trench across the Southeast Court from north to south was dug, and the south line of Basal Terrace 1, with its heightened cornice, was found. The plinth for another building was also uncovered in this area. Although a pit was dug in the center of the plinth, only loose rubble was found.

The North Temple platform in the Ball Court was the subject of intensive study. The first platform or terrace was opened, and the plaque in the pavement of the Ball Court exposed. At first, the plaque was thought to be the lid to a cache, but its removal disclosed nothing but more loose rubble.

Continuing the excavations near the northwest corner of Platforms 1 and 2 revealed the base line of Platform 1 and, farther north, the west wall of the Main Stairs and the north wall foundation of the northwest face of Platform 3. Slightly south of the northwest corner of Platform 1 and below its surface, a shieldlike incised graffito was found in the plaster face of the platform. A painted black band extended north and around the corner from this design.

In front of the large cave, the facing of Platform 3 was entirely missing from the stairs to the northwest corner except for the lower veneer-faced courses, which were interpreted as being part of the terrace supporting the Main Stairs. Many of the stones from this facing of Platform 3 were found in the debris, and were used to rebuild part of the wall to act as a buttress against the broken north facing, which ended in the approximate plane of the west face of the Main Stairs.

284

This broken facing had already been partly pointed in the 1932 season.

Excavation along the west side of the Main Stairs revealed the poor condition of the terrace supporting the west casing. The debris in the cave had apparently supported the west casing, and the removal of this debris led to further slippage of an already weakened wall. The first indication of imminent collapse occurred when one stone was sheared in half by the force of the imperceptible movement of the supporting terrace. Repairs already begun in the cave under the southwest corner of the Main Stairs and the adjoining area of Platform 3 were immediately extended beneath the stairs. This emergency operation had been under way only half an hour when the stairs terrace facing buckled. The facing was discovered to be only a very thin veneer over a loose stone fill. To repair the damage, timbers were placed against the casing to hold the mass in position while sections of the supporting terrace were removed and rebuilt. The original facing stones were not reused; instead, stones with longer tenons but with approximately the same face dimensions were substituted.

The buckling had caused old cracks to reopen and a new one to appear in the upper quarter of the stairs and extending into the area of Platform 3 above the cave. The direction of the cracks in Platform 3 and the existence of the cave under the southwest corner of the stairs indicated that the buckling had caused an overturning to the south as well as to the west. For this reason, the buttress was built to replace the missing area of the north wall of Platform 3.

Since the west section and the west casing of the Second Story Stairs were in hazardous condition, it was necessary to remove both. Before the stairs and casings were removed, all the face stones were numbered, photographed, and drawings made, so that they could be later replaced in their original positions.

The lower section of the west end of the Main Stairs had been missing, and the upper part had been in danger of slipping before the excavations were begun. While I was numbering the stones in the few rows above the missing section, several gave way, and I was carried down in a mass of large stones. My injuries were confined to leg lacerations, and I was able to return to the task within two weeks. Fortunately, this was the only serious injury suffered by anyone in the entire course of the project, in spite of the potential hazards in working on a building with loose masonry. In my absence, Russell Smith supervised and completed removal of the stairs without further difficulty.

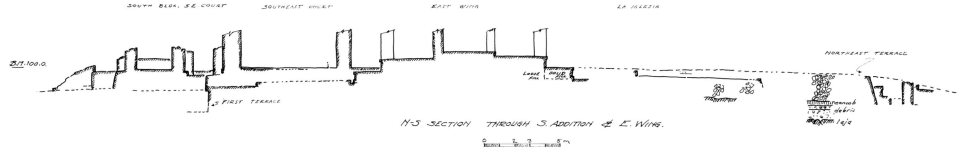

East Wing and South Addition section, excavation survey

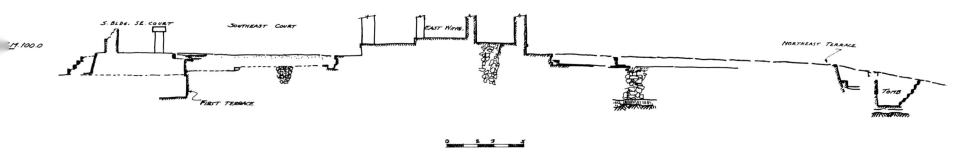

Northeast Terrace and burial vault, East Wing and Southeast Court section, excavation survey

The collapsed lower steps of the stairs terrace were rebuilt. Most of the steps above were missing; those remaining had slipped forward and downward. Part of the stairs coping had to be removed and replaced. The casing was rebuilt as it was found; its surface plane was not parallel to that of the stairs arrises, which had moved forward.

For additional reinforcing, five lengths of narrow-gauge railroad rails were embedded into the rebuilt masonry under the stairs at the sixth, ninth, fifteenth, twentieth, and twenty-sixth steps from the top.

Only the west third of the steps was removed and replaced. The remainder were later cleaned and pointed.

The entire section of Platform 5 under the west casing of the Second Story Stairs and around the collapsed area was removed and rebuilt. A temporary buttress wall was built between the shell of Platform 3 and the north face of Platforms 1 and 2; most of this wall was removed after the work on the stairs had been completed. On the Second Story Stairs itself, it was necessary to rebuild only the west casing; the east casing and the rest of the structure needed only repointing.

After the work on the stairs and adjoining structures had been completed, excavations were continued in the area bounded by the

285

stairs and the northwest sections of Platforms 3 and 4. The remains of the wall of Platform 4 were cleaned and repaired.

On the section of Basal Terrace 1 at the south side of Platform 4, disintegration had been caused by roots and animals, and in several places the footings were weak. The top of the west end of Platform 4 had tilted away from Platform 3. To correct these conditions, suitable repairs were made.

In the areas to the southeast, tracing the basal terraces revealed the southeast corner of Basal Terrace 4; tracing the latter to the north led to the discovery of Basal Terrace 3 and its south face slightly north of the Southeast Annex.

The floors of the South Addition to the East Wing were cleaned and traced, and the existence of a former bench noted. Work in this area was also helpful in determining the nature of the doors to Room 15. A pit was later dug through the floor of this room, to facilitate the study of the east end of Platform 4. The plinth course under the Southeast Court was discovered to have been constructed earlier than had the platform but to have been removed when the platform was built. This study of the east foundations of Platform 4 also resulted in a partial solution of the problem of the heightening of the basal terraces.

Extensive work was undertaken on the possible east and west additions to the Southeast Annex. The Northwest Addition to the East Wing was cleaned, and its north side studied.

The building remains west of La Iglesia and on the level of the East Wing Basement were carefully cleaned and studied before they were filled in again.

Renewed work on the Northeast Terrace led to further excavation of the North Building, beginning on the east and progressing west. This excavation, in turn, resulted in the discovery of the tomb that had been built after the entire northeast area had been filled, probably at about the time of the construction of the outer building of the Temple of the Wall Panels. Examination of this tomb, with its apparently secondary burials, offered an inviting respite from the arduous labor of excavation, study, and repair of the complex.

The lateral addition to the Main Stairs Terrace was encountered at the west end of the North Building. The east face was traced north to the northeast corner and then west for a few meters to a point at which the north line disappeared after rising over loose stone from a

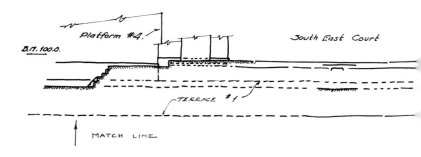

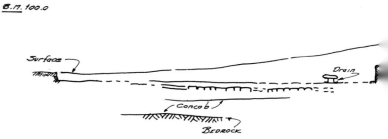

battered corner to a single-stone course. Although this terrace was not completely excavated, it was discovered that in the length of the east face it changed from a vertical terrace on the south to a battered one on the north. Complete excavation of this face might have revealed the precise point of transition and the possibility that several other phases of the terrace existed.

After the repairs to the stairs, the supporting basal terrace, and the west end had been completed, the Second and Third Stories, the outer facings of the platforms, the East Wing, La Iglesia, and the Southeast Annex were all pointed. Where water seepage was found to be endangering the buildings, new roofs were applied by removing several centimeters of the disintegrated cap and replacing it with a

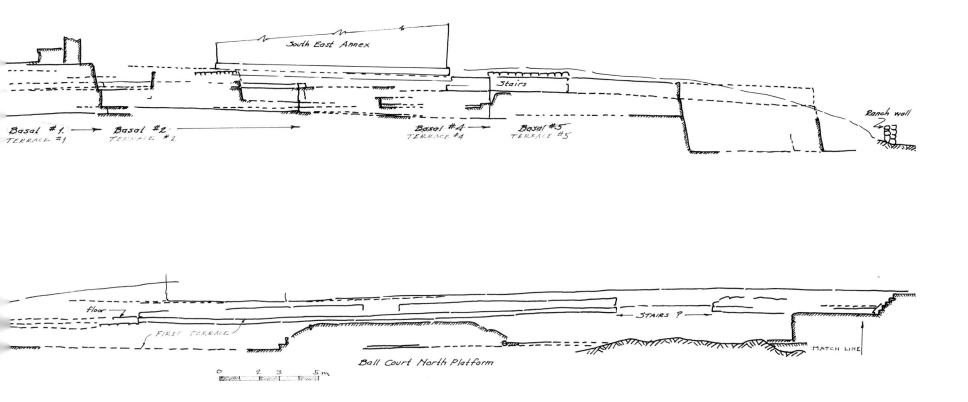

Basal terraces, south elevation, excavation survey

new surface of plaster. Only faint traces of the original roof surfaces were found in any of the repaired areas.

Two pits were dug into the surface of Platform 5, one on the approximate center line of the East Wing into Platform 4. It was hoped that some traces of the former roof of the East Wing could be found, possibly in the form of plaster marks on the face of Platform 3. Excavation was carried below the level of the present roof of the East Wing, but no evidence of the earlier roof was found. The pit, dug slightly east of the stairs, did reveal the northeast corner of Platform 2 and the cornice breaks on its north and east faces. This corner was surrounded by the loose fill of Platform 3. The solid masonry cap of Platform 3 was flush with the surface of Platform 2. The loose masonry

fill was apparently extended upward at the same time as the shell was, because as much as one-third of the length of the outer stones of the fill was embedded in mortar. The stones of both the fill and the shell are laid more or less flat.

The weep hole east of the stairs in Platform 3 was found in digging the pit to the northeast corner of Platform 2.

The east face of Basal Terrace 1 was first encountered in a test pit east of the northeast corner of the East Wing. A floor extended east from the base of the terrace until it joined bedrock. West of this same corner, the upper part of another test pit, dug between the First and Second additions to the East Wing Basement, contained lime-filled reused rubble; the lower part contained only clean buff-colored stone

287

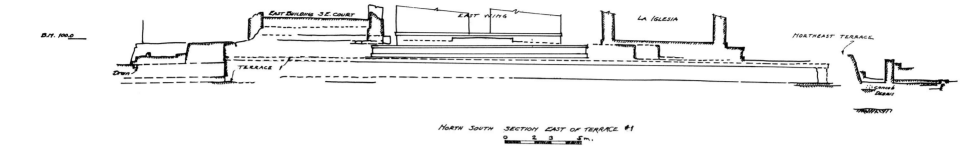

Basal Terrace 1, east elevation, excavation survey

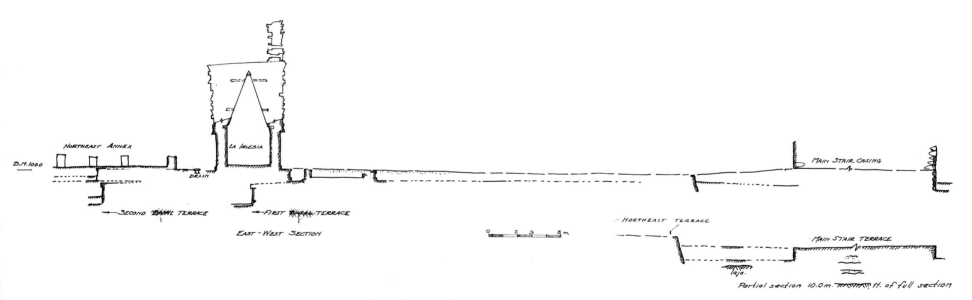

La Iglesia to Main Stairs sections, excavation survey

down to bedrock. The solid condition of the masonry was noted, but the wall face was not identified at that time. An effort to trace the east face of Basal Terrace 1 by digging a pit within La Iglesia led to the tracing of the additions to the East Wing Basement. Except for the south line of the first addition, which extends under the East Building of the Southeast Court, all these additions were completely traced.

Finding the east line of Basal Terrace 1 led to the discovery of the southeast corner slightly east of the South Building of the Southeast Court. An excavation extending north of La Iglesia revealed the remains of the north end of the east face of Basal Terrace 1 and traces of the bedding marks for the rough northeast corner. The floor extending north from the base of the East Wing Basement addition supporting La Iglesia was broken away slightly south of the line of demolition of the basal terrace beneath it. The south end of the east face of the Northeast Terrace rose above the debris, and sloped down to the north approximately from the line of the break in the floor.

In order to define the probable north line of Basal Terrace 1, a north-south trench was dug, beginning in front of the line of the north faces of the platforms, extending north on the line of the west door of the East Wing, and bringing the north limit of the trench to slightly inside the probable north line of Basal Terrace 1. This trench revealed two distinct fills, the division line being north of the line of the platforms. South of the division between the fills, two face stones—apparently the only remains of a weep hole or drain—were found below the surface. The short distance from these face stones north to the loose fill was occupied by a section of masonry with mortar binding. South of the face stones were evidences of the floor level in the plane of the base of the East Wing Basement, traces of the floor itself near the surface, and a small-stone fill containing bits of earth and plaster. Below the floor level, the loose masonry fill was covered by soscob and mortar. Immediately under the soscob, a possible construction level was discernible in places.

Later, another pit was dug in the approximate north line of Basal Terrace 1. The lower part of this pit contained black earth and large, immovable stones that were probably part of the bedrock. Above the level of the black earth was a stratum of old lime mortar containing many colored fragments of hard plaster. Above this clearly defined level was another stratum of soscob mixed with old mortar, which was capped with a level of cancob. The interstices of the lower part of

these stones were filled with black earth; at the surface was a thin layer of earth mixed with small aggregate.

Another north-south trench was dug west of the northwest corner of the Northeast Terrace in a further effort to find some trace of the north line of Basal Terrace 1. Above the bedrock was a stratum of cancob and soscob, above which was a layer of stones with some soscob in the interstices. A probable floor line above this was on approximately the same level as the floor at the base of the Main Stairs Terrace. This fact almost certainly precluded the possibility of evidence of Basal Terrace 1 above this level; no traces of it has been found below. Above the probable floor line was a layer of earth, small stones, and old mortar. The bottom of this layer of debris was above the top of a similar layer of debris found in the first north-south trench, on the east. Over this debris, a fill of loose stones, on the level of the Main Stairs Terrace, was capped with what seemed to have been the remains of a floor level—possibly the floor of the lateral extension to the Main Stairs Terrace. The upper part of the loose stone and earth was probably filled at some stage of construction of the low plinth courses extending from the Temple of the Wall Panels.

Trenches dug southwest and northwest of the platforms revealed no traces of walls or floors that could be directly connected with known levels. On the southwest, the drain from the west end of the north zone of the Ball Court led into what was probably a sump or catch basin. On a level below this, there were remains of what seemed to have been an earlier drain, at the end of which was a fill that had probably been a sump.

Northwest of the complex, and west of the northwest corner of Platform 4, trenches revealed minor remains of floor levels.

Efforts were made to find traces of the sacbe (paved road), from the south, which terminated near the west end of the complex. The northernmost evidences of this road were west of the south end of the Ball Court and southwest of the Southwest Mound.

At the bottom of a pit, dug east of the north end of the East Building of the Southeast Court, a plinth was found with its east face apparently parallel with, and related to, Basal Terrace 1. The face of the plinth was east of the basal terrace. Traces of the level of the lateral extensions of the basal terrace revealed that the loose fill below was of large, clean, rough stones, whereas that above contained much lime and was obviously of reused material.

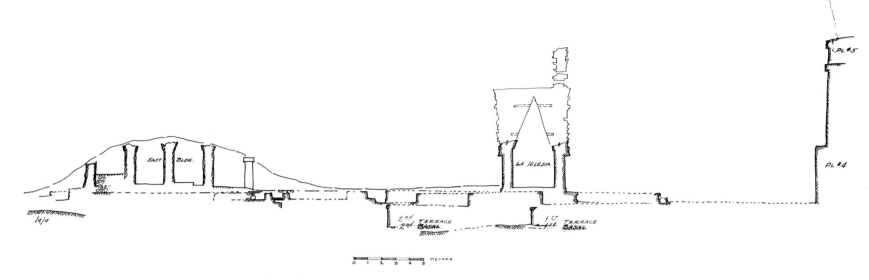

East Building through La Iglesia sections, excavation survey

In Room 17, a pit was dug down to the surface of Platform 3, in an effort to find evidence of possible earlier structures. Although this pit extended north and south, it revealed nothing more than a construction level surface of the platform. A north-south crack found in the surface of the platform was apparently part of the one pointed in the vault of Room 17.

In Room 22, an excavation down between the east and center-line doors was extended as a tunnel terminating in the inner faces of the stones forming the facings for the north and south lines of the Second Story Basement. In this tunnel were found four well-cut blocks, two masses of solid masonry, and the transverse weep holes of the basement.

In Rooms 1 and 4 of the East Wing, excavations revealed the solid masonry shell and loose fill construction of the East Wing plinth. This solid section extended down to the surface level of the East Wing Basement, which was similarly constructed and the solid section of which was of the same width as the exposed section. There were no

290

apparent indications in the loose masonry of levels of the basal terrace, basement, and plinth. In Room 4, a pit was excavated, the upper part of which contained small stones and some debris; the loose stones below became larger toward the bottom. In the east end of Room 4, a layer of ash and charcoal was found below the floor. In Room 1, a pit was dug without revealing any change in the fill. In the northeast corner of Room 1, the interior northeast corner of the solid shell was found equidistant from both the north and the east walls.

The lack of levels revealed in the excavations in the East Wing floors led to the conclusion that the basal terrace, basement, and plinth were all built at the same time.

Repairs of the collapsed area west of the Second Story stairs necessitated removal of the sections of Platform 5 immediately bordering the breaks. A new facing of masonry was installed to support the loose fill of the platform and to prevent further collapse. The west face of the broken area showed that several kinds of fill had been used. From the edge of the Second Story Basement and extending through more than one-third of the fill, a loose combination of both large and small rough stones had been used to the full height of the basement and then sloping downward almost to its north limit. Between this section and the solid facing of the platform, a fill of small stone, soscob, and mortar extended to more than half the required height. This fill, apparently the residue from the demolition of an earlier building from which only the face stones had been reused, abutted both the outer retaining wall and the loose fill against the basement. A third distinct kind of fill—large stones combined with earth, which may have been humus that had found its way downward after the disintegration of the floor above—extended this section up to the required level. This same condition of the masonry was not found in other areas of Platform 5, although no such large complete cross sections were exposed. Elsewhere in Platform 5, the fill was of loose stones apparently placed in position carelessly, with no effort made to lay them flat or properly to fill the interstices.

The complete study of Platforms 1 and 2 required that their casings be entered in order to define the floor level between the two and to examine the construction. An excavation was made through the rough west end of Platform 2, extended down into Platform 1 in search of a floor that could not be found, and continued as a tunnel and shaft into the center of the mass.

The excavation into the center of the platform was accomplished by using the solid masonry cap over the platform as the ceiling of the tunnel. The loose fill could not be easily removed because of the danger of the collapse of the stones above. The shaft to bedrock was made possible by keeping the opening nearly circular and by using mortar and spalls to maintain a solid shell around the shaft as it extended downward. By supporting the loose fill in this manner, the operation was easily and safely completed.

The shell of Platform 2 was apparently a continuation of that of Platform 1. No levels could be distinguished between the loose stone fills, and no surface was found on Platform 2. The loose stone fill extended above the exterior top line of the platform. Perhaps a building plinth or basement had been planned for Platform 2; if so, no through capping would have been intended, as was true in the foundations of the East Wing.

After the interior of the platform had been thoroughly studied, the tunnel and shaft were refilled. If they are ever to be reopened,

shoring should be provided for both, because dumping the loose stones into the excavation might have damaged the arch action obtained while the ceiling of the tunnel had been supported by timbers in several questionable sections.

Upon completion of the repairs to the dangerous areas of the Main Stairs, it was possible to accomplish more complete excavations at the bottom of the stairs and on both sides. The debris at the foot of the stairs was removed, bringing to light a Chac Mool and several spools from the Third Story cornice. A plaque, with a well-shaped mano on it, was found embedded in the pavement against the center line of the lowest riser.

Excavations at the northeast corner of the stairs revealed both the stairs terrace and the terrace connecting the stairs with the Northeast Terrace. Both these terraces were completely traced. The stairs terrace was broken away in three places along its north line. A square area of face stones was discovered flush with the surface over the north face.

A pit was dug into the center line of the stairs at a spot where no steps remained. This excavation revealed the step down in the stairs terrace back of the fifth riser. The rubble of the terrace behind the first five risers was loose, whereas that of the Main Stairs was solid. The loose fill extended down to the level of the top of the third riser. The excavation was not carried further south; when it was extended downward, however, no demarcation could be found at the terrace surface level, thereby confirming the other evidence that the lowest risers were related to the terrace in front of the stairs.

North of the stairs, a pit was dug downward from the surface to bedrock. Here the bedrock was covered with russet-red earth, above which was a stratum of black earth, which was, in turn, covered by a gray layer of soscob, earth, and plaster floor or wall fragments. Above this was a layer of loose stones mixed with soscob in the lower part. This stone layer had been apparently brought to a level in anticipation of further construction.

A course of stones mixed with gravel and soscob topped with firm soscob provided a base for a few centimeters of loose black earth. The area above this could be considered the Main Stairs Terrace fill, consisting of large, loose rubble topped by small stones and gravel mixed with earth that had filtered down from above after the pavement had disappeared.

Basal Terrace 2 was traced north of the Northeast Annex, and was eventually discovered in the form of its lower course only beneath the east end of the North Building. The cornice of the terrace broke off south of the south wall of the North Building. The northernmost trace of the foundation was found north of the south wall of the building and beneath the bench in the east end of the building. The lower floor level of the terrace was below the floor of the North Building. The top of the low plinth found under the North Building portal was above the level of the lower floor of the basal terrace, whereas the floor south of the plinth was below. The upper floor, abutting the base of the basal terrace and partly broken away, was above the level of the lower floor of the terrace and only slightly above the floor of the North Building.

Future excavation below the east end of the North Building might reveal traces of the northeast corner or north line of Basal Terrace 2.

Basal Terrace 3 was discovered abutting Basal Terrace 2 slightly north of the Southeast Annex. Basal Terraces 4 and 5 were also found, and the latter was partly analyzed. Neither Terrace 3 nor 5 was traced along its foundation line to the full extent east. Completion of this work at some time in the future might reveal some interesting results. Basal Terrace 5 probably returned upon Terrace 3 as Terrace 4 did. Terrace 3 would probably prove the more interesting. Finding its east and north limits would be of great assistance in clarifying the east end of the entire complex of Las Monjas.

Work east of the Northeast Annex was increased after the study of the basal terraces.

A tunnel was constructed along the line of the upper step-up in the west footing line in Platform 3, in a further effort to find traces of a West Wing similar to the East Wing. It had been hoped that some of the plinth course facing of a West Wing might be found under the platform, but the tunnel failed to reveal any traces. For the entire length of the tunnel, the solid masonry of the platform retained its step-up over the loose rubble, which was somewhat similar to that found in the excavations in the East Wing, consisting of many small nut- and fist-size stones filling the interstices of large, irregular stones. On the other hand, both the plinth and the basement of the East Wing had solid casings confining the rubble, which were not found on the west.

Before the floor relationships in the Ball Court could be studied, a thorough cleaning with brush and trowel had to be undertaken. Efforts were made to determine the number and character of floors from each

construction period. This study assisted in establishing the sequences of construction and remodeling. At this time, Fred Parris began the work of drawing the sculpture of the Ball Court. Each panel was removed for drawing, and later reset in the same plaster bed from which it had been removed. Removal of these panels also assisted the study of the Ball Court floors. The North Temple terraces of the Ball Court were cleaned, repaired, and then left partly exposed.

The study of the vaulting of the East Wing and the possible changes between the vault zones of Rooms 1 and 2 led to the cutting of a hole in the vault end of Room 2. The vault soffit of Room 2 was found to extend beyond the vault-end wall—apparently according to standard Maya practice. No discernible change was found in the solid masonry backing between the vault end of Room 2 and the backing for the vault soffit of Room 1. The excavation exposed the end of a beam hole of Room 1 (the center of a set of three). From the west end of this beam hole, a lateral hole extended north to the north beam hole of the group of three.

THE 1934 SEASON

The third season of work on Las Monjas was confined chiefly to completing the measured drawings and plans and studying every detail of the buildings, from the footings to the stone and fresco ornamentation. Several mounds abutting the previously excavated basal terraces and the late buildings obviously required excavation before the project could be considered complete.

Late in the season, permission and funds were forthcoming for the excavation of the important mound east of the East Wing. That work was undertaken and completed in the few remaining months of the season.

Except for the work at the East Mound, little excavation was undertaken. Pits and trenches were often found necessary to solve problems and answer questions that arose in the course of completing the plans, elevations, and final study of the complex. Several trenches were dug in a renewed but futile attempt to find a west wing. A pit was dug back of Platform 1, and a trench at the west side of the Main Stairs. The tunnel and shaft into the center of the interior platforms were reopened to allow further study of the rough basal terrace found there in the 1933 season.

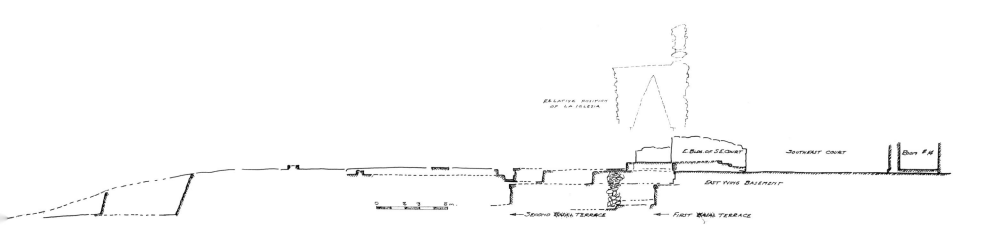

Southeast Terraces through Southeast Court section, excavation survey

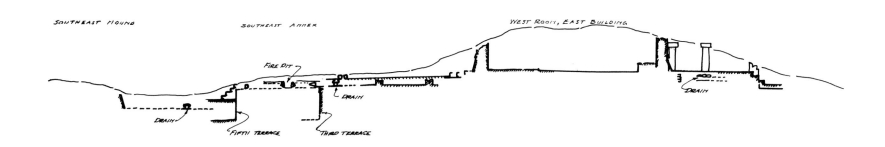

East Building through Basal Terraces 1 and 5 section, excavation survey

In some of the rooms, small holes were cut into the floors to permit investigation of floor series and depths of confining walls.

In all these excavations, the same care was taken to protect floors and walls as had been the rule in former seasons. When all material had been thoroughly studied, the excavations were refilled.

The East Mound contained a large, multiple-room, colonnaded entrance building with additions on the north. The entrance, with its four columns, was at the west, facing the facade of the East Wing of the main building. From this entrance portico, a wide area, with two columns similar to those at the entrance, opened onto a vestibule. A door at the rear of the vestibule led to a hall, from which there were entrances to three inner sanctuaries. The east room was similar in size and position to the hall and vestibule, whereas the north and south rooms were longer and extended east and west to the north and south of the vestibule, hall, and the east room. The north room had an exit through the north wall near the east end.

The first addition to the East Building on the north was a single-room structure, with columns set into the basal slope of the building for support of the south half of its east-west vault. The next addition was built around the earlier one, and closed the east court on the north. This structure was called the Northeast Annex.

In the debris of the mound, sculptured disks with streamers were discovered which had evidently fallen from their original positions in the upper parts of the facades. In the outer rooms, many metates were found which had obviously been placed there for ceremonial, rather than practical, purposes. Many shards as well as several nearly complete ceramic specimens were found in the debris.

Completion of work on the East Mound facilitated the tracing of the basal terraces in that area. Floors and remains of walls found below the base level of the East Mound could not be completely studied because of the shortage of both time and funds.

As had been done earlier in the Southeast Court mounds, the walls in the East Mound were simply repaired as found. No restoration was attempted beyond installing new wood lintels where stones had been found in situ over doorways. In these instances, the vaults had fallen before the wood lintels had decayed, and had filled the doorways with debris from the vaults; as a result, when the wood lintels finally did collapse, the stones above dropped only a short distance, if at all.

Other repairs included installing a new protective roof over the part of the south chamber of the Second Story where the large section of frescoes was still in position. Another new roof was built over a part of the East Wing where a depressed area had allowed rainwater to accumulate and later to filter through and damage the room below.

The last few weeks of work on the project were spent in a complete checking of all repairs and refilled excavations. The entire complex was cleaned of all debris and left in a condition suitable for turning over to the Department of Archeology of the Mexican government.

In this final season, many detailed drawings of masks and sculptured elevations—such as those on La Iglesia and the Southeast Annex—were completed.

The north, south, and west elevations of the main building were measured and drawn at a scale of 1 to 100. These drawings were accurate to within ten centimeters on the masonry of the platforms, and even more accurate—as much as line would allow—on the sculptured details. This precision should prove most valuable for future study of the platforms, since each of these had peculiarities of construction that were difficult to explain in writing.

Elevations and sections were made also of all the excavated structures, from which restorations drawings and comparative studies could derive.

Elevations were made of the side and end walls of each of the many kinds of rooms, which provided accurate information about such items as beam holes, cord holders, and details of the masonry.

Many previously unobserved remains of paintings, graffiti, and sculpture were discovered in the detailed analytic description that was written at firsthand throughout the entire three seasons of work on the complex. Among the late finds were the paired painted capstones of the East Wing rooms. One pair of these capstones was removed and copied before being returned to its original position.

APPENDIX C : THE MAJOR ARCHITECTURAL DEVELOPMENT PHASES OF LAS MONJAS COMPLEX

FIRST STAGE

The low terrace beneath Platform 1 and the wall line found in the pit to the east of East Building's Southeast Court represented the earliest known constructions of Las Monjas complex. The wall line may have belonged to a later structure than Platform 1, but neither was explored sufficiently to determine the relationship.

SECOND STAGE

The construction of Basal Terrace 1 and Platform 1 represented the first known major structures. No remains of the stairs to this platform were encountered, although the cornice breaks indicated the location. There was a stairs terrace to the north, but no definite tie existed between Platform 1 and that terrace. The top of this terrace was above the level of the base of Platform 1.

THIRD STAGE

There were no remains of a floor on Platform 1 to show that it had ever stood independently as a completed structure, and Platform 2 may have been built or planned before Platform 1 was completed. In fact, the masonry rubble of Platform 1 and Platform 2 appeared to have been contiguous. However, no floor remains were found on top of Platform 2, which must have stood with its top completed, since it was the central motif flanked by an East Wing and West Wing. These wings were planned with Platform 2. A stairs location was found, but no stairs to Platform 2.

Platform 1 section (top); Platforms 1 and 2 section (center); Platform 3 section (bottom).

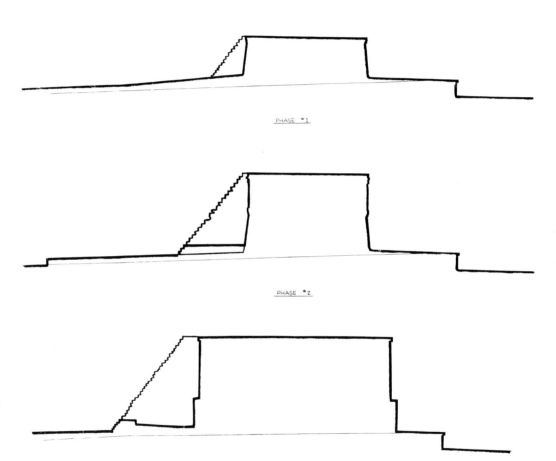

FOURTH STAGE

Platform 3 was built completely covering Platform 2. On the east, it encompassed one series of rooms of the East Wing, the walls of which were torn down to their first course. On the west, the foundation line of Platform 3 assumed the shape of the plinth and basement of a West Wing similar to those of the East Wing, but no other evidence of the West Wing was found. The foundations of Platform 3 seemed to indicate that there may have been a West Wing (or, at the very least, foundations for a West Wing) and that this wing was torn down before Platform 3 was built. There were slight traces of East Wing walls within Platform 3, where walls had been torn down to make space for expansion of the platform. The question here is whether the West Wing remained standing following the construction of Platform 3, and why more of the foundations of the West Wing were destroyed than those of the East Wing. We do not know how far the East Wing plinth entered Platform 3; nor could we find evidence of a north face of a possible West Wing. It may be that the builders of Platform 3 removed all the facings of plinths and terraces to be covered.

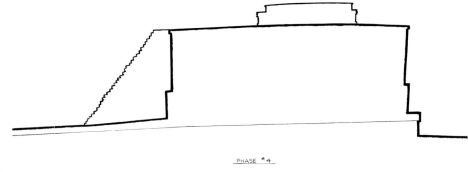

Platform 4 section

FIFTH STAGE

Platform 4 was built after all evidence of a West Wing had been removed. This platform covered a second series of rooms of the East Wing. It was the same height as Platform 3, but had its mid-height setback one course higher, and had also raised the top of Basal Terrace 1 several courses along the south side. Temporarily at least, the Basal Terrace was not raised to the east, the east foundation of Platform 4 stepping down to the old level. This level, the present surface of the Southeast Court, was not raised until construction of Basal Terrace 4, that small section under the east portion of the Southeast Annex. The two so-called Iglesia terraces to the east of the East Wing precede the period of raising of the basal level.

On Platform 4 was the first evidence of a platform superstructure. A trace of a floor carried through at the top of this base, but this may have been only a construction level, and the base, plinth, and walls to the cornice of the Second Story Building may have been planned as a unit. The base and walls of the Second Story seemed to have been contemporaneous.

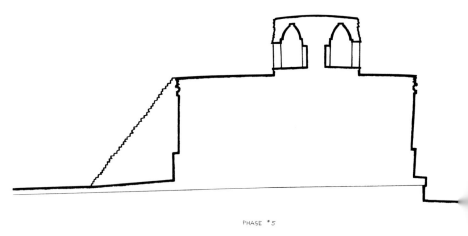

Platforms 4 and 5 section, with Second Story

296

Sixth Stage

Platform 5 increased the height of the main body of the complex by the addition of an encircling course of masks. The base of a building on Platform 4 was encased in the construction. The existing Second Story may have belonged to the Platform 4 era, but its masonry was not as refined as that of the encased base upon which it rested.

Seventh Stage

This stage included construction of the Third Story and its stairs. The changes in the East Wing, its South Addition, the Southeast Annex, and La Iglesia all appeared to have been later than Platforms 3 and 4. The Ball Court, Southeast Court, and East Building complex were built after the introduction of timber lintels, and had the general appearance of the late Mexican buildings of the main plaza at Chichén Itzá.

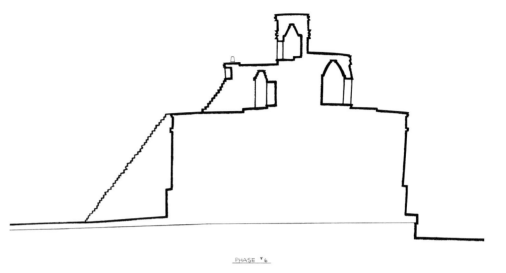

PHASE ⁴6

Platforms 4 and 5 section, with Second and Third Story

GLOSSARY

Maya art and architecture have generally been described using terminologies dating back to, and before, William Chambers' *Treatise of Civil Architecture* (1759), where the "Orders of the Ancients" prevailed. In the present work, an attempt has been made to clarify such uses and to freely apply others. Herein, "base" certainly does not resemble the "Attic Base," with its Torus, Scotia, and Plinth, although we have freely used the terms "plinth" and "stylobate" much as they came from Chambers and others.

In many cases, it was difficult to assign a term consistently, often because the original function of the architectural element changed with the growth of Las Monjas complex.

It is hoped that this section will aid the reader and perhaps help to clarify the terms generally in use in Central America. No doubt some will find grounds for disagreement. Perhaps another, wider-ranging, glossary, and one not so obviously based upon Las Monjas at Chichén Itzá, will be published in the near future.

Adorno: A row of sculptured stones set in the roof just back of the top cornice line. Similar to "antefix" in classical architecture.

Ashlar: Smooth facing stones with short tenons and requiring few if any spalls. Some Maya ashlar was so precisely cut that no mortar was required; others had narrow chinks and slightly rounded faces.

Basement: The lower finish course or band, generally from 0.50 to 0.75 m high, upon which a building or room was constructed.

Bedrock: The undisturbed native limestone upon which a complex of terraces, platforms, and buildings was built.

Black earth: Probably humus or milpa (cornfield) fire debris.

Boot stone: A vault facing stone with a boot shape—the face being the heel, and the lower portion of the tenon the sole of the boot.

Boveda: Same as boot stone.

Building: A structure containing rooms.

Capstone: Maya vaults were either pointed or had a flat, narrow top. Often the center stone or, if peaked, central pair of stones had painted inscriptions.

Chink: The small opening, space, or interstice between facing stones. These were generally filled with small stones called spalls (sometimes referred to as chinks).

Chinking: The filling of the joints in masonry with spalls.

Concob: A Maya name given to a mixture of humus, soscob, and other debris found on the bedrock and sometimes within the terraces and platforms. It was generally very dark, giving the appearance that the area may have been burned over, as with modern milpas.

Cord holders: Either small stone rings, with tenons or slots, or holes cut or drilled into the edges of finished masonry, especially about doorways, although often in the cornices. When on the inner faces of door jambs, they were paired on opposite jambs, usually near the floor, at mid-height, or near the lintel. Although no supporting evidence exists, they appear to have been used to hold cords across doorways. In cornice bands, they were generally equally spaced and could have been used for cords festooning the building. In general, they were from one to several centimeters in diameter.

Cornice: The projecting band or bands of masonry forming the cap for a masonry wall. Simple forms existed generally on terraces, basements, and platforms. More elaborate forms existed on room structures. The term "medial cornice" applied to splayed masonry at the level of the vault offset. The "upper cornice" was above the plain or elaborate frieze facing of the upper or vault zone of the building. In classical architecture, the medial cornice would be referred to as the "architrave."

Drains: Channels provided in the fill of terraces and platforms to remove water from courts or from beneath roof spouts. Considering the occasional heavy tropical rains, most drains were large enough to serve only one area after a storm.

End markers: A narrow guilloche design in stone set with top surface in the plane of the playing area in line with the end walls of the ball courts at Las Monjas and La Casa Colorada in Chichén Itzá.

Flying facade: A decorative wall built above the roof and in line with the front wall of the building. Usually composed of stylized masks or other geometrical masonry work.

Frescoes: Paintings on the plaster finish of rooms, depicting scenes and representations of deities and rulers. These did not appear to have been wet-plaster frescoes in the classical sense. Fragments of such paintings were found in places on the exterior walls.

Frets: Usually continuous bands composed of stones or carvings and appearing to have been developed from the stylization of serpent forms. Other frets occurred in stylized masks, as at the corners of the mouth element where they appeared to represent a bifurcated tongue. In masks, there were also frets over the earplug and also on either side of the main body of the mask.

Frieze: The decorative area at the upper zone of the face of a room structure or, as in Las Monjas, the upper addition to the main platforms.

Graffiti: Lines in the plaster, most often cut in the fresh mortar but sometimes scratched into firm plaster. Some such line work depicted recognizable subjects.

Gravel: Fairly hard, loose limestone usually graded from the size of sand to around one centimeter. Same as European or American gravel except in the nature of the material.

Masks: Stylized panels of masonry work composed of sculptured stones which, when set in place, represent a Maya deity. Generally the masks were plastered and colored. In some Maya areas, masks were made of plaster with rough stone backing.

Masonry: Facing stones of terraces, platforms, and buildings having the interstices, or chinks, between stones filled with spalls and generally with lime mortar. Also a term used in referring to the stone fill within a structure.

Mortar: A cementitious material made from lime and the soscob or lime gravel found in the area. Used for setting masonry, for plaster, for paving, and for roof finishing. Today, Maya masons use the same material for the same purposes. Roofs are rubbed down with corn-grinding stones and water to produce a watertight surface.

Paintings: Usually referring to frescoes, although also applied to the accent polychrome colorings of sculptural reliefs.

Plaster: Lime mortar applied to the interior and exterior of buildings and to terraces, platforms, floors, and roofs.

Platform: An elevated structure with stairs, built upon a terrace for the purpose of supporting a building containing rooms.

Playing bench: A shelf at the base of the side walls of a ball court. Early ones had low, sloping faces and sloping tops. Las Monjas court falls between this type and the high vertical face with flat ledge of the large, late ceremonial court in Chichén Itzá.

Plinth: A course of finish masonry resting upon the surface of a terrace, platform, or basement, having as its top line the floor level of the room or rooms.

Rings: A rather broad term applied to small ring-type cord holders and to large ball-court scoring circles, and to similar

299

stones, having openings of around twenty centimeters, used as architectural motifs on casings of stairs.

Roof comb: A decorative wall built above a roof at the center line of the building. Usually composed of stylized masks or other geometrical masonry work.

Rubble: Usually loose limestone, from fist- to head-size, used as the fill behind the facing stones of terraces and platforms. Rubble set in lime mortar was used as the backing for short-tenon facing stones of the upper zones of buildings and occasionally back of terrace and platform facings.

Soscob: A Maya name given to a loose limestone gravel found in pockets or caves. Used as the aggregate for lime mortar.

Spall: Small, thin stones used to fill the interstices between facing stones. In some architectural works, referred to as "chinks."

Stairs casing: The finished end wall of a stairs.

Stairs coping: A finished top of a stairs casing following the slope of the stairs. Sometimes carved with serpent representations or decorated with protruding stones similar to those over the mouth of a stylized mask and thought to represent the nose.

Structure: Either a platform or a building having rooms.

Task wall: A rough masonry wall probably erected to limit the then-current construction program of a terrace but not built with care or plastered.

Tenon: The part of a facing stone projecting into the wall or masonry. In general, terraces and platforms had facing stones with tenons projecting well into the structure, whereas vaults and walls of the buildings, or rooms, had short tenons. This generalization of course applies only to Las Monjas at Chichén Itzá, and even then has obvious variations.

Terrace: A leveled area upon which structures such as buildings and platforms or pyramids were erected. The periphery was usually rough-faced masonry with a plaster finish face. The fill was usually loose rubble, with small stones and gravel forming the surface, which was generally finished with a hard plaster, colored red or ochre. Sometimes referred to as a basal terrace.

Vault: The Maya vault was not a true thrust vault in the classic sense, nor was it a true corbel type of vault. It was more like a V-grooved section of solid masonry set upside down on two walls and exerting no lateral force upon them. The exterior facing was often applied over the rough core of the vault and obviously added to its stability.

Weep holes: Holes in the solid or loose fill of a structure having their orifices in the exterior walls of the terrace, platform, or building they served. Since some were in loose fill, they would not hold water; they must have been thought necessary to ventilate the interior masonry.

REFERENCES

Blom, Frans. *The Conquest of Yucatan.* Boston and New York, Houghton Mifflin, 1936.

Charnay, Désiré. *The Ancient Cities of the New World: Being Travels and Explorations in Mexico and Central America from 1857–1882.* London, Chapman and Hall, 1887.

Hagen, Victor Wolfgang von. *Maya Explorer: John Lloyd Stephens and the Lost Cities of Central America and Yucatán.* Norman, University of Oklahoma Press, 1947.

Holmes, W. H. *Archaeological Studies among the Ancient Cities of Mexico.* Chicago, Field Columbian Museum Publication 8, 1895.

Le Plongeon, Augustus. *Sacred Mysteries among the Mayas: The Story of Central American Antiquities and Their Relation to the Sacred Mysteries of Egypt, Greece, Chaldea, and India.* New York, 1886.

Maudslay, Anne Cary, and Alfred Percival Maudslay. *A Glimpse at Guatemala, and Some Notes on the Ancient Monuments of Central America.* London, John Murray, 1899.

Morley, Sylvanus Griswold. *The Ancient Maya.* Third edition, revised by George W. Brainerd. Stanford, California, Stanford University Press, 1956.

Norman, Benjamin N. *Rambles in Yucatan.* New York, 1843.

Stephens, John L. *Incidents of Travel in Yucatan.* London, John Murray, 1843.

Thompson, J. Eric S. *The Rise and Fall of Maya Civilization.* Norman, University of Oklahoma Press, 1954.

Wauchope, Robert. *Lost Tribes and Sunken Continents: Myth and Legend in the Study of American Indians.* Chicago, University of Chicago Press, 1962.

Wauchope, Robert. *They Found the Buried Cities: Exploration and Excavation in the American Tropics.* Chicago, University of Chicago Press, 1965.

Willard, Theodore A. *The Lost Empires of the Itzaes and Mayas: An American Civilization, Contemporary with Christ, Which Rivaled the Culture of Egypt.* Glendale, California, Arthur H. Clark, 1933.